THE PULSE

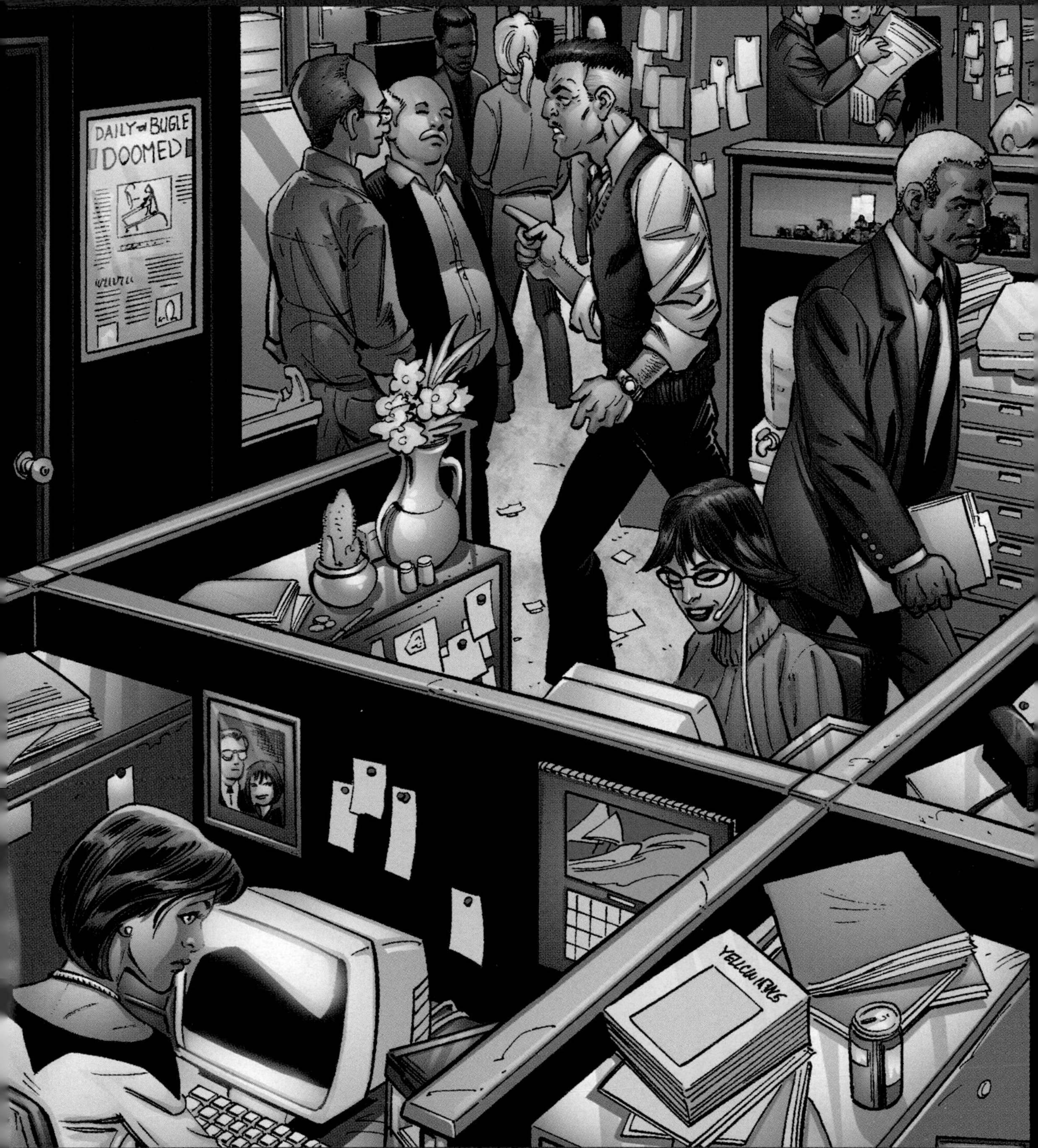
DAILY BUGLE
DOOMED

THIN AIR

THIN AIR

Writer: Brian Michael Bendis

Penciler: Mark Bagley

Inker: Scott Hanna

Colorists: Pete Pantazis with Brian Reber

Letterer: Virtual Calligraphy's Cory Petit

Cover Art: Mike Mayhew with Avalon's Andy Troy

Assistant Editors: Marc Sumerak & Nicole Wiley

Editor: Andy Schmidt

The Pulse created by Brian Michael Bendis

Collections Editor: Jeff Youngquist

Assistant Editor: Jennifer Grünwald

Book Designer: Carrie Beadle

Creative Director: Tom Marvelli

Editor in Chief: Joe Quesada

Publisher: Dan Buckley

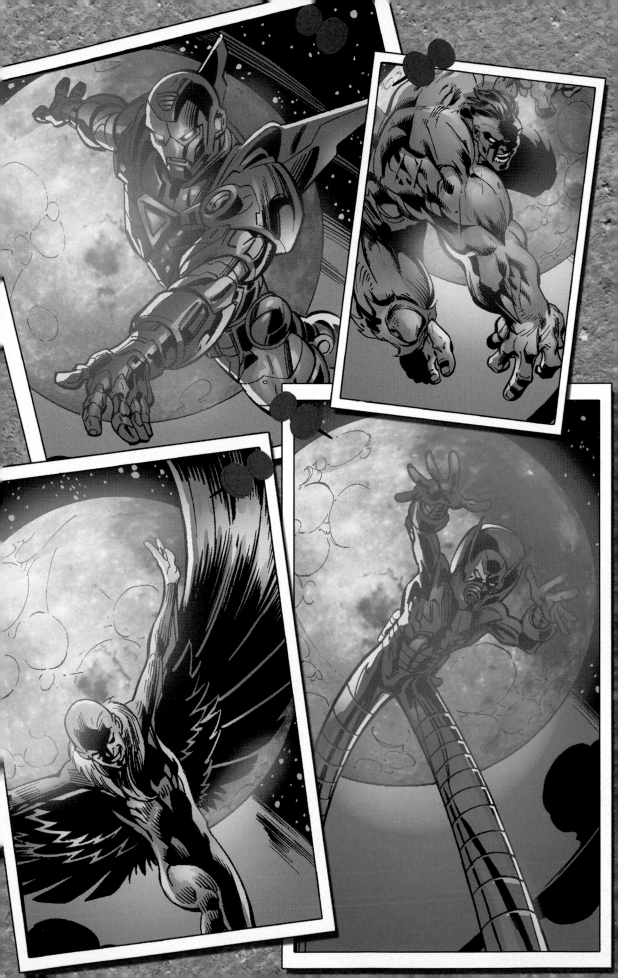

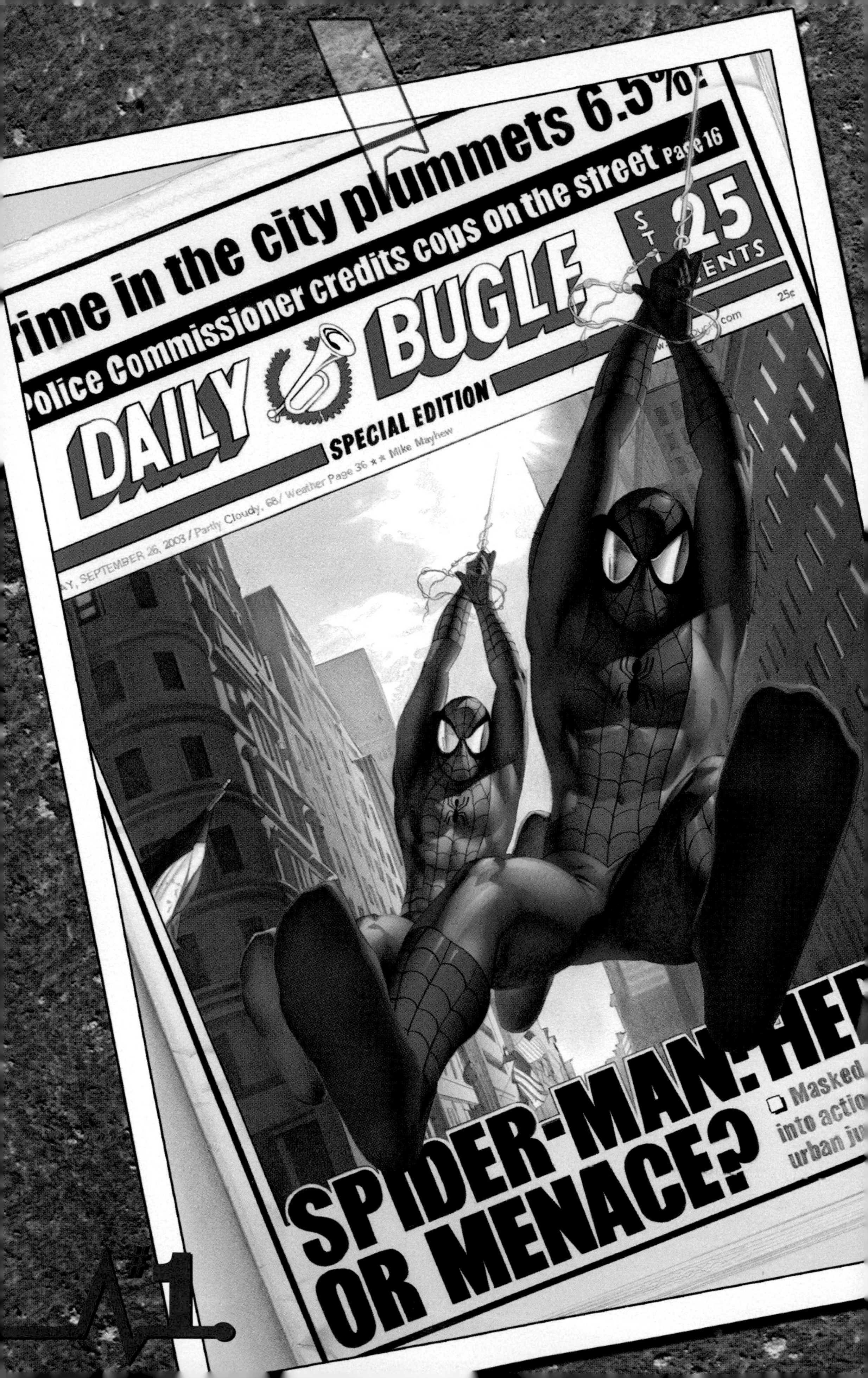

rime in the city plummets 6.5%:
Police Commissioner credits cops on the street Page 16
DAILY BUGLE
SPECIAL EDITION
25 CENTS
25¢
Mike Mayhew
AY, SEPTEMBER 26, 2003 / Partly Cloudy, 68/ Weather Page 36
SPIDER-MAN: HE
OR MENACE?
Masked
into actio
urban ju
#1

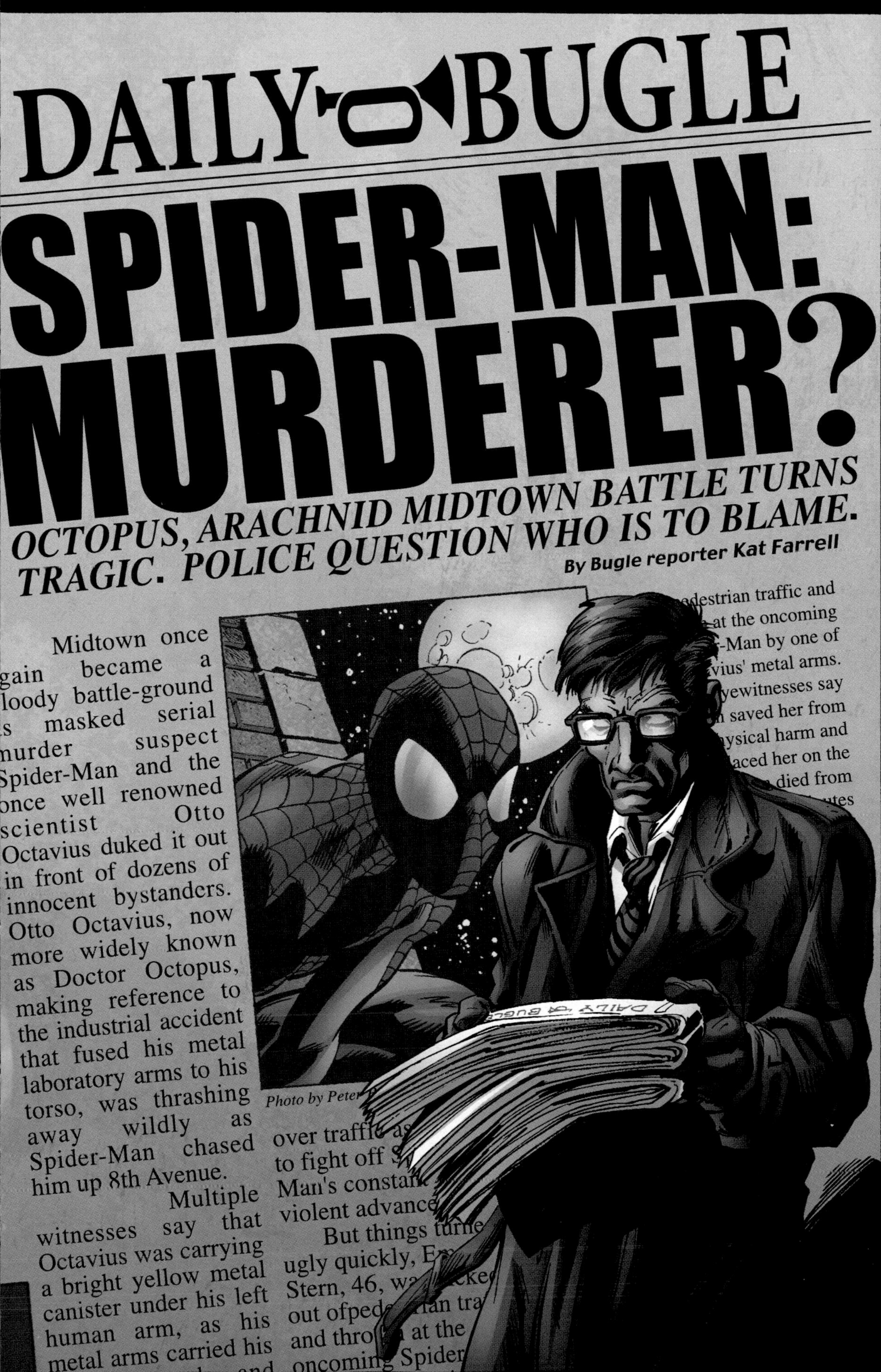

DAILY BUGLE

SPIDER-MAN: MURDERER?

OCTOPUS, ARACHNID MIDTOWN BATTLE TURNS TRAGIC. POLICE QUESTION WHO IS TO BLAME.

By Bugle reporter Kat Farrell

Photo by Peter P...

Midtown once again became a bloody battle-ground as masked serial murder suspect Spider-Man and the once well renowned scientist Otto Octavius duked it out in front of dozens of innocent bystanders. Otto Octavius, now more widely known as Doctor Octopus, making reference to the industrial accident that fused his metal laboratory arms to his torso, was thrashing away wildly as Spider-Man chased him up 8th Avenue.

Multiple witnesses say that Octavius was carrying a bright yellow metal canister under his left human arm, as his metal arms carried his

over traffic as to fight off S Man's consta violent advance

But things turne ugly quickly, E Stern, 46, wa ocke out of pede rian tra and thro a at the oncoming Spider

edestrian traffic and at the oncoming -Man by one of vius' metal arms. yewitnesses say n saved her from ysical harm and aced her on the died from tes

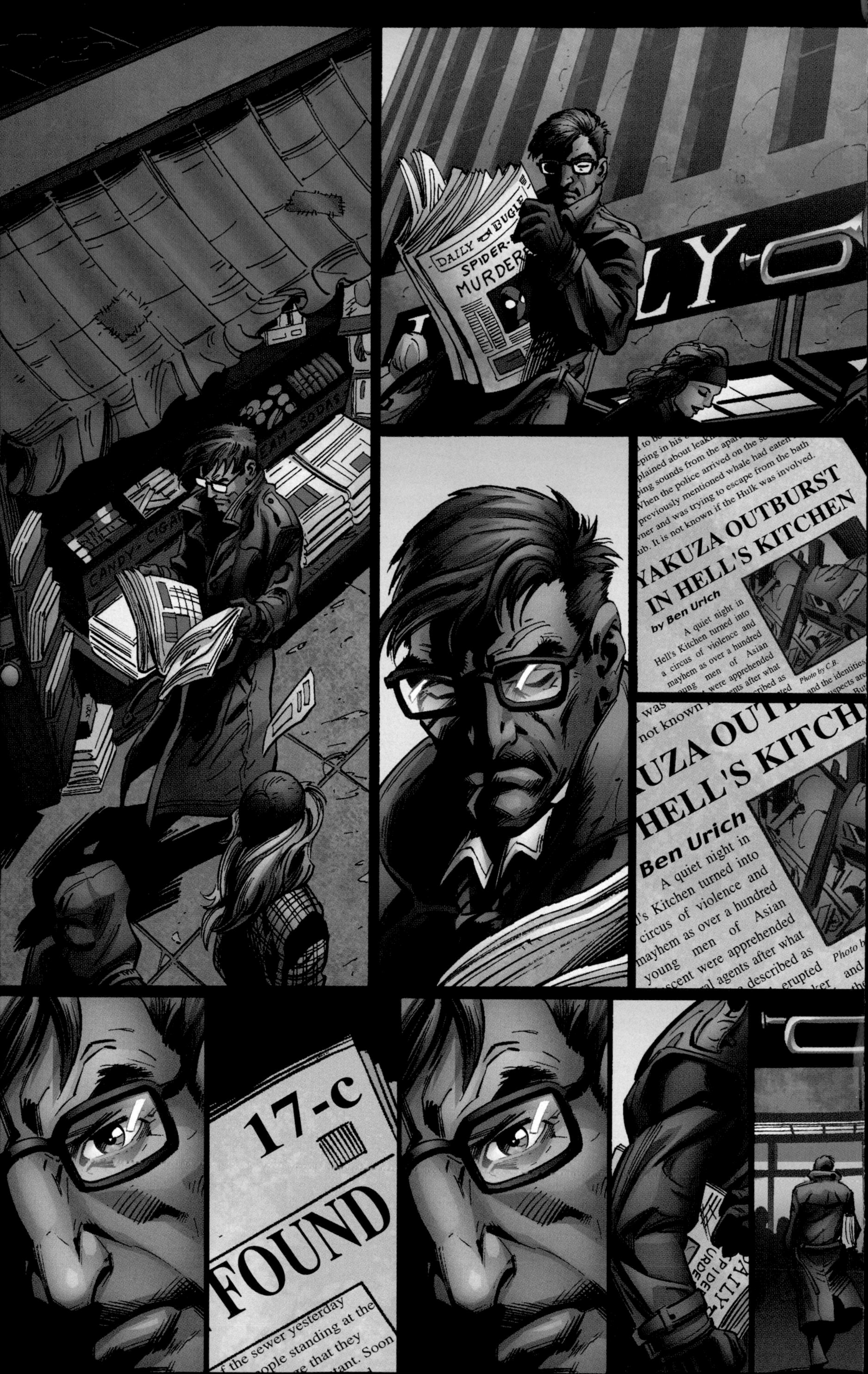

CANDY
DAILY BUGLE
SPIDER-
MURDER
When the police arrived on the
previously mentioned whale had eaten
owner and was trying to escape from the bath
It is not known if the Hulk was involved.
YAKUZA OUTBURST
IN HELL'S KITCHEN
by Ben Urich
A quiet night in Hell's Kitchen turned into a circus of violence and mayhem as over a hundred young men of Asian
were apprehended
Photo by C.B.
Ben Urich
A quiet night in
Kitchen turned into
circus of violence and
mayhem as over a hundred
young men of Asian
were apprehended
described as
17-c
FOUND
the sewer yesterday
people standing at the
that they
Soon

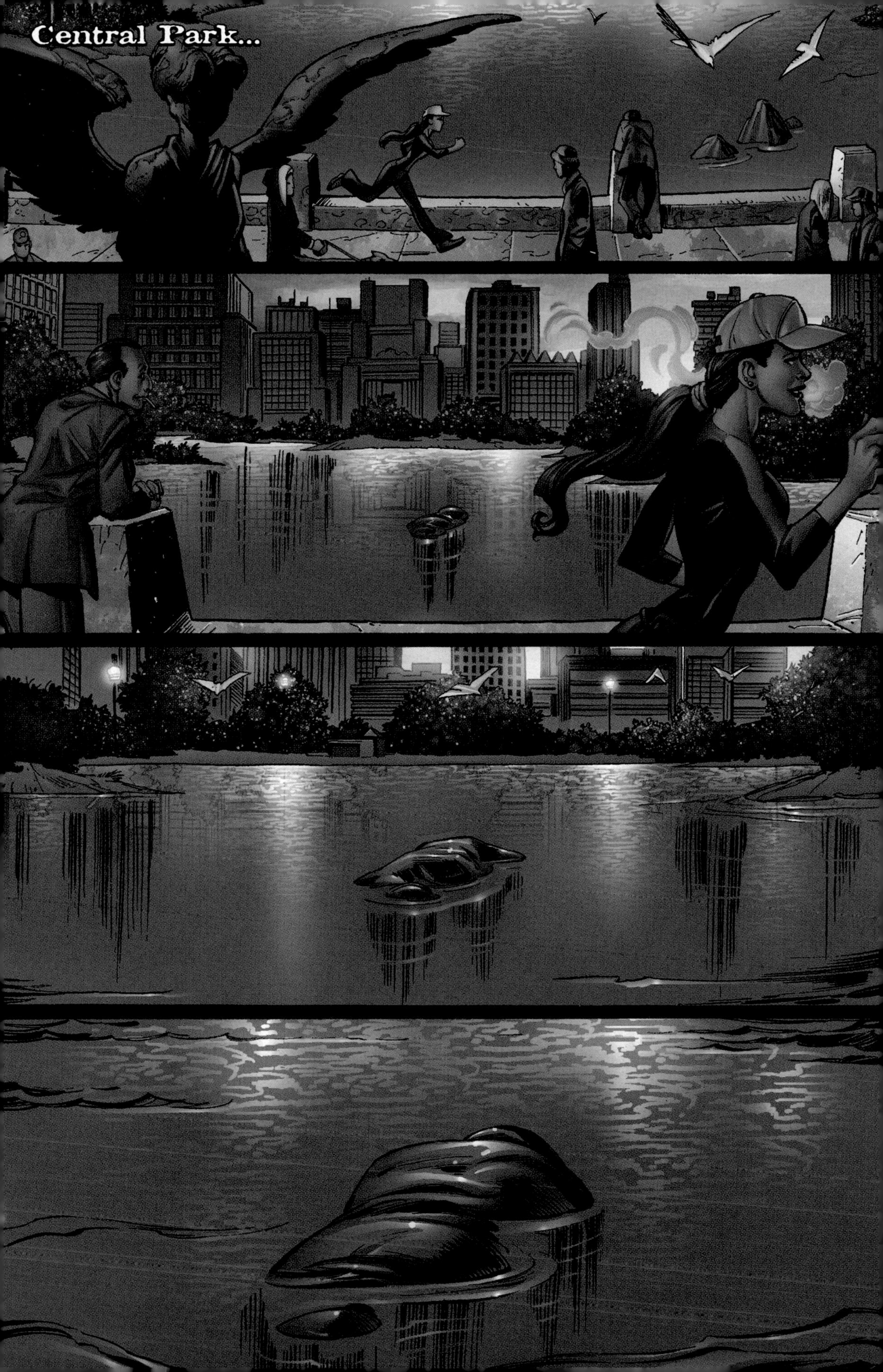
Central Park...

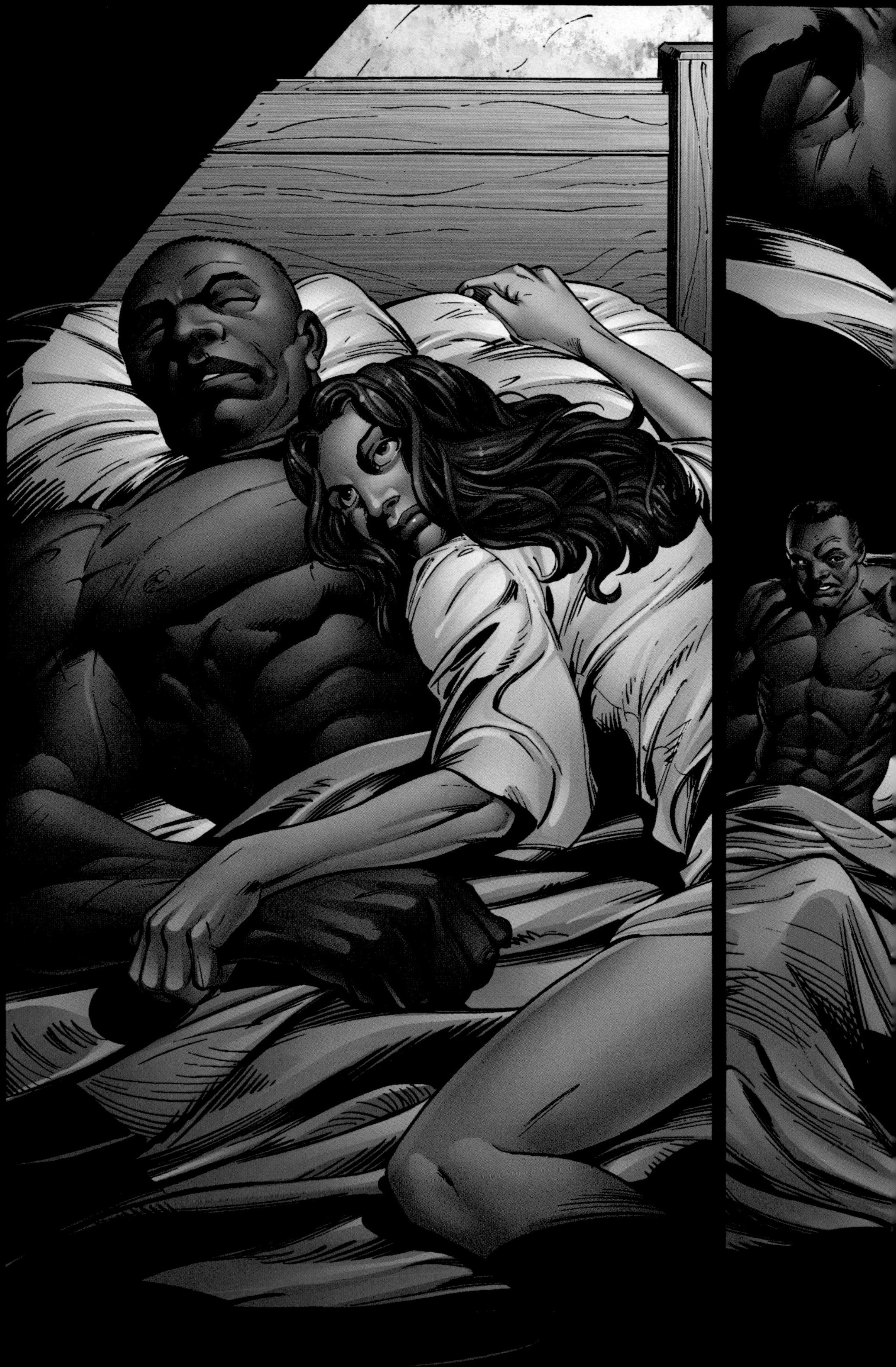

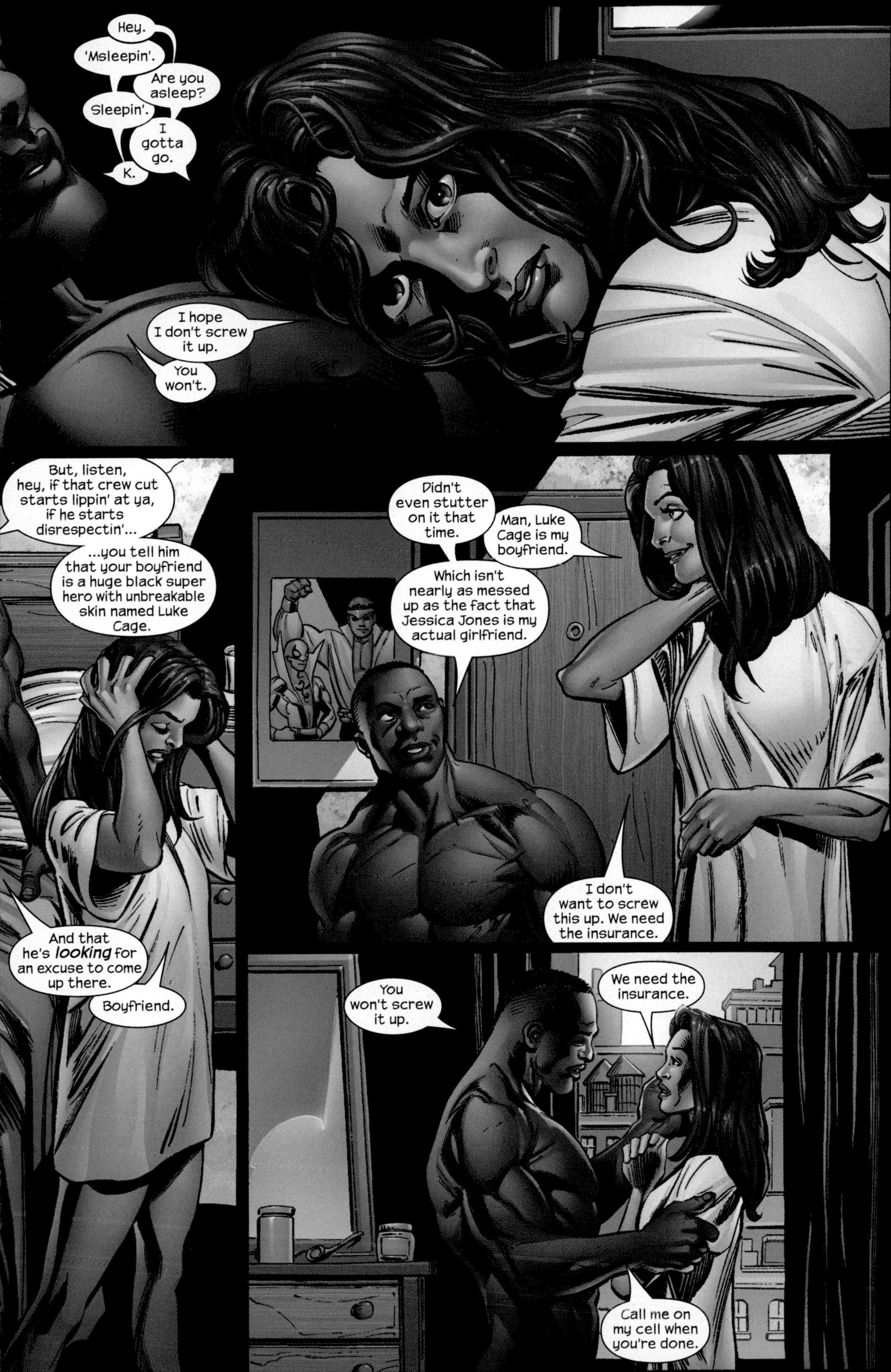
Hey.
'Msleepin'.
Are you asleep?
Sleepin'.
I gotta go.
K.
I hope I don't screw it up.
You won't.
But, listen, hey, if that crew cut starts lippin' at ya, if he starts disrespectin'...
...you tell him that your boyfriend is a huge black super hero with unbreakable skin named Luke Cage.
And that he's *looking* for an excuse to come up there.
Boyfriend.
Didn't even stutter on it that time.
Man, Luke Cage is my boyfriend.
Which isn't nearly as messed up as the fact that Jessica Jones is my actual girlfriend.
I don't want to screw this up. We need the insurance.
You won't screw it up.
We need the insurance.
Call me on my cell when you're done.

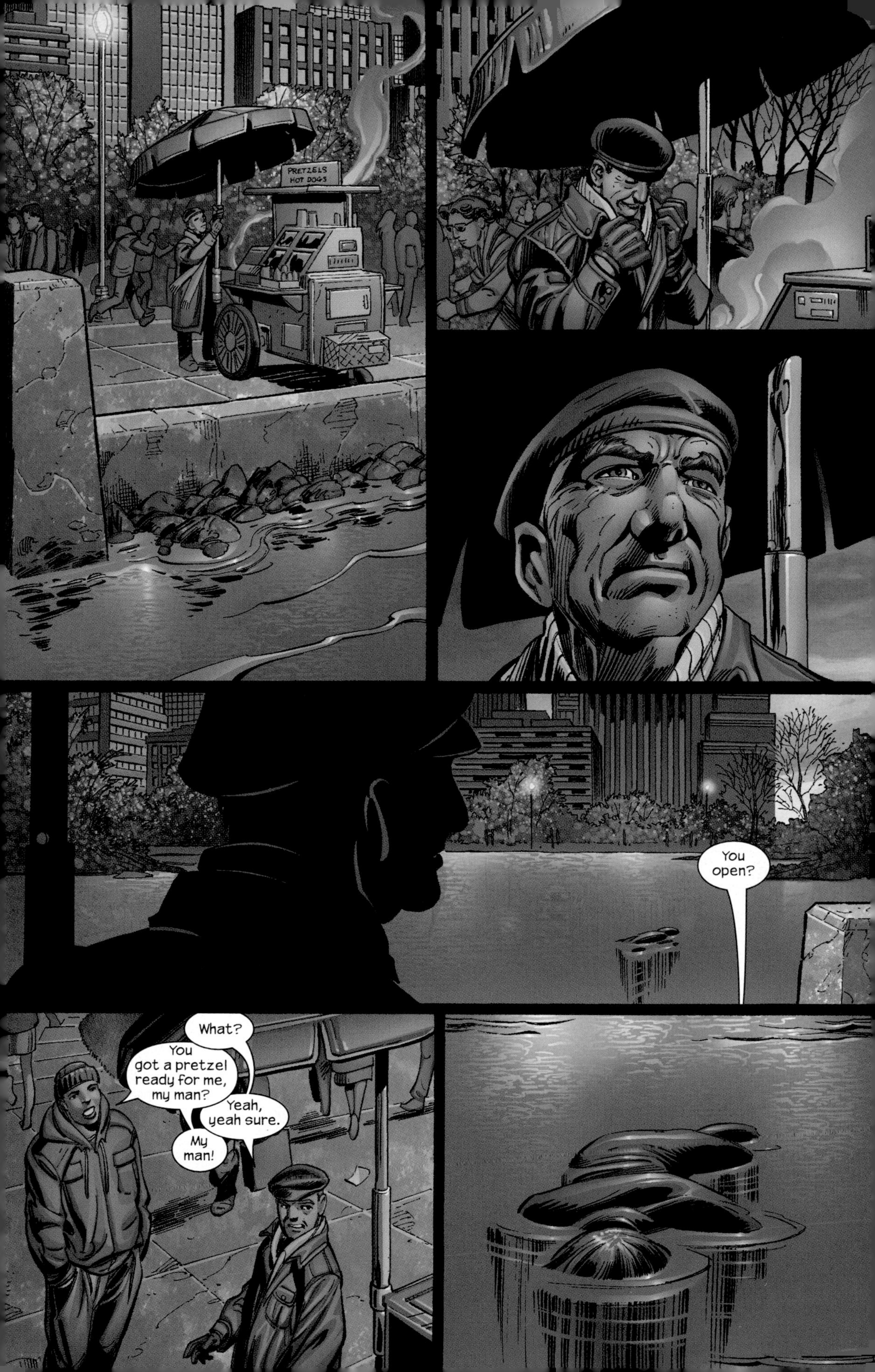
PRETZELS HOT DOGS
You open?
What?
You got a pretzel ready for me, my man?
Yeah, yeah sure.
My man!

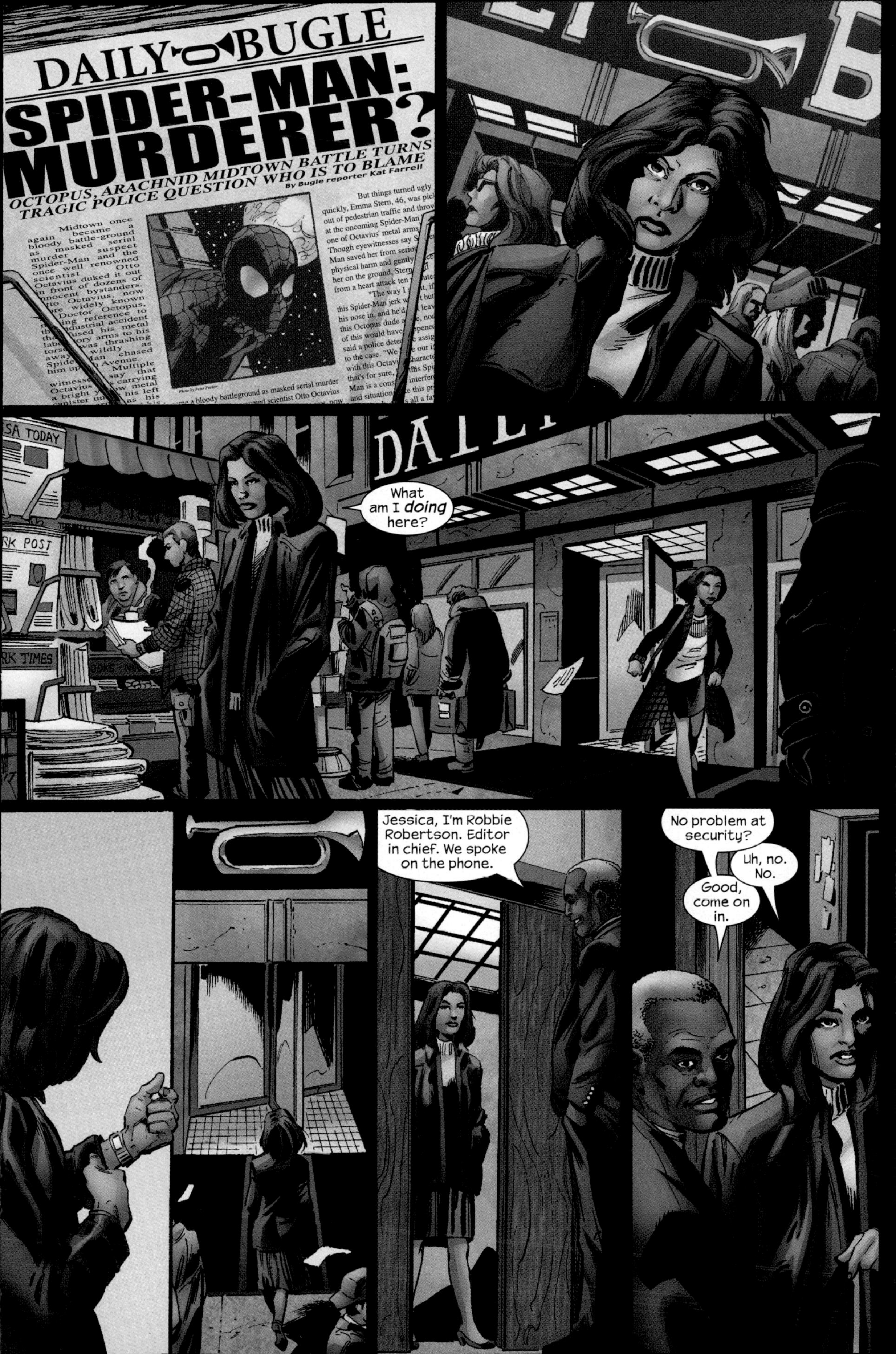
DAILY BUGLE
SPIDER-MAN: MURDERER?
OCTOPUS, ARACHNID MIDTOWN BATTLE TURNS TRAGIC POLICE QUESTION WHO IS TO BLAME
By Bugle reporter Kat Farrell
Photo by Peter Parker
What am I doing here?
Jessica, I'm Robbie Robertson. Editor in chief. We spoke on the phone.
No problem at security?
Uh, no. No.
Good, come on in.

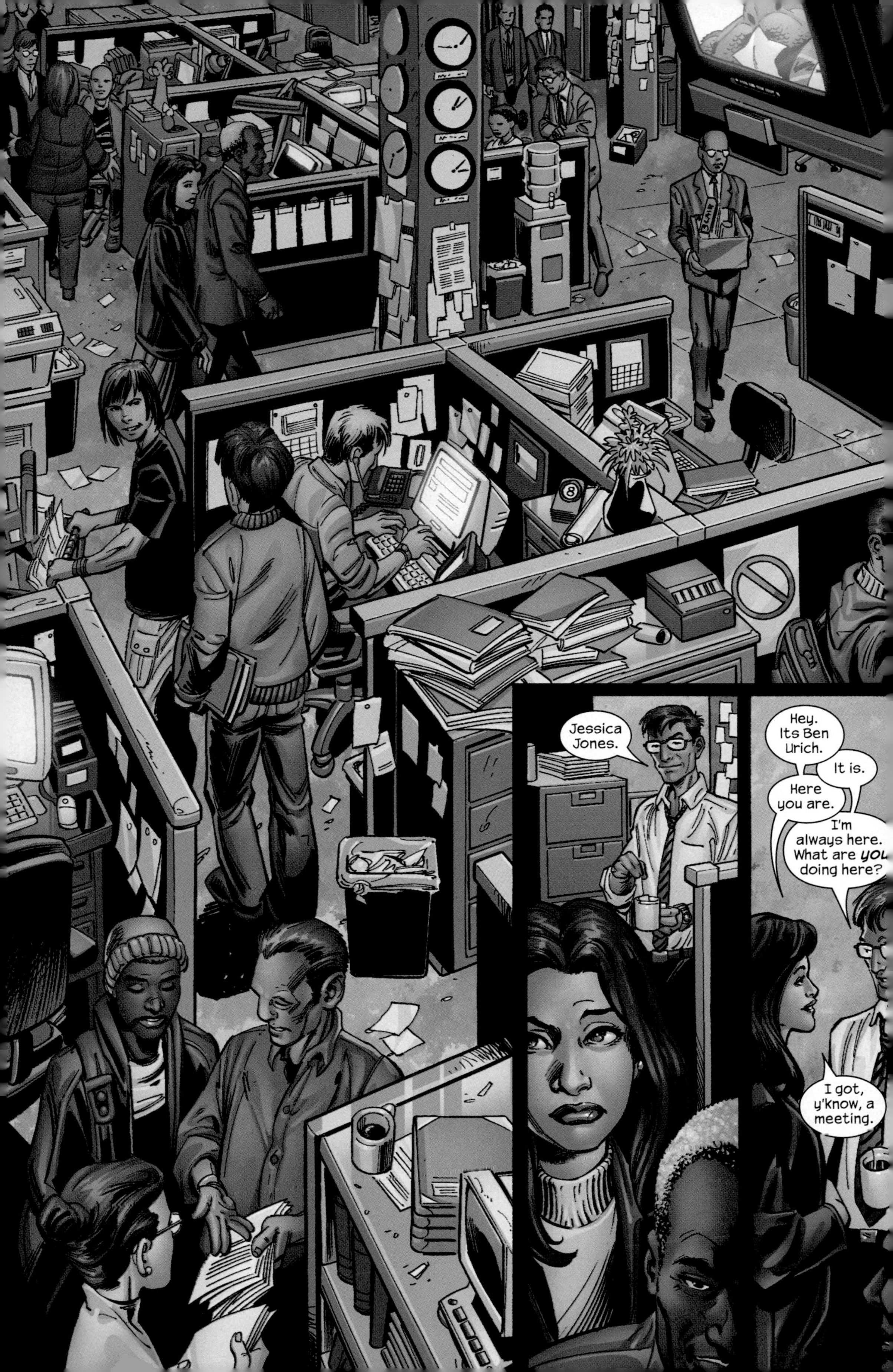

Jessica Jones.
Hey. Its Ben Urich.
It is.
Here you are.
I'm always here. What are *YOU* doing here?
I got, y'know, a meeting.

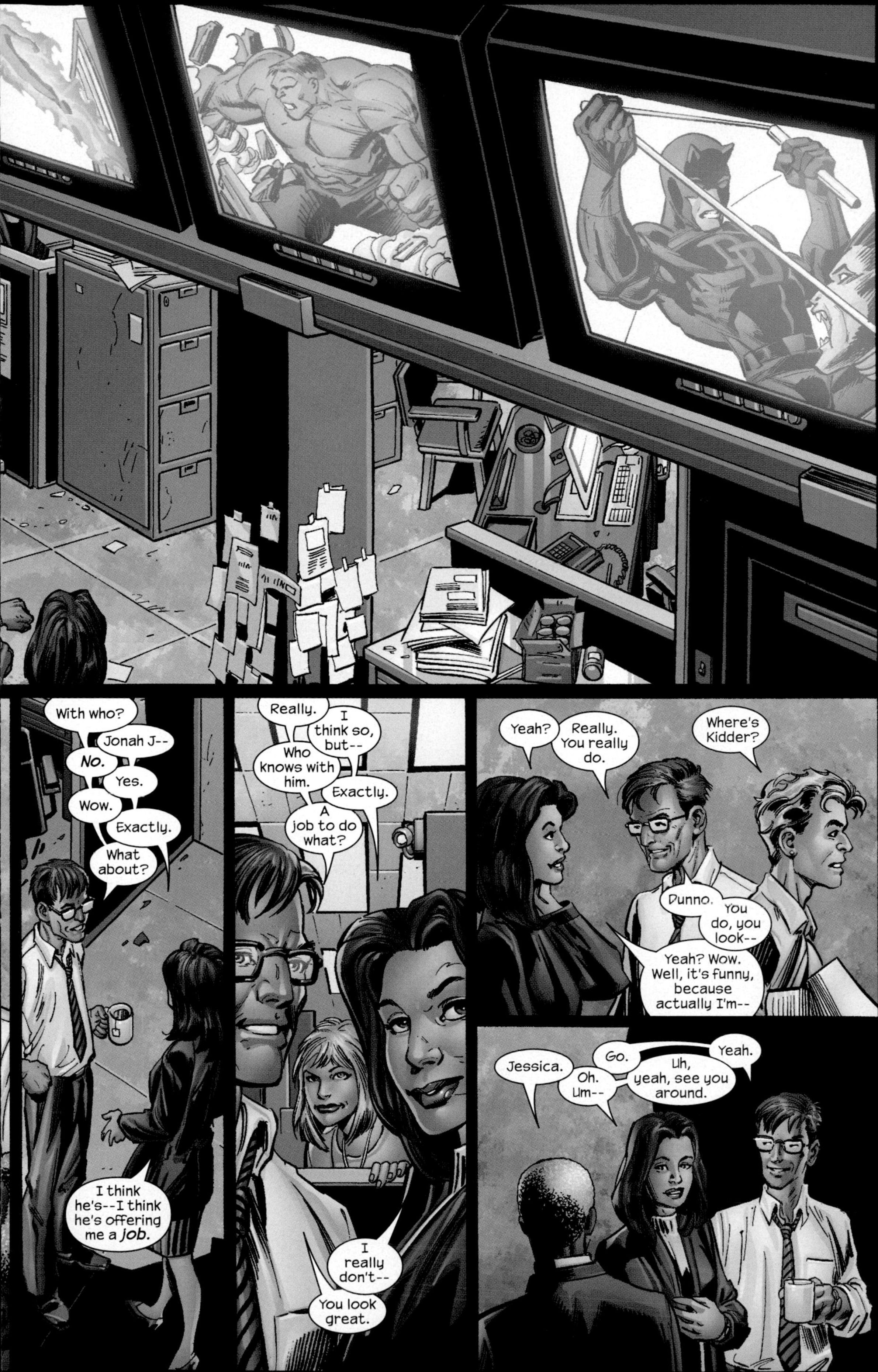
With who?
Jonah J--
No.
Yes.
Wow.
Exactly.
What about?
I think he's--I think he's offering me a job.
Really.
I think so, but--
Who knows with him.
Exactly.
A job to do what?
I really don't--
You look great.
Yeah?
Really. You really do.
Where's Kidder?
Dunno.
You do, you look--
Yeah? Wow. Well, it's funny, because actually I'm--
Jessica.
Oh. Um--
Go.
Uh, yeah, see you around.
Yeah.

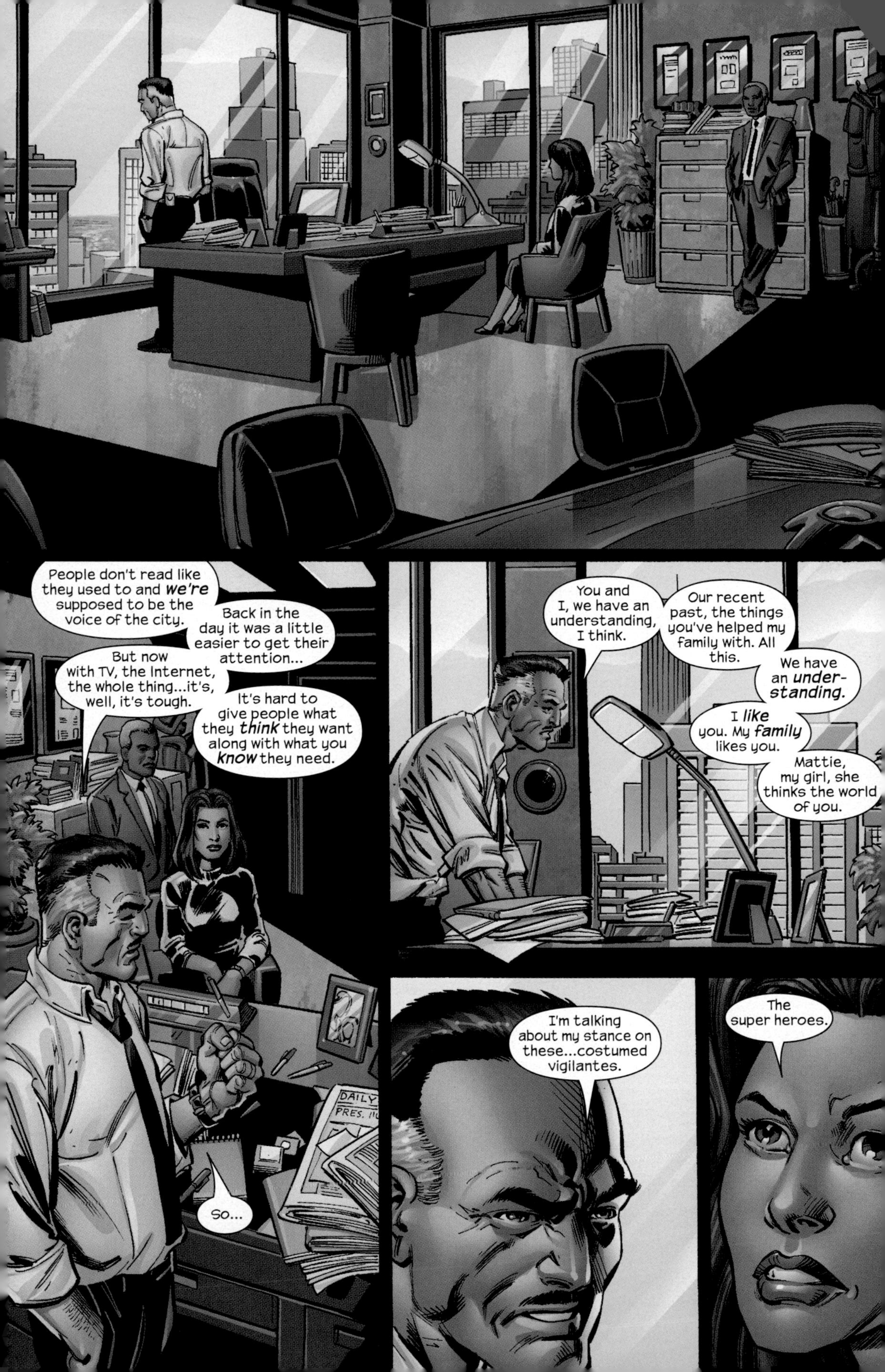
People don't read like they used to and we're supposed to be the voice of the city.
Back in the day it was a little easier to get their attention...
But now with TV, the Internet, the whole thing...it's, well, it's tough.
It's hard to give people what they think they want along with what you know they need.
So...
You and I, we have an understanding, I think.
Our recent past, the things you've helped my family with. All this.
We have an under-standing.
I like you. My family likes you.
Mattie, my girl, she thinks the world of you.
I'm talking about my stance on these...costumed vigilantes.
The super heroes.

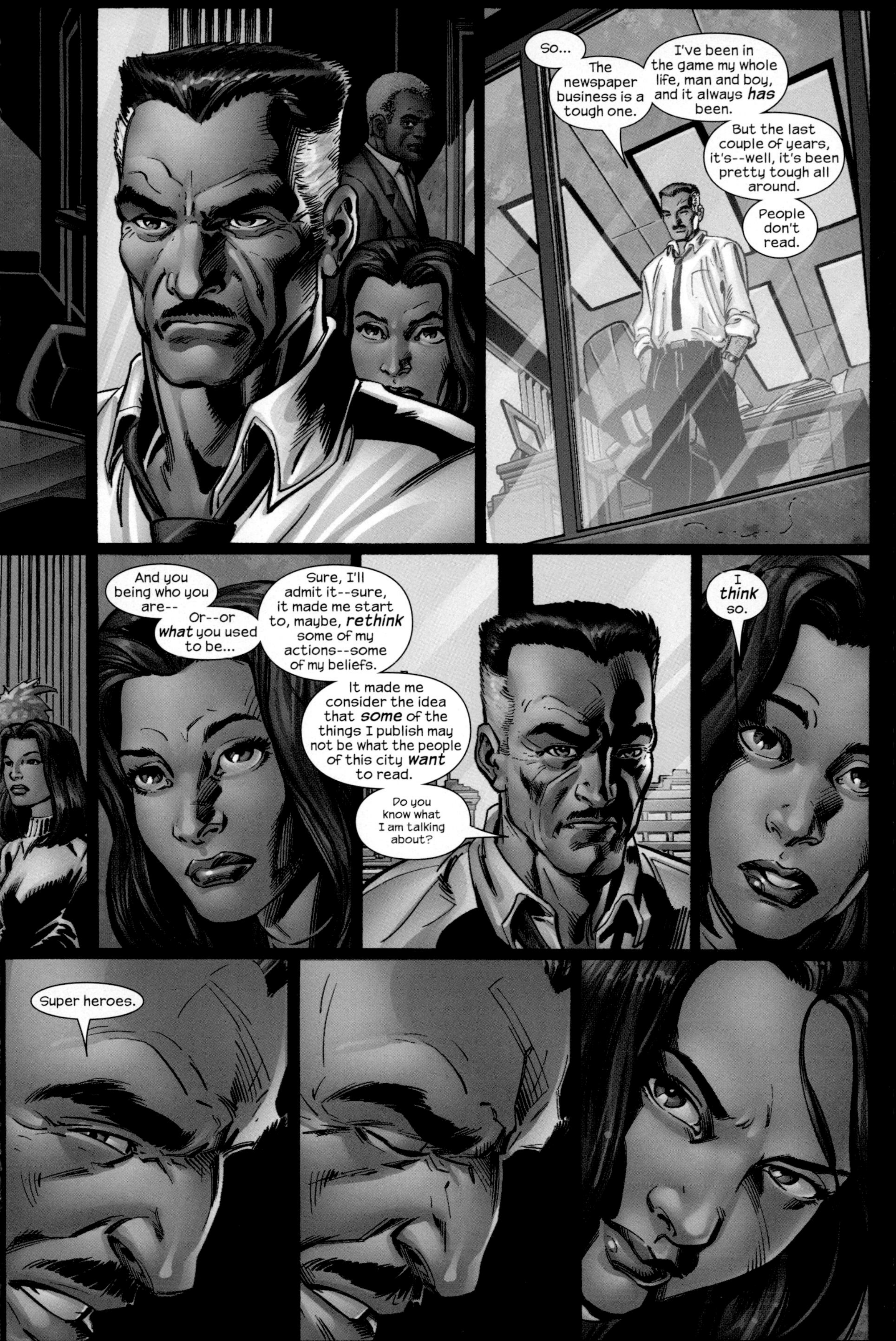
So...
The newspaper business is a tough one.
I've been in the game my whole life, man and boy, and it always *has* been.
But the last couple of years, it's--well, it's been pretty tough all around.
People don't read.
And you being who you are--
Or--or *what* you used to be...
Sure, I'll admit it--sure, it made me start to, maybe, *rethink* some of my actions--some of my beliefs.
It made me consider the idea that *some* of the things I publish may not be what the people of this city *want* to read.
Do you know what I am talking about?
I *think* so.
Super heroes.

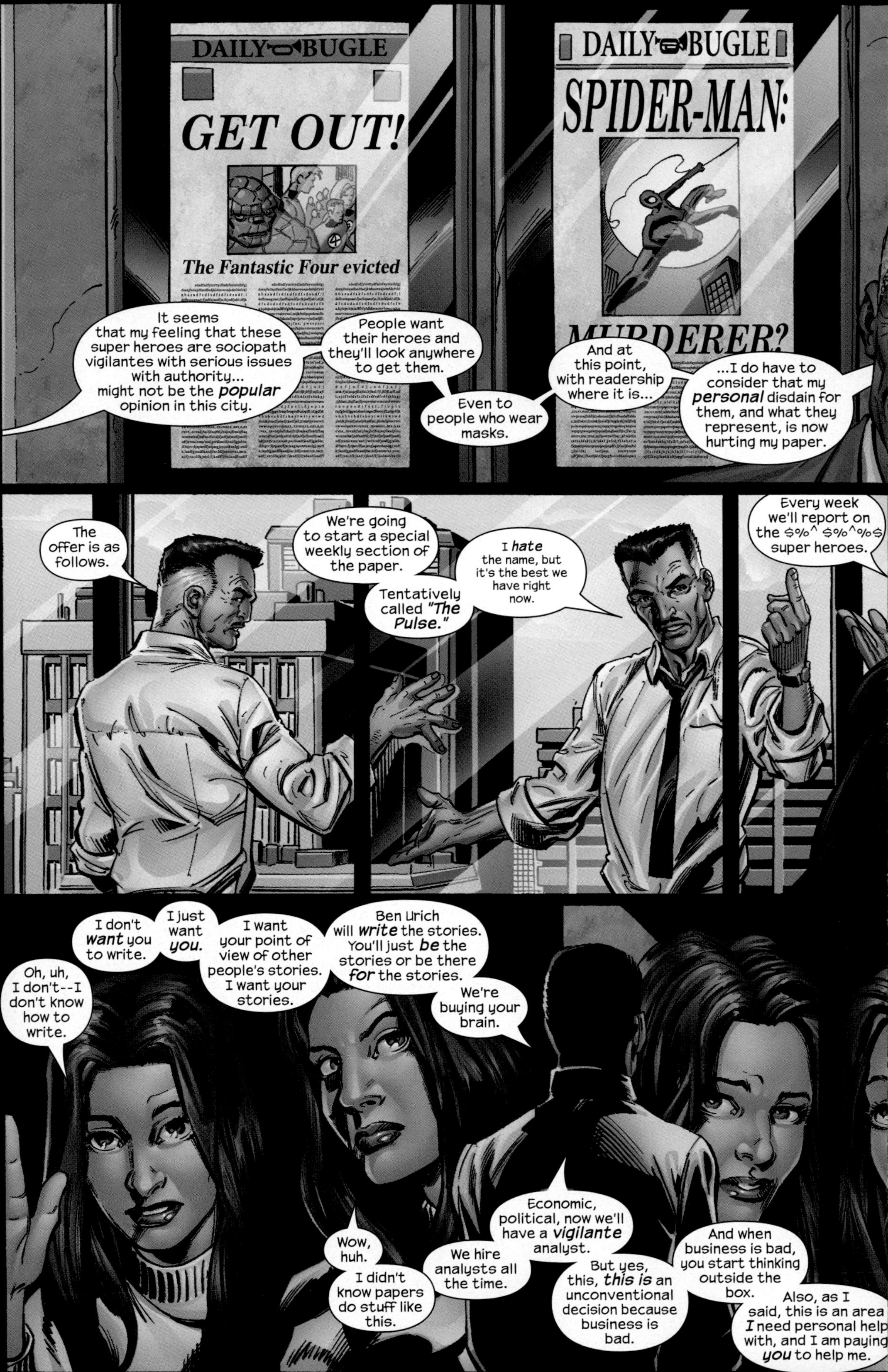
DAILY BUGLE
GET OUT!
The Fantastic Four evicted
DAILY BUGLE
SPIDER-MAN:
MURDERER?
It seems that my feeling that these super heroes are sociopath vigilantes with serious issues with authority... might not be the *popular* opinion in this city.
People want their heroes and they'll look anywhere to get them.
Even to people who wear masks.
And at this point, with readership where it is...
...I do have to consider that my *personal* disdain for them, and what they represent, is now hurting my paper.
The offer is as follows.
We're going to start a special weekly section of the paper.
Tentatively called *"The Pulse."*
I *hate* the name, but it's the best we have right now.
Every week we'll report on the $%^ $%^%$ super heroes.
Oh, uh, I don't--I don't know how to write.
I don't *want* you to write.
I just want *you.*
I want your point of view of other people's stories. I want your stories.
Ben Urich will *write* the stories. You'll just *be* the stories or be there *for* the stories.
We're buying your brain.
Wow, huh.
I didn't know papers do stuff like this.
We hire analysts all the time.
Economic, political, now we'll have a *vigilante* analyst.
But yes, this, *this is* an unconventional decision because business is bad.
And when business is bad, you start thinking outside the box.
Also, as I said, this is an area *I* need personal help with, and I am paying *you* to help me.

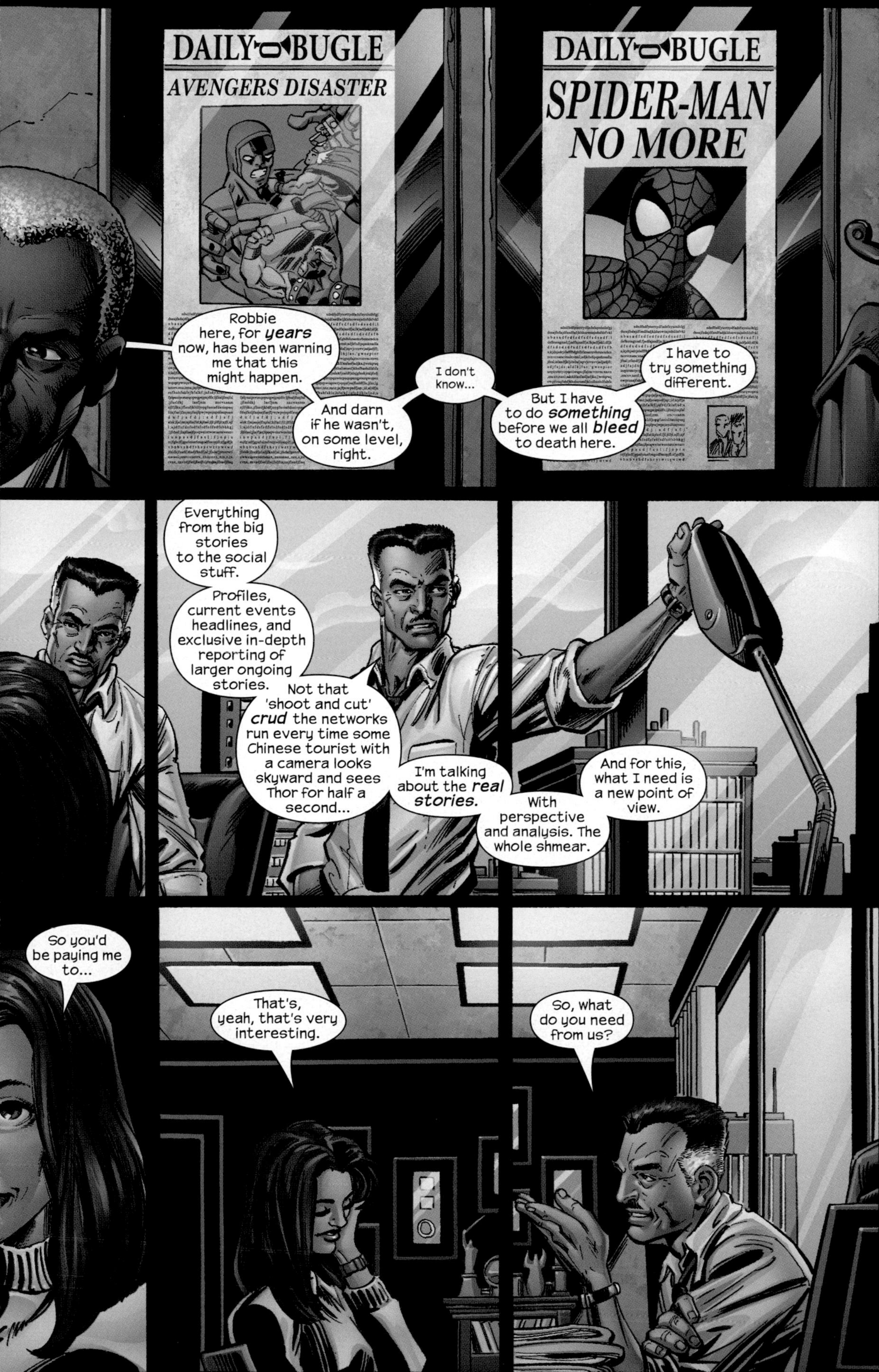
DAILY BUGLE
AVENGERS DISASTER
DAILY BUGLE
SPIDER-MAN NO MORE
Robbie here, for years now, has been warning me that this might happen.
And darn if he wasn't, on some level, right.
I don't know...
But I have to do something before we all bleed to death here.
I have to try something different.
Everything from the big stories to the social stuff.
Profiles, current events headlines, and exclusive in-depth reporting of larger ongoing stories.
Not that 'shoot and cut' crud the networks run every time some Chinese tourist with a camera looks skyward and sees Thor for half a second...
I'm talking about the real stories.
With perspective and analysis. The whole shmear.
And for this, what I need is a new point of view.
So you'd be paying me to...
That's, yeah, that's very interesting.
So, what do you need from us?

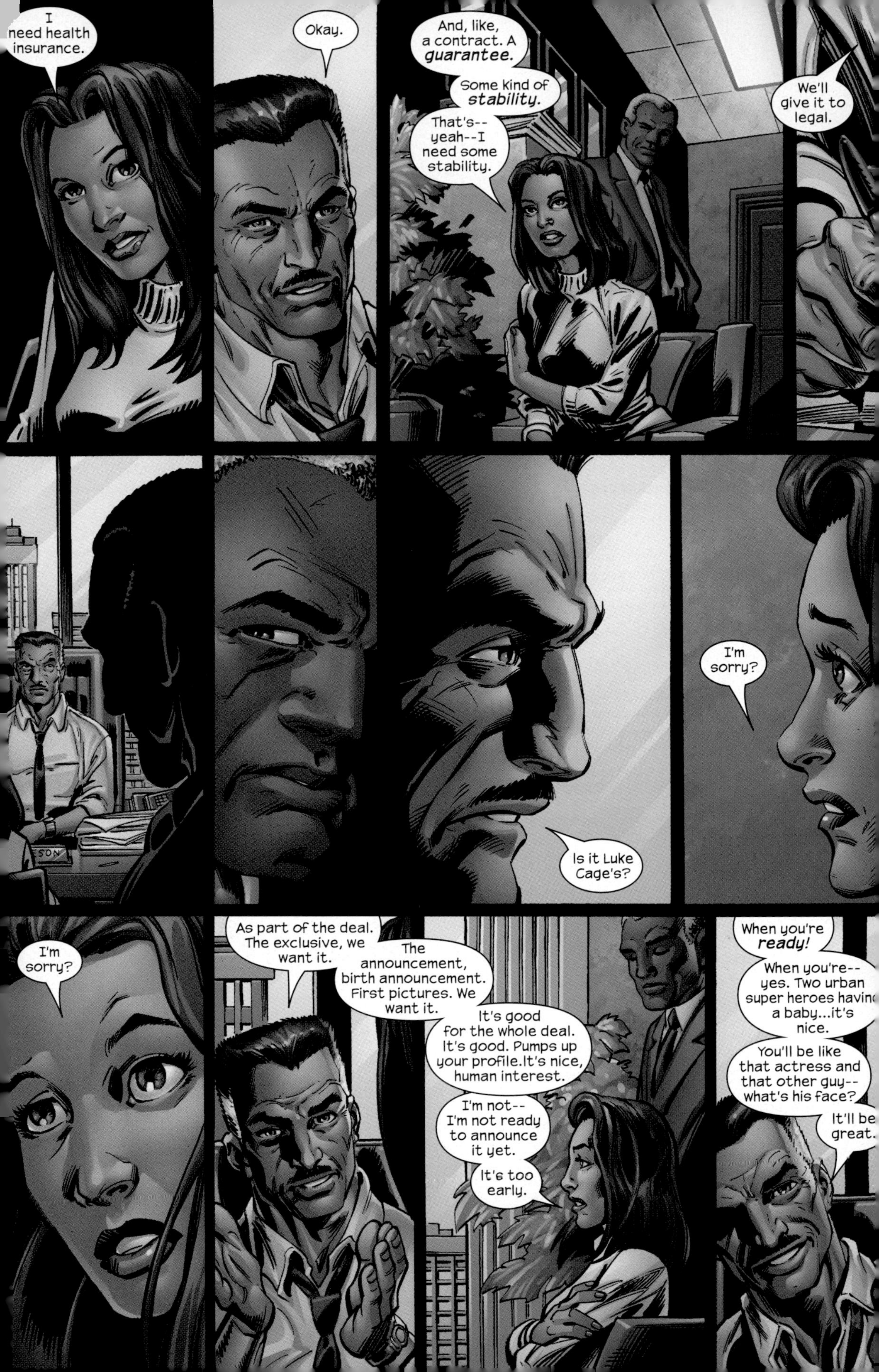
I need health insurance.
Okay.
And, like, a contract. A *guarantee.*
Some kind of *stability.*
That's-- yeah--I need some stability.
We'll give it to legal.
Is it Luke Cage's?
I'm sorry?
I'm sorry?
As part of the deal. The exclusive, we want it.
The announcement, birth announcement. First pictures. We want it.
It's good for the whole deal. It's good. Pumps up your profile.It's nice, human interest.
I'm not-- I'm not ready to announce it yet.
It's too early.
When you're *ready!*
When you're-- yes. Two urban super heroes havin a baby...it's nice.
You'll be like that actress and that other guy-- what's his face?
It'll be great.

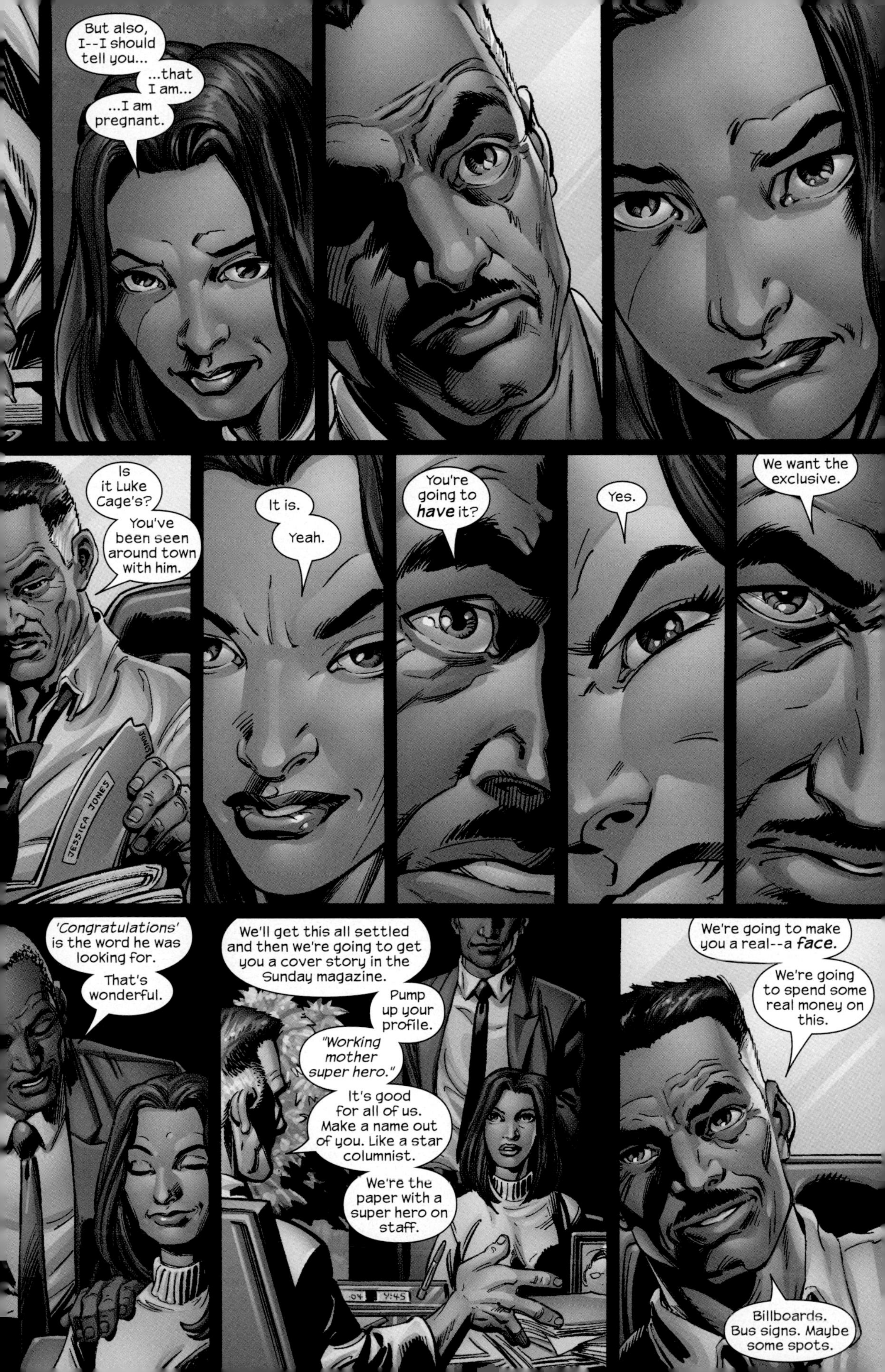
But also, I--I should tell you...
...that I am...
...I am pregnant.
Is it Luke Cage's?
You've been seen around town with him.
JESSICA JONES
It is.
Yeah.
You're going to *have* it?
Yes.
We want the exclusive.
'Congratulations' is the word he was looking for.
That's wonderful.
We'll get this all settled and then we're going to get you a cover story in the Sunday magazine.
Pump up your profile.
"Working mother super hero."
It's good for all of us. Make a name out of you. Like a star columnist.
We're the paper with a super hero on staff.
We're going to make you a real--a *face.*
We're going to spend some real money on this.
Billboards. Bus signs. Maybe some spots.

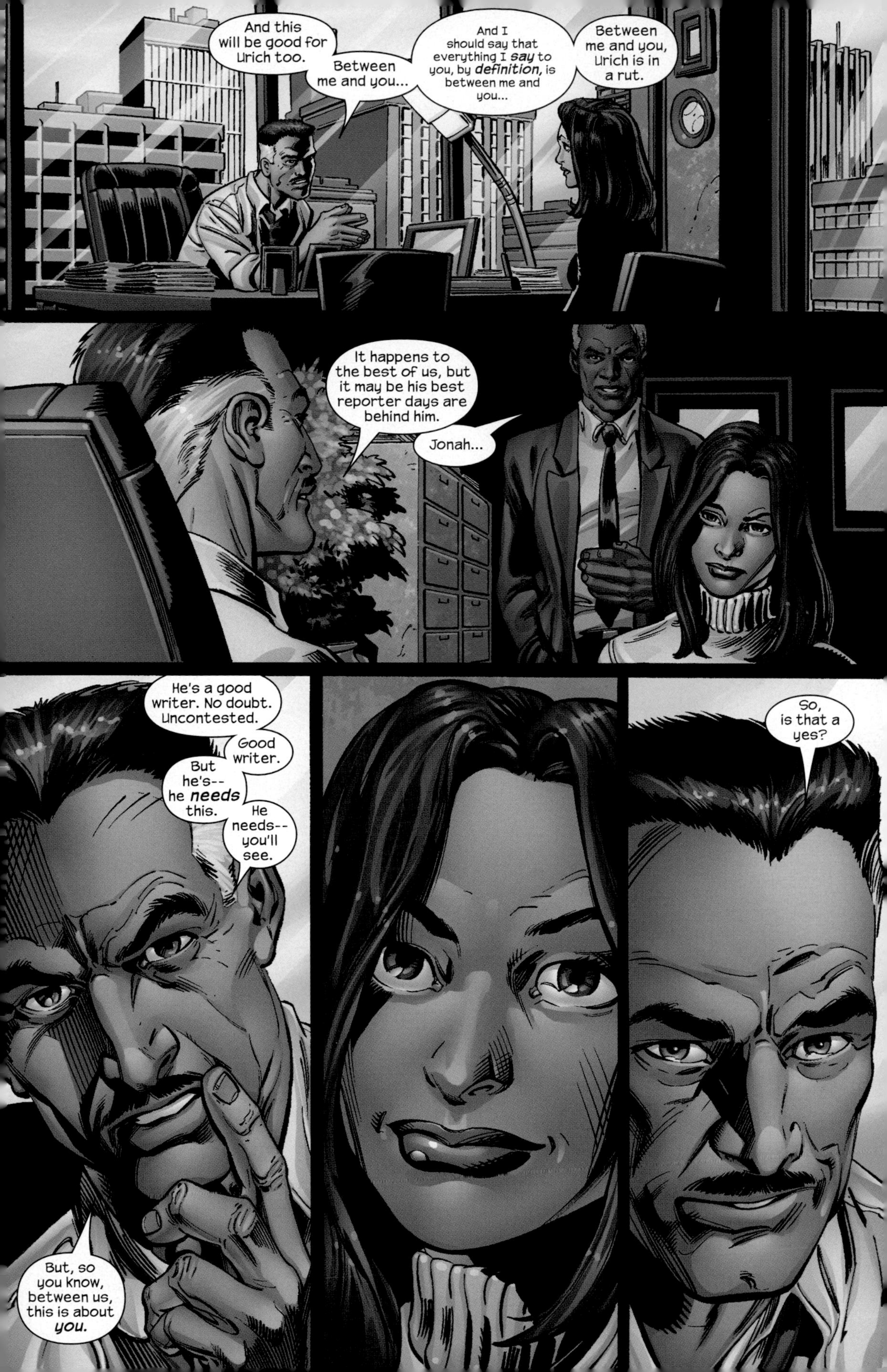
And this will be good for Urich too.
Between me and you...
And I should say that everything I *say* to you, by *definition,* is between me and you...
Between me and you, Urich is in a rut.
It happens to the best of us, but it may be his best reporter days are behind him.
Jonah...
He's a good writer. No doubt. Uncontested.
Good writer.
But he's-- he *needs* this.
He needs-- you'll see.
But, so you know, between us, this is about *you.*
So, is that a yes?

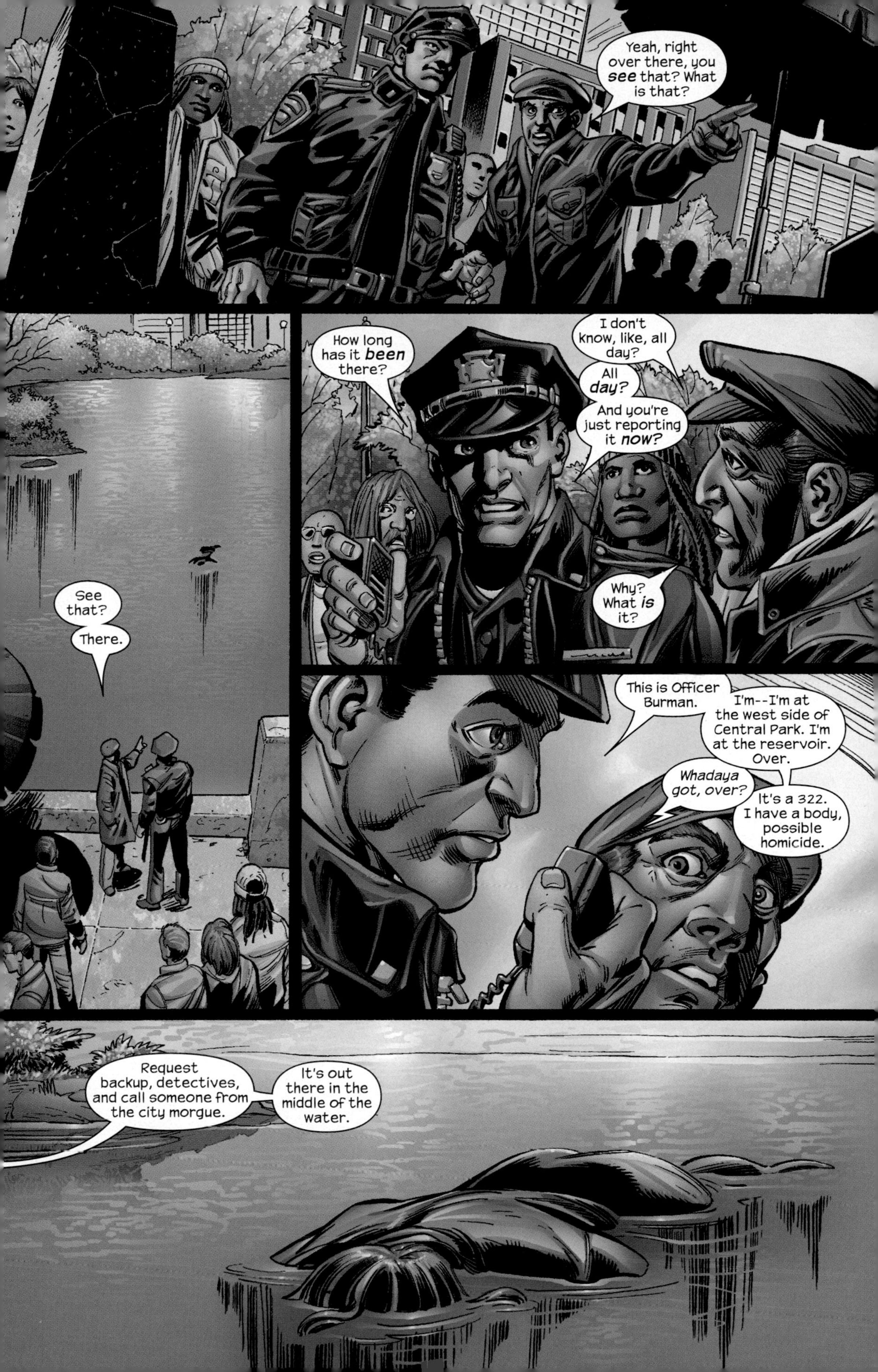
Yeah, right over there, you *see* that? What is that?
See that?
There.
How long has it *been* there?
I don't know, like, all day?
All *day?*
And you're just reporting it *now?*
Why? What *is* it?
This is Officer Burman.
I'm--I'm at the west side of Central Park. I'm at the reservoir. Over.
Whadaya got, over?
It's a 322. I have a body, possible homicide.
Request backup, detectives, and call someone from the city morgue.
It's out there in the middle of the water.

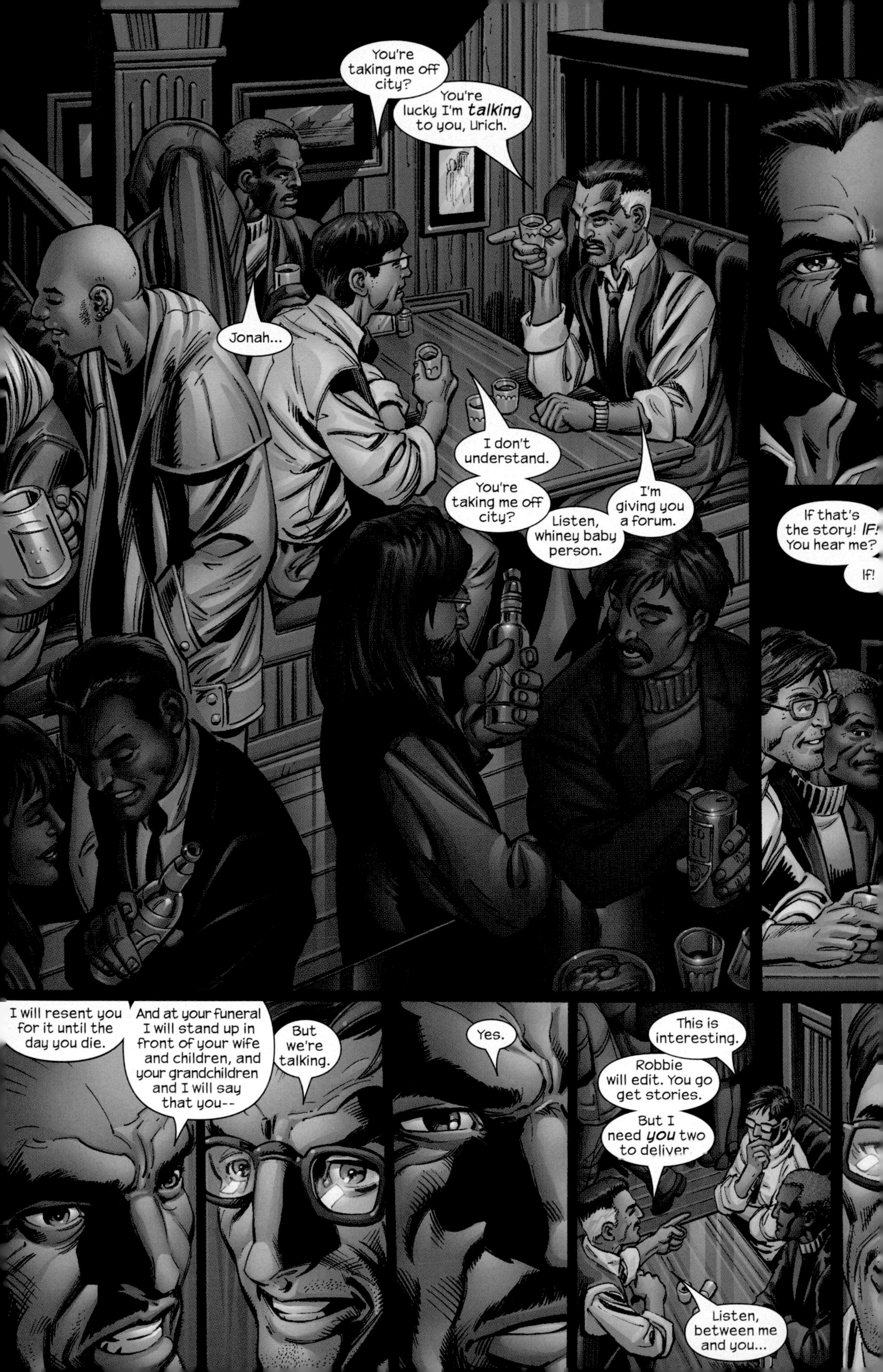
You're taking me off city?
You're lucky I'm ***talking*** to you, Urich.
Jonah...
I don't understand.
You're taking me off city?
I'm giving you a forum.
Listen, whiney baby person.
If that's the story! *IF!* You hear me?
If!
I will resent you for it until the day you die.
And at your funeral I will stand up in front of your wife and children, and your grandchildren and I will say that you--
But we're talking.
Yes.
This is interesting.
Robbie will edit. You go get stories.
But I need ***you*** two to deliver.
Listen, between me and you...

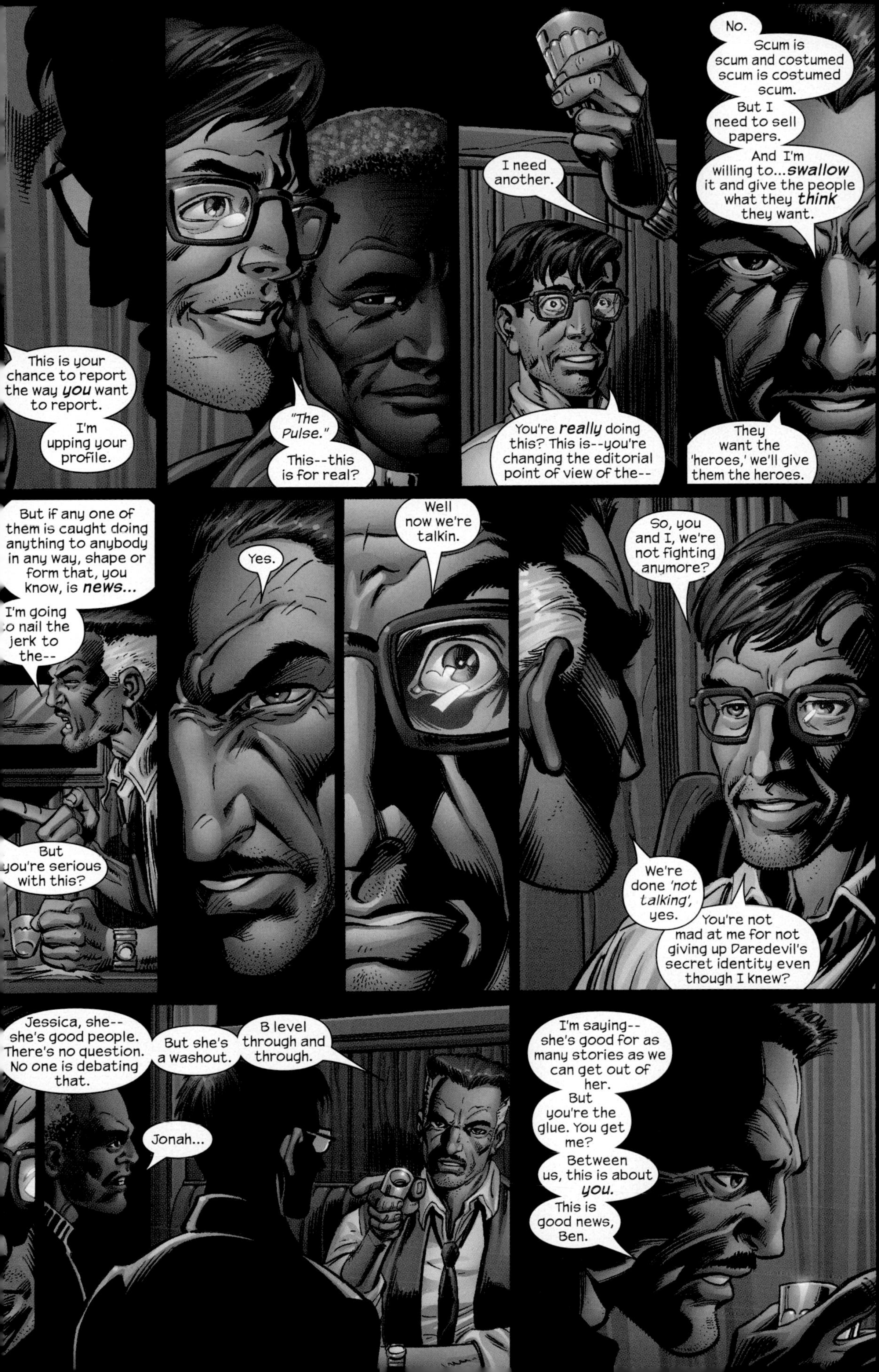
This is your chance to report the way *you* want to report.
I'm upping your profile.
"The Pulse."
This--this is for real?
I need another.
You're *really* doing this? This is--you're changing the editorial point of view of the--
No.
Scum is scum and costumed scum is costumed scum.
But I need to sell papers.
And I'm willing to...*swallow* it and give the people what they *think* they want.
They want the 'heroes,' we'll give them the heroes.
But if any one of them is caught doing anything to anybody in any way, shape or form that, you know, is *news...*
I'm going to nail the jerk to the--
But you're serious with this?
Yes.
Well now we're talkin.
So, you and I, we're not fighting anymore?
We're done *'not talking'*, yes.
You're not mad at me for not giving up Daredevil's secret identity even though I knew?
Jessica, she--she's good people. There's no question. No one is debating that.
But she's a washout.
B level through and through.
Jonah...
I'm saying--she's good for as many stories as we can get out of her.
But you're the glue. You get me?
Between us, this is about *you.*
This is good news, Ben.

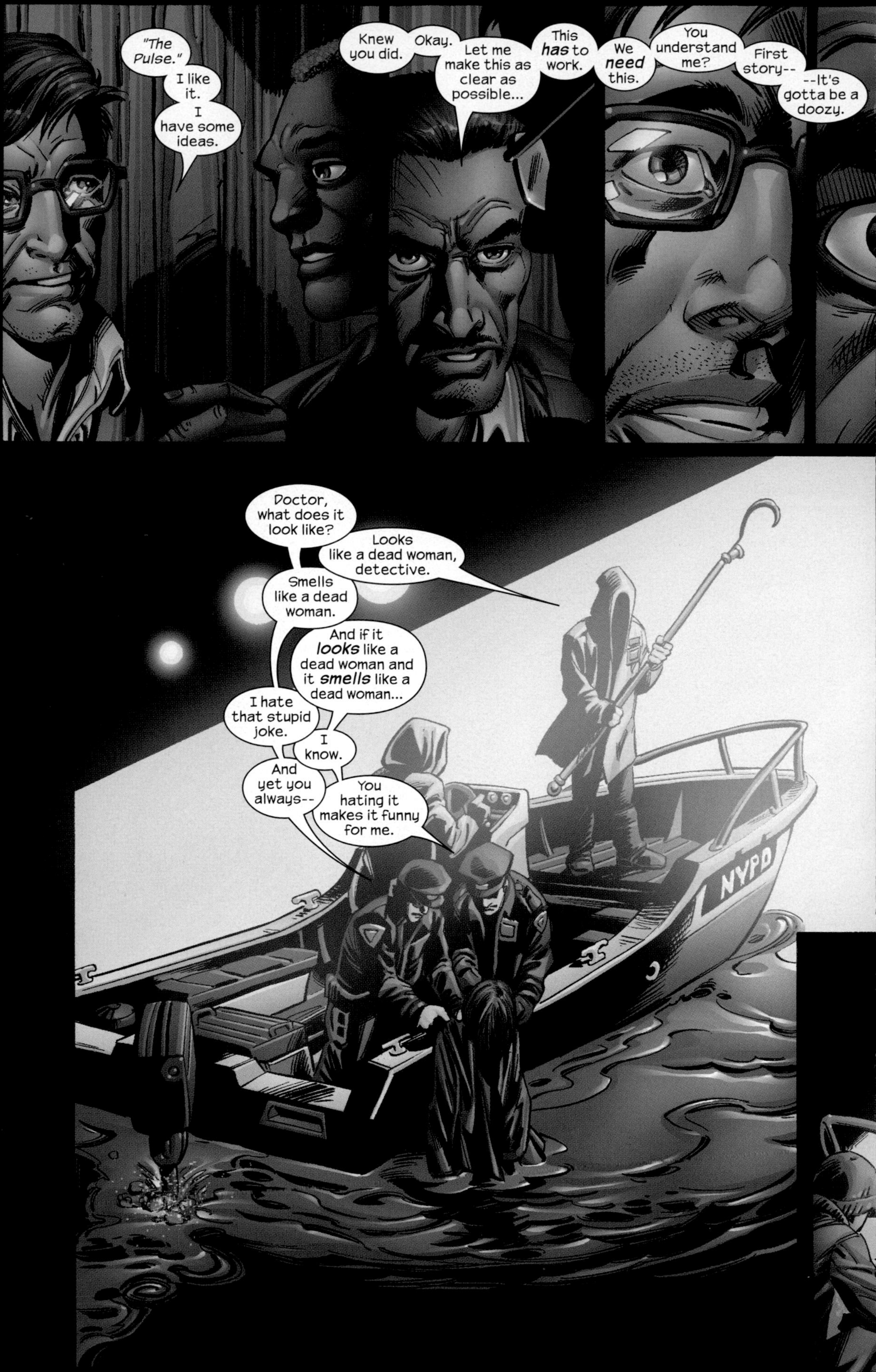
"The Pulse."
I like it.
I have some ideas.
Knew you did.
Okay.
Let me make this as clear as possible...
This *has* to work.
We *need* this.
You understand me?
First story--
--It's gotta be a doozy.
Doctor, what does it look like?
Looks like a dead woman, detective.
Smells like a dead woman.
And if it *looks* like a dead woman and it *smells* like a dead woman...
I hate that stupid joke.
I know.
And yet you always--
You hating it makes it funny for me.
NYPD

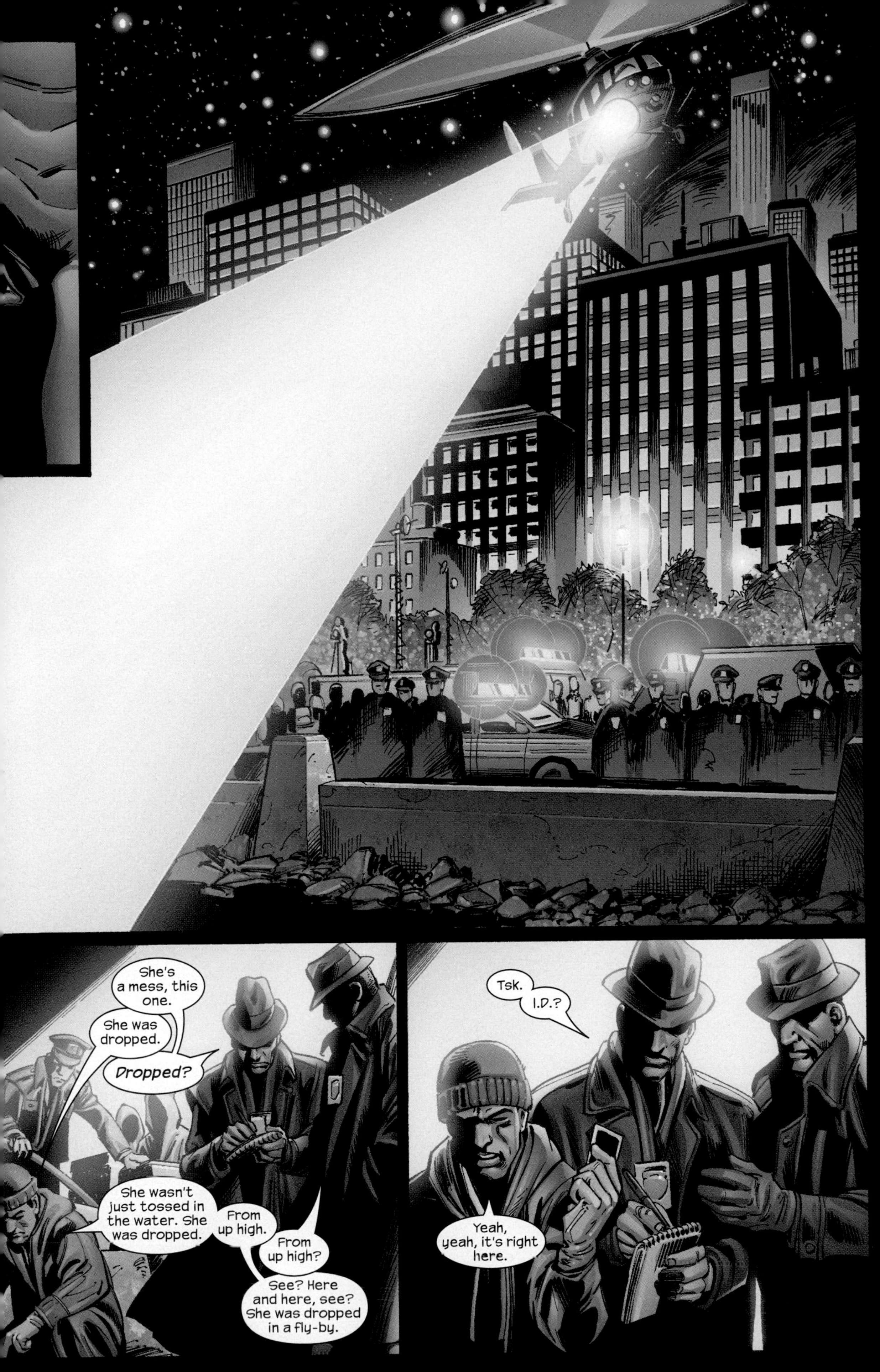
She's a mess, this one.
She was dropped.
Dropped?
She wasn't just tossed in the water. She was dropped.
From up high.
From up high?
See? Here and here, see? She was dropped in a fly-by.
Tsk.
I.D.?
Yeah, yeah, it's right here.

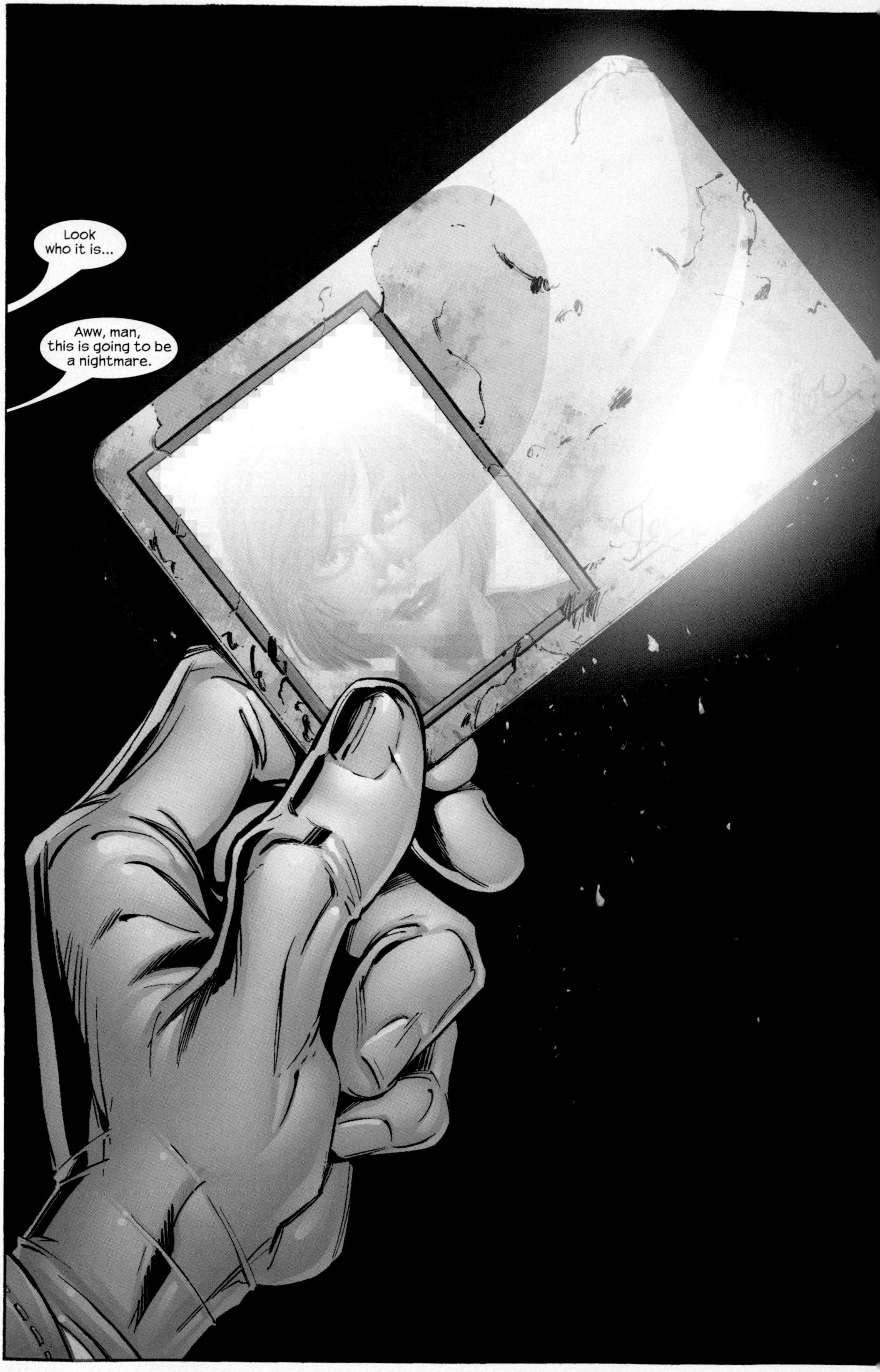
Look who it is...
Aww, man, this is going to be a nightmare.

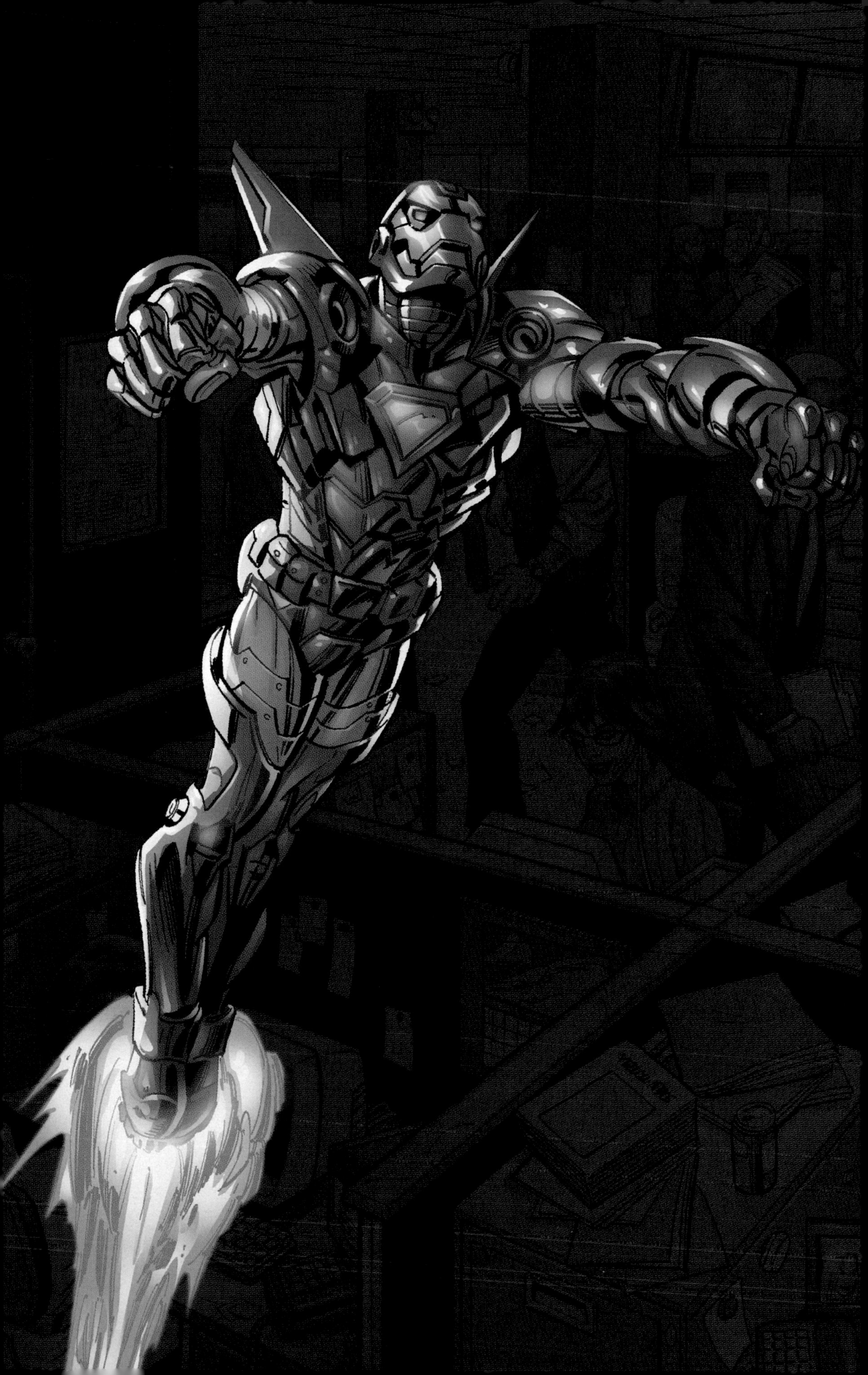

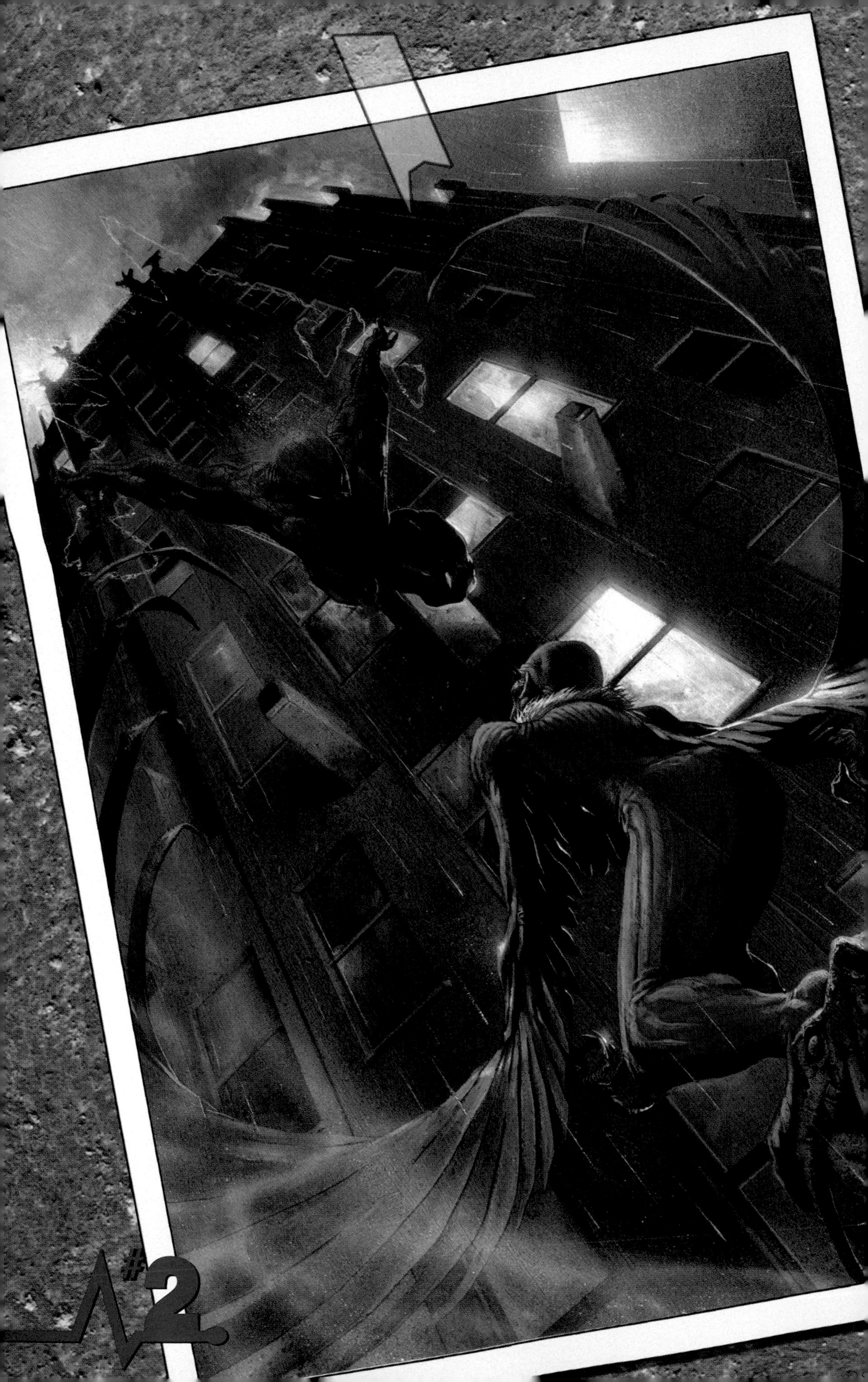
#2

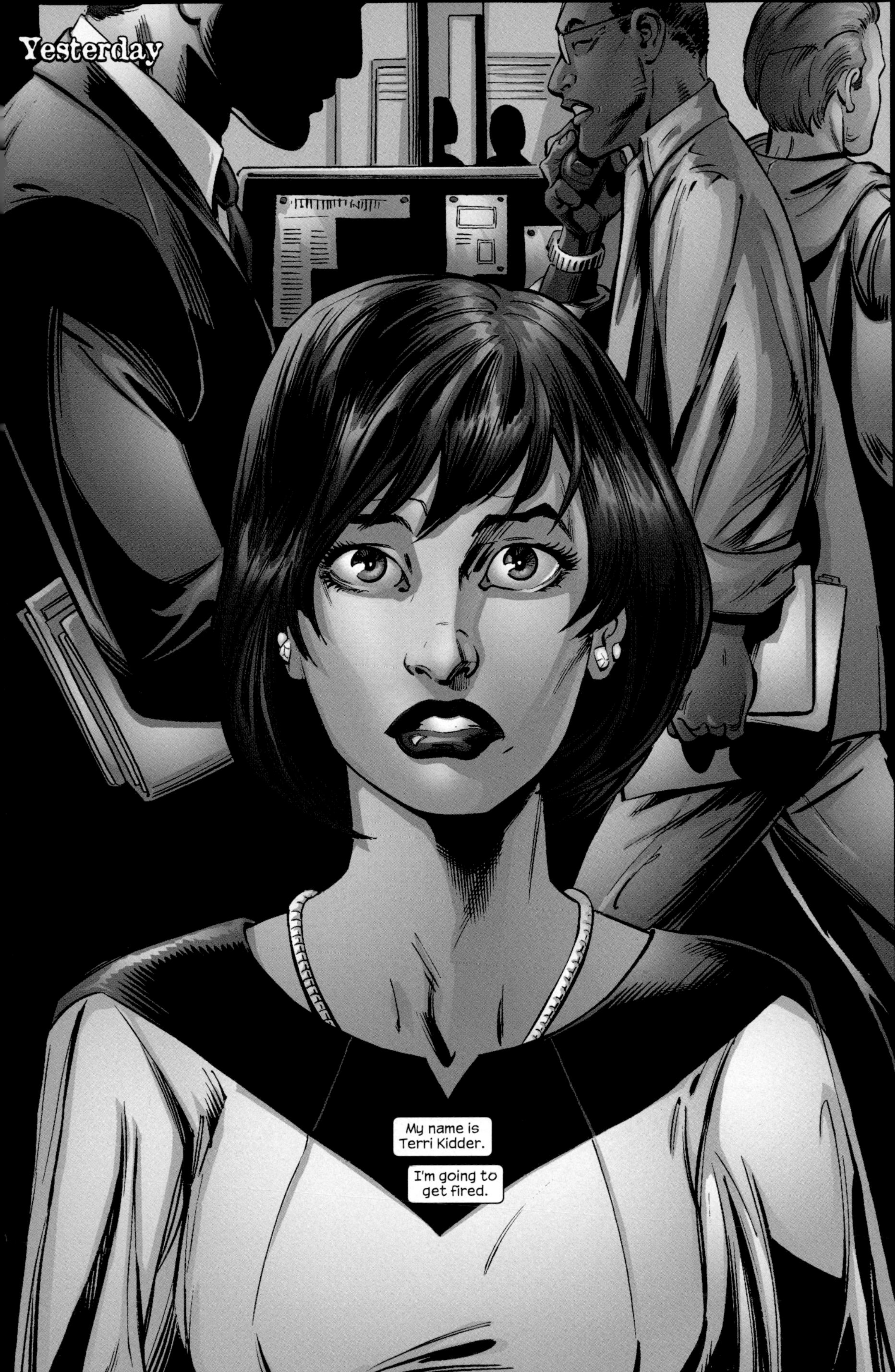
Yesterday
My name is Terri Kidder.
I'm going to get fired.

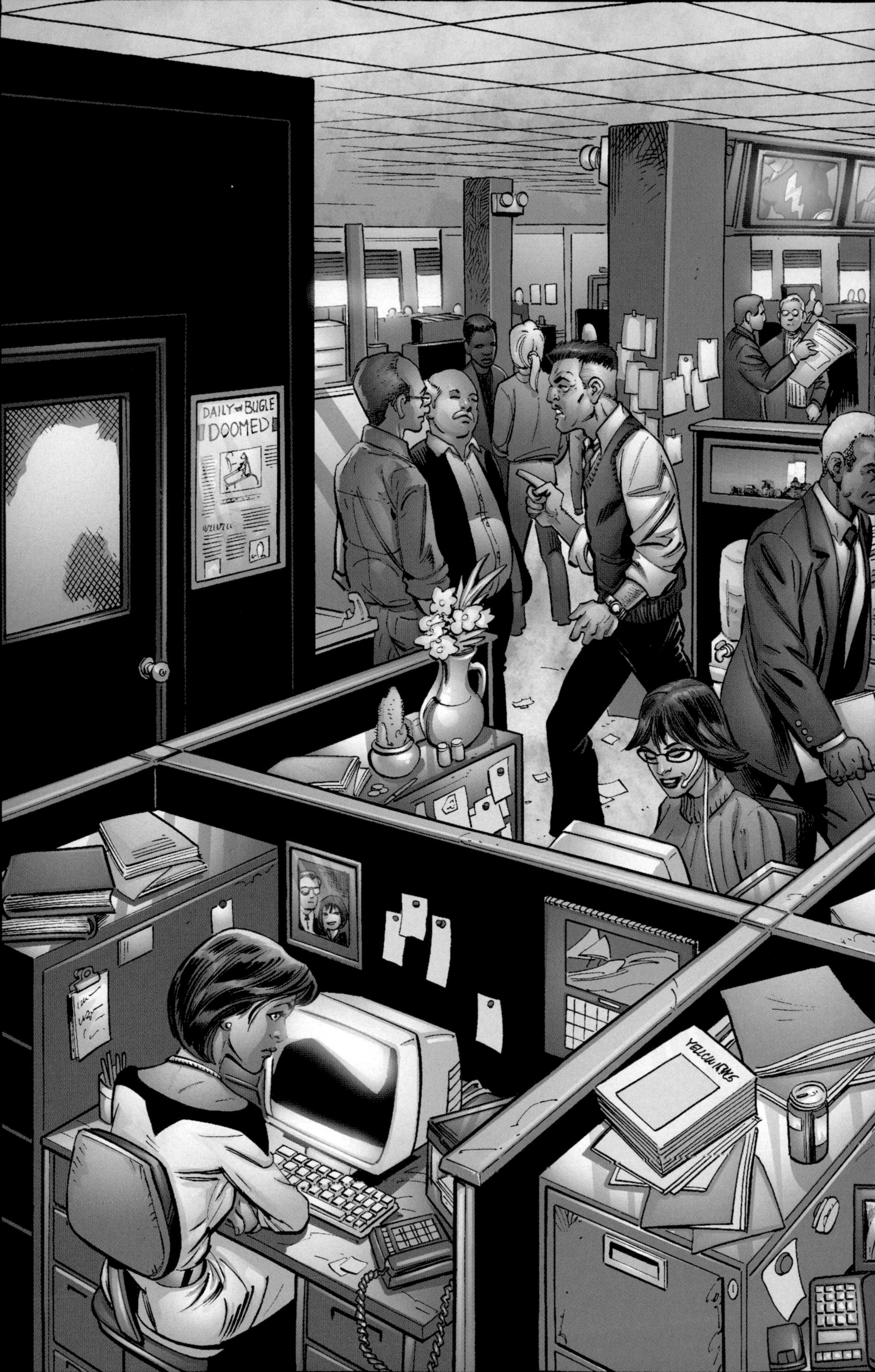
DAILY BUGLE
DOOMED

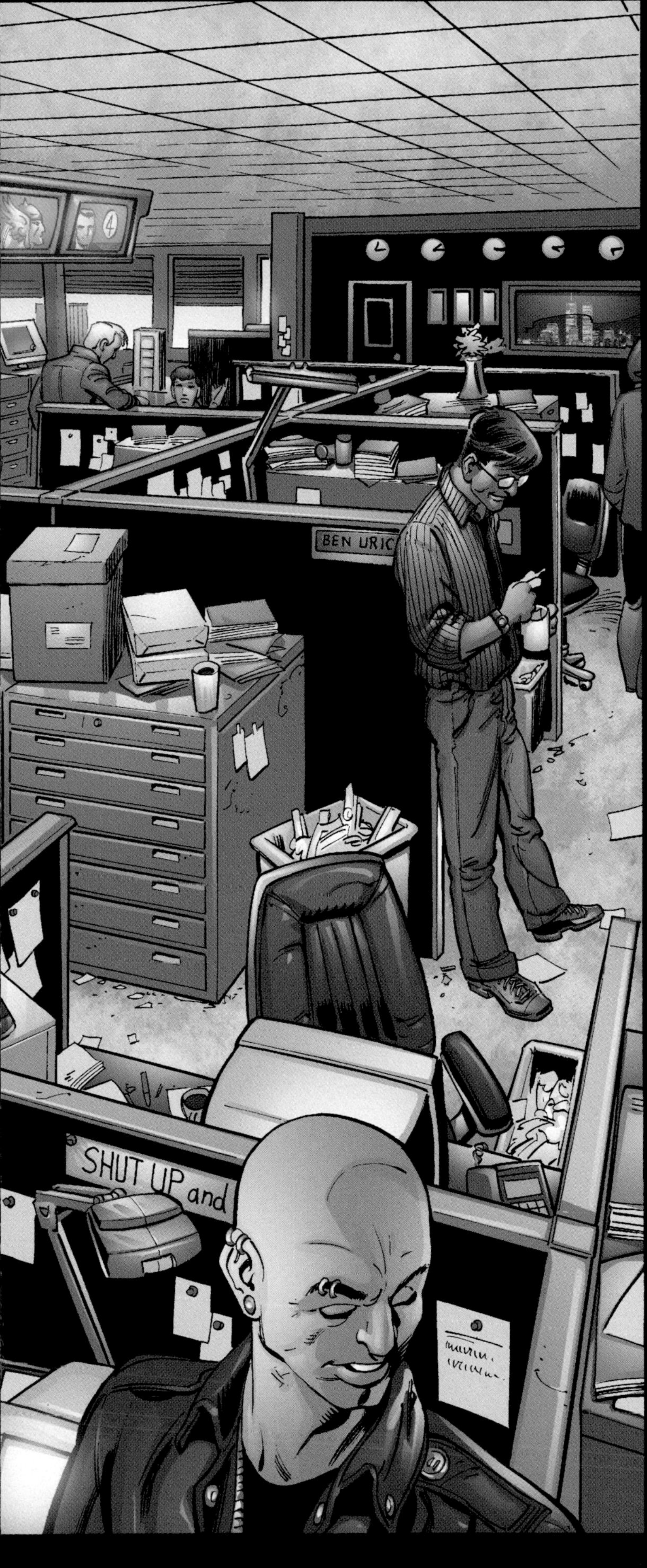
BEN URIC
SHUT UP and

I am.

I can feel it.

It's three o' clock
and I have no story.

I need a story. That's
what this stupid job is.
It's ***all*** it is.

Finding a story. Getting
a story. Feeding a story.
Making a story.

Four kabillion
people in this
city.

Every one of them cheating, robbing,
killing, stabbing, someone out of
something somewhere...and I have
no story!

Half the people in this ***room*** are
probably closet ***mutants*** and
I have no story.

I've been here two weeks
and I haven't found one story
worth publishing.

But I have to find ***something***
or I am out on my toosh by Friday.

No joke. I am
so gone it's not
even funny.

But I've never worked for a paper like
this. My last job was at one of those
big, old-fashioned, great metropolitan
newspapers...

...and if you're, basically, ***everyone*** I
know...you're asking: "Why on earth
would you leave a job at a big,
respected newspaper to come work
at a tabloid like the frakakta Daily Bugle?'

And by tabloid I'm not talking about
'Princess Di's head is kidnapped by
Aliens' or--or 'Reed Richards is sleeping
with Madonna,' no.

'Tabloid' gets a crap reputation
because people don't know what
the ***word*** means.

Tabloid is the format. The folded
newspaper format. And it's the only
thing we have in common with those
pieces of rag trip.

No. This is a real tabloid newspaper.

And I ***wanted*** to work here...in
New York City. For exactly ***this***
kind of paper.

My other job felt shallow and--and
uninspired. Look at this place! Look
how alive it is.

We are the voice of the ***people.***
We're the voice of the common man.
The commuter. The coffee gut.

We speak for ***everyone*** in a language
they want and understand.

Me personally? No. I'm not speaking
for ***anyone*** because I have ***no story!***

I'm just not used to the
politics of this place yet.

I mean, ***every*** place has
them, the politics. I just don't
understand how this place works.

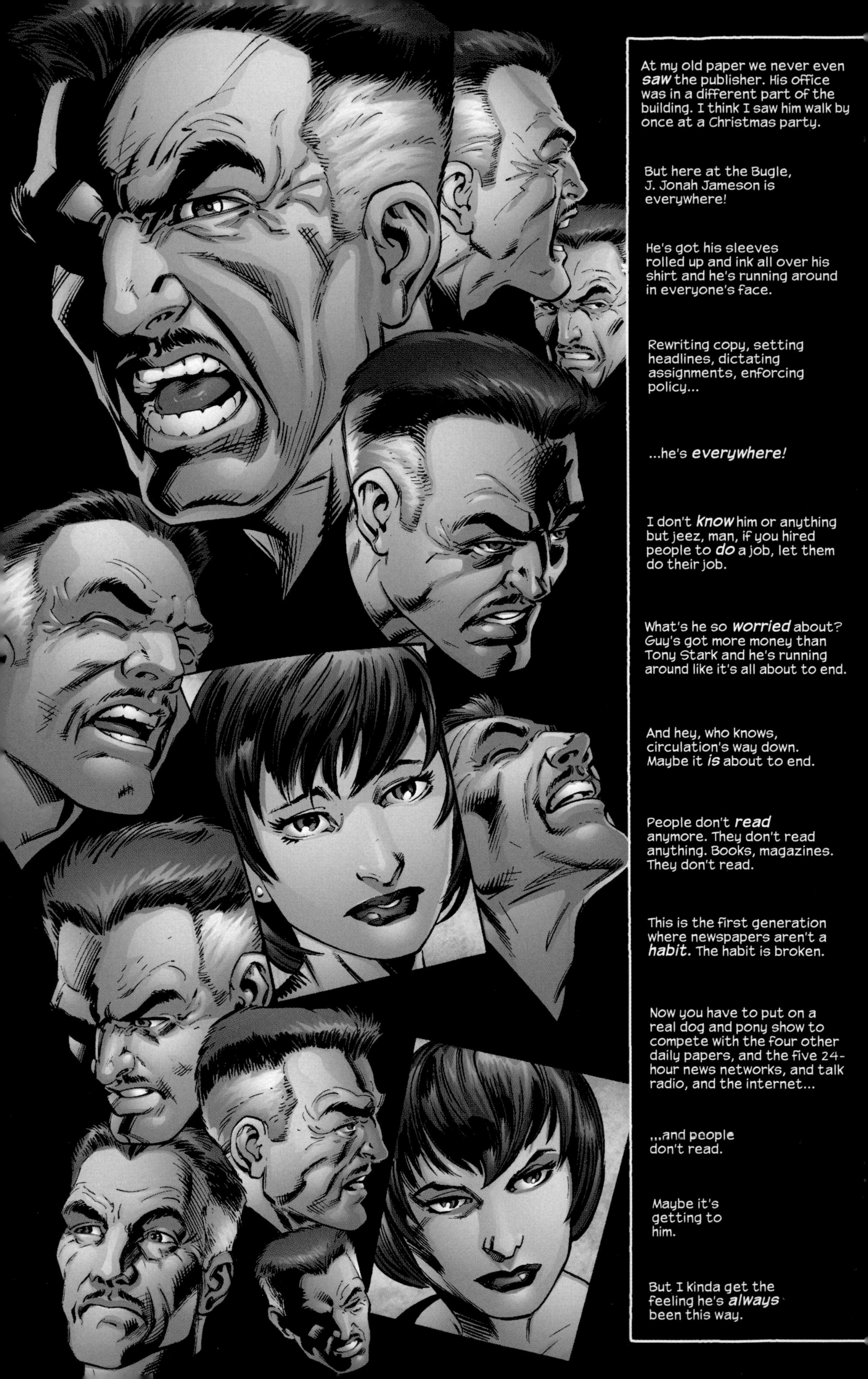
At my old paper we never even saw the publisher. His office was in a different part of the building. I think I saw him walk by once at a Christmas party.
But here at the Bugle, J. Jonah Jameson is everywhere!
He's got his sleeves rolled up and ink all over his shirt and he's running around in everyone's face.
Rewriting copy, setting headlines, dictating assignments, enforcing policy...
...he's everywhere!
I don't know him or anything but jeez, man, if you hired people to do a job, let them do their job.
What's he so worried about? Guy's got more money than Tony Stark and he's running around like it's all about to end.
And hey, who knows, circulation's way down. Maybe it is about to end.
People don't read anymore. They don't read anything. Books, magazines. They don't read.
This is the first generation where newspapers aren't a habit. The habit is broken.
Now you have to put on a real dog and pony show to compete with the four other daily papers, and the five 24-hour news networks, and talk radio, and the internet...
...and people don't read.
Maybe it's getting to him.
But I kinda get the feeling he's always been this way.

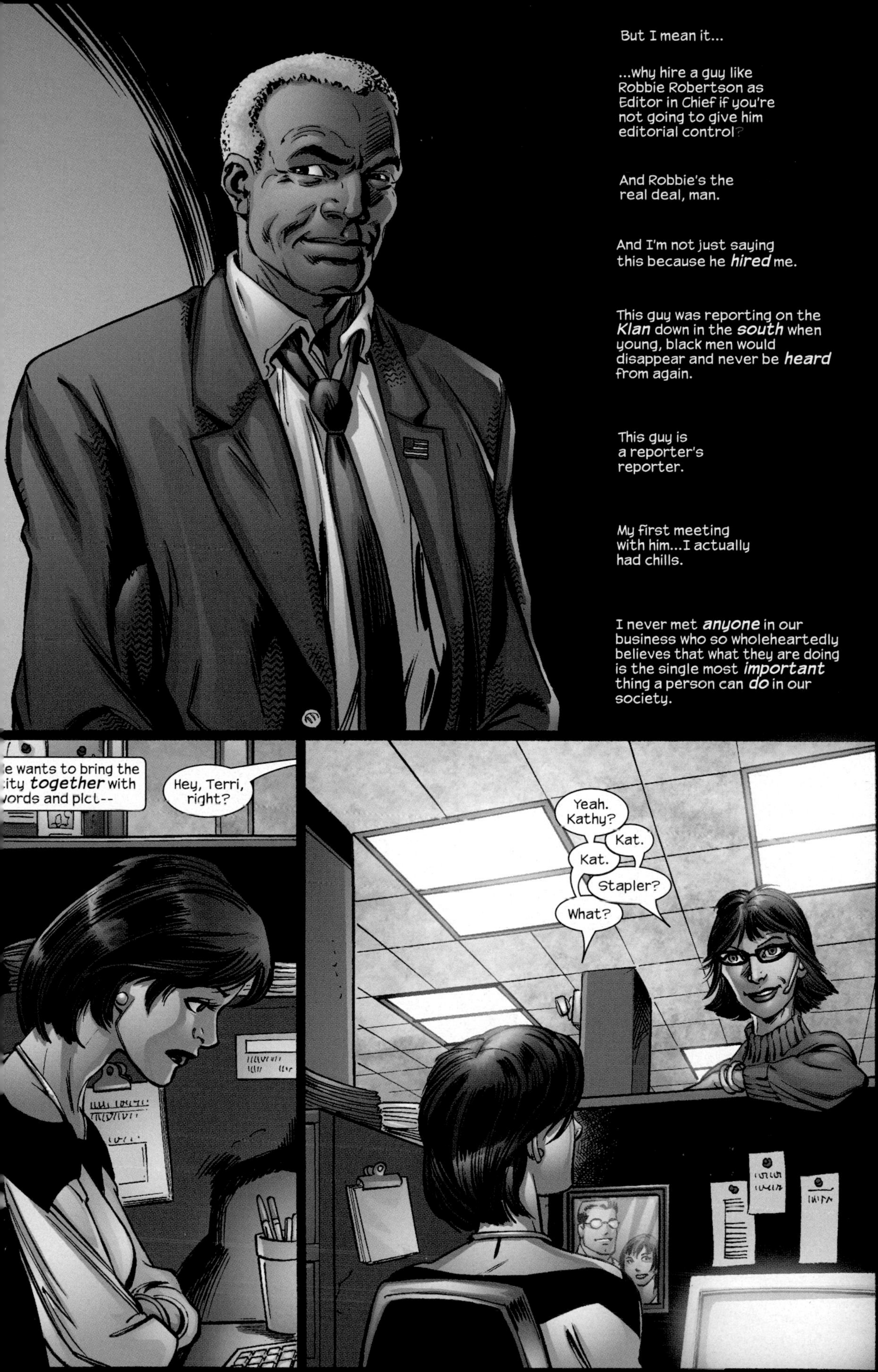
But I mean it...
...why hire a guy like Robbie Robertson as Editor in Chief if you're not going to give him editorial control?
And Robbie's the real deal, man.
And I'm not just saying this because he *hired* me.
This guy was reporting on the *Klan* down in the *south* when young, black men would disappear and never be *heard* from again.
This guy is a reporter's reporter.
My first meeting with him...I actually had chills.
I never met *anyone* in our business who so wholeheartedly believes that what they are doing is the single most *important* thing a person can *do* in our society.
e wants to bring the ity *together* with vords and pict--
Hey, Terri, right?
Yeah. Kathy?
Kat.
Kat.
Stapler?
What?

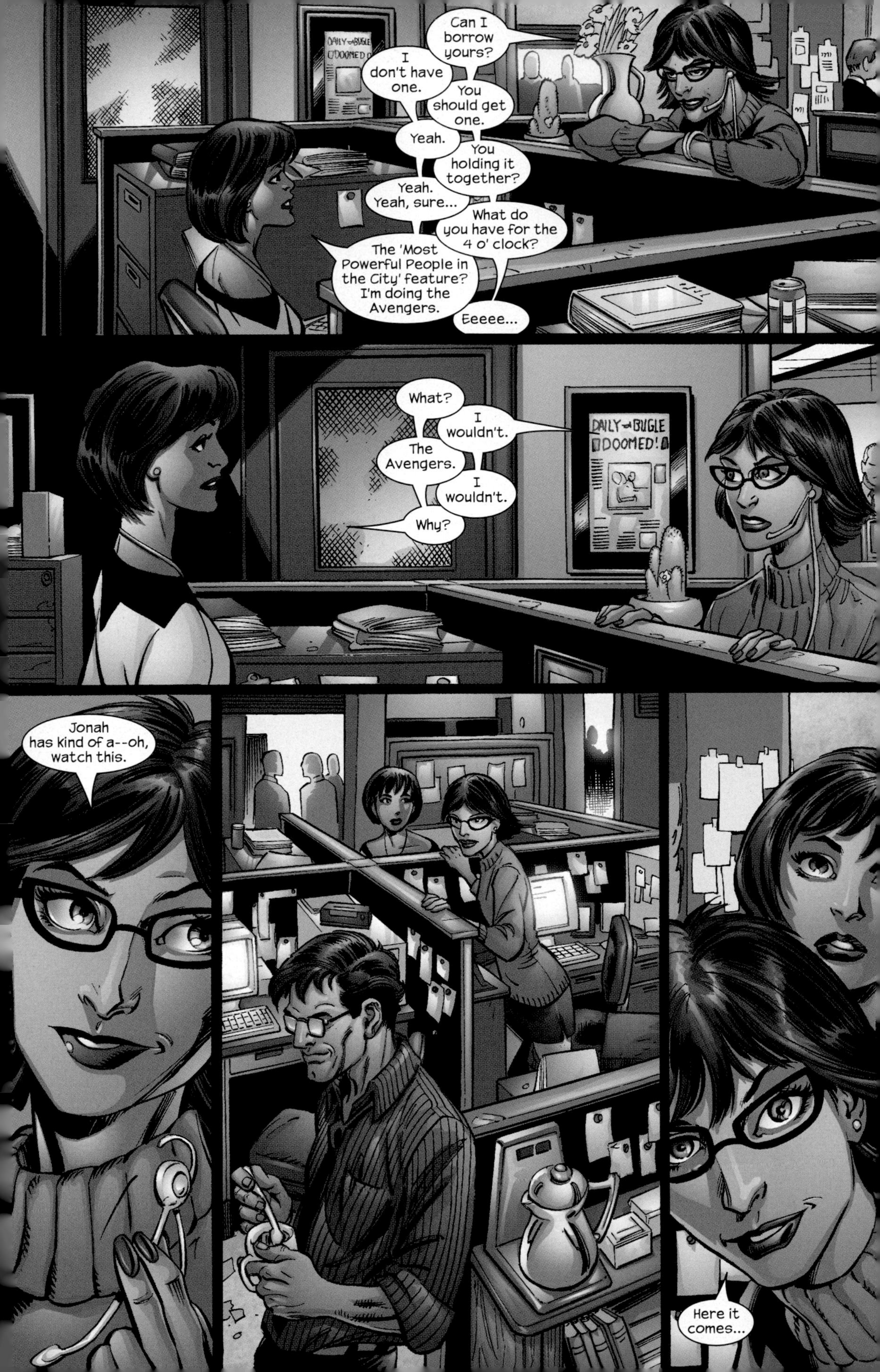

Can I borrow yours?
I don't have one.
You should get one.
Yeah.
You holding it together?
Yeah. Yeah, sure...
What do you have for the 4 o' clock?
The 'Most Powerful People in the City' feature? I'm doing the Avengers.
Eeeee...
DAILY BUGLE
DOOMED!
What?
I wouldn't.
The Avengers.
I wouldn't.
Why?
Jonah has kind of a--oh, watch this.
Here it comes...

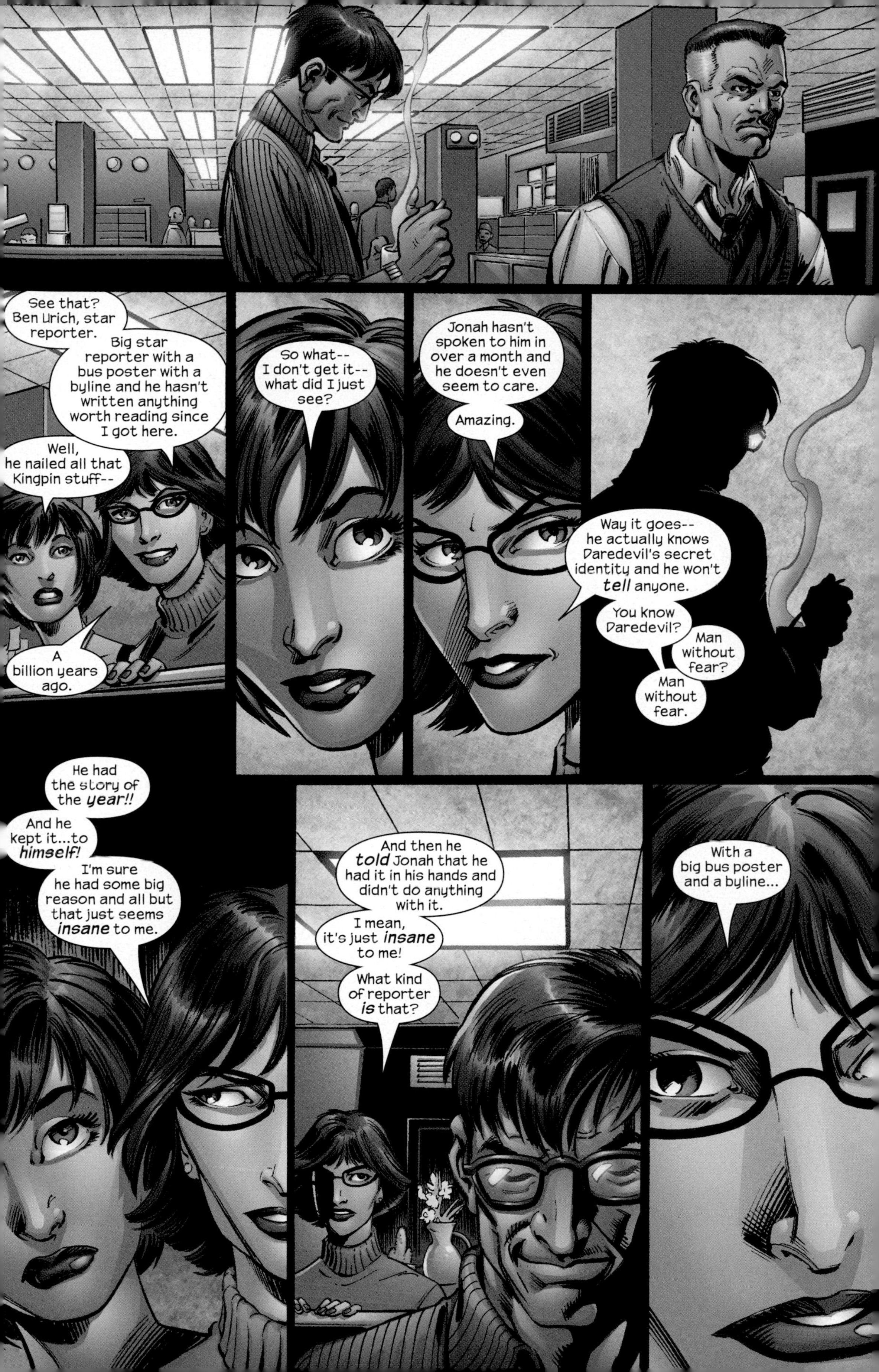
See that? Ben Urich, star reporter.
Big star reporter with a bus poster with a byline and he hasn't written anything worth reading since I got here.
Well, he nailed all that Kingpin stuff--
A billion years ago.
So what-- I don't get it-- what did I just see?
Jonah hasn't spoken to him in over a month and he doesn't even seem to care.
Amazing.
Way it goes-- he actually knows Daredevil's secret identity and he won't tell anyone.
You know Daredevil?
Man without fear?
Man without fear.
He had the story of the year!!
And he kept it...to himself!
I'm sure he had some big reason and all but that just seems insane to me.
And then he told Jonah that he had it in his hands and didn't do anything with it.
I mean, it's just insane to me!
What kind of reporter is that?
With a big bus poster and a byline...

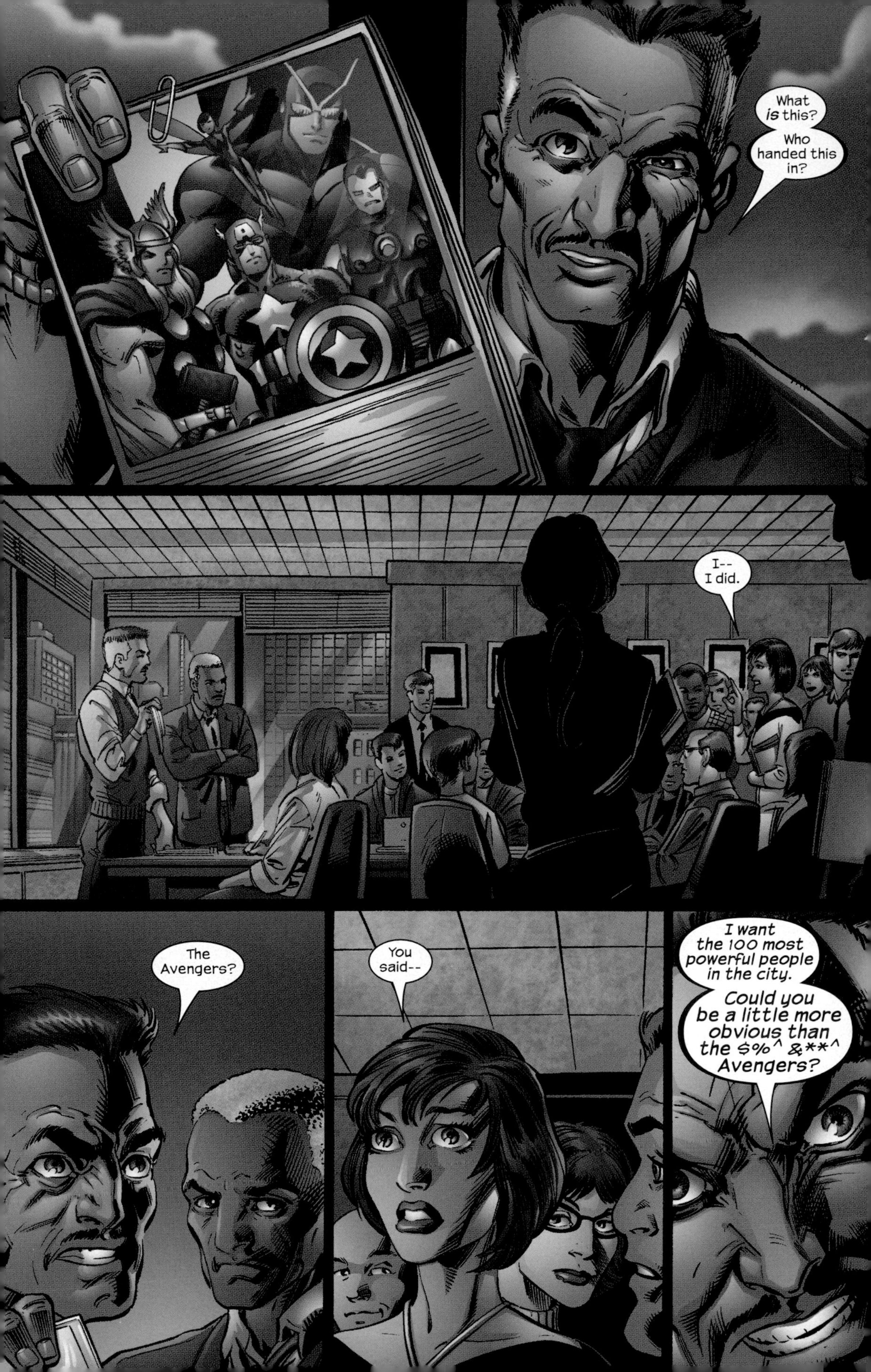
What *is* this?
Who handed this in?
I-- I did.
The Avengers?
You said--
I want the 100 most powerful people in the city.
Could you be a little more obvious than the $%^ &**^ Avengers?

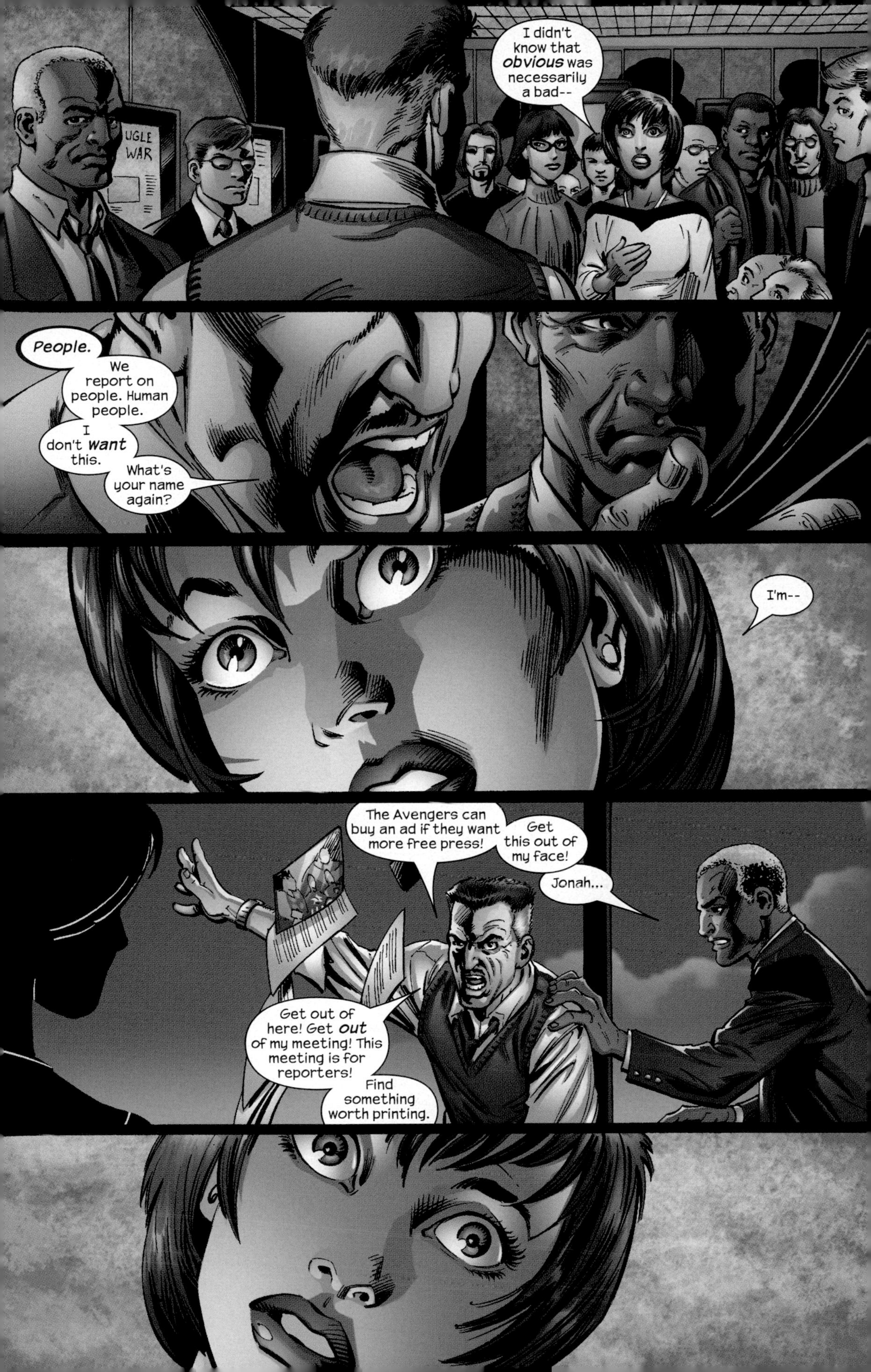

I didn't know that obvious was necessarily a bad--
People.
We report on people. Human people.
I don't want this.
What's your name again?
I'm--
The Avengers can buy an ad if they want more free press!
Get this out of my face!
Jonah...
Get out of here! Get out of my meeting! This meeting is for reporters!
Find something worth printing.

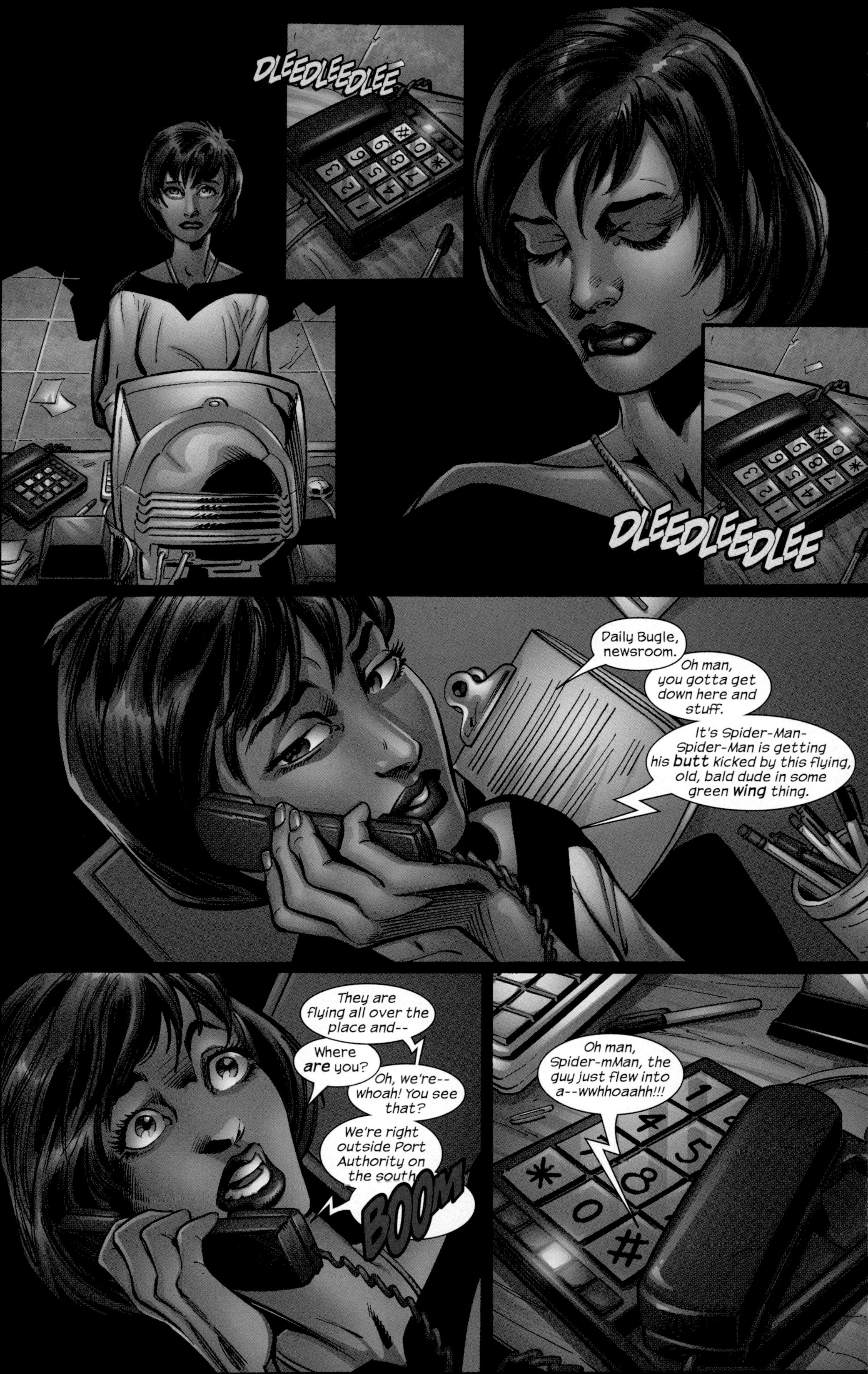
DLEEDLEEDLEE
DLEEDLEEDLEE
Daily Bugle, newsroom.
Oh man, you gotta get down here and stuff.
It's Spider-Man- Spider-Man is getting his **butt** kicked by this flying, old, bald dude in some green **wing** thing.
They are flying all over the place and--
Where **are** you?
Oh, we're-- whoah! You see that?
We're right outside Port Authority on the south
BOOM
Oh man, Spider-mMan, the guy just flew into a--wwhhoaahh!!!

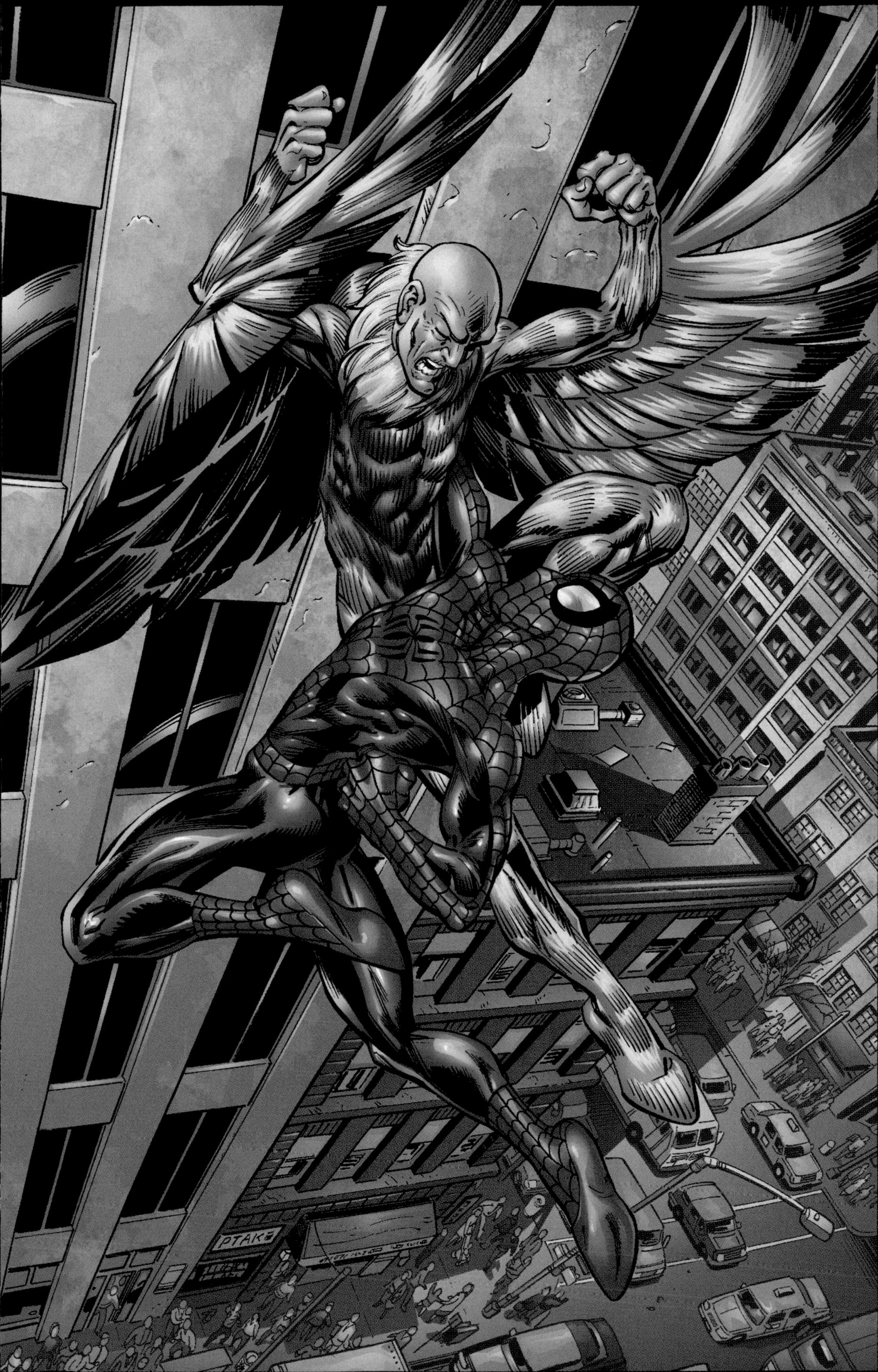

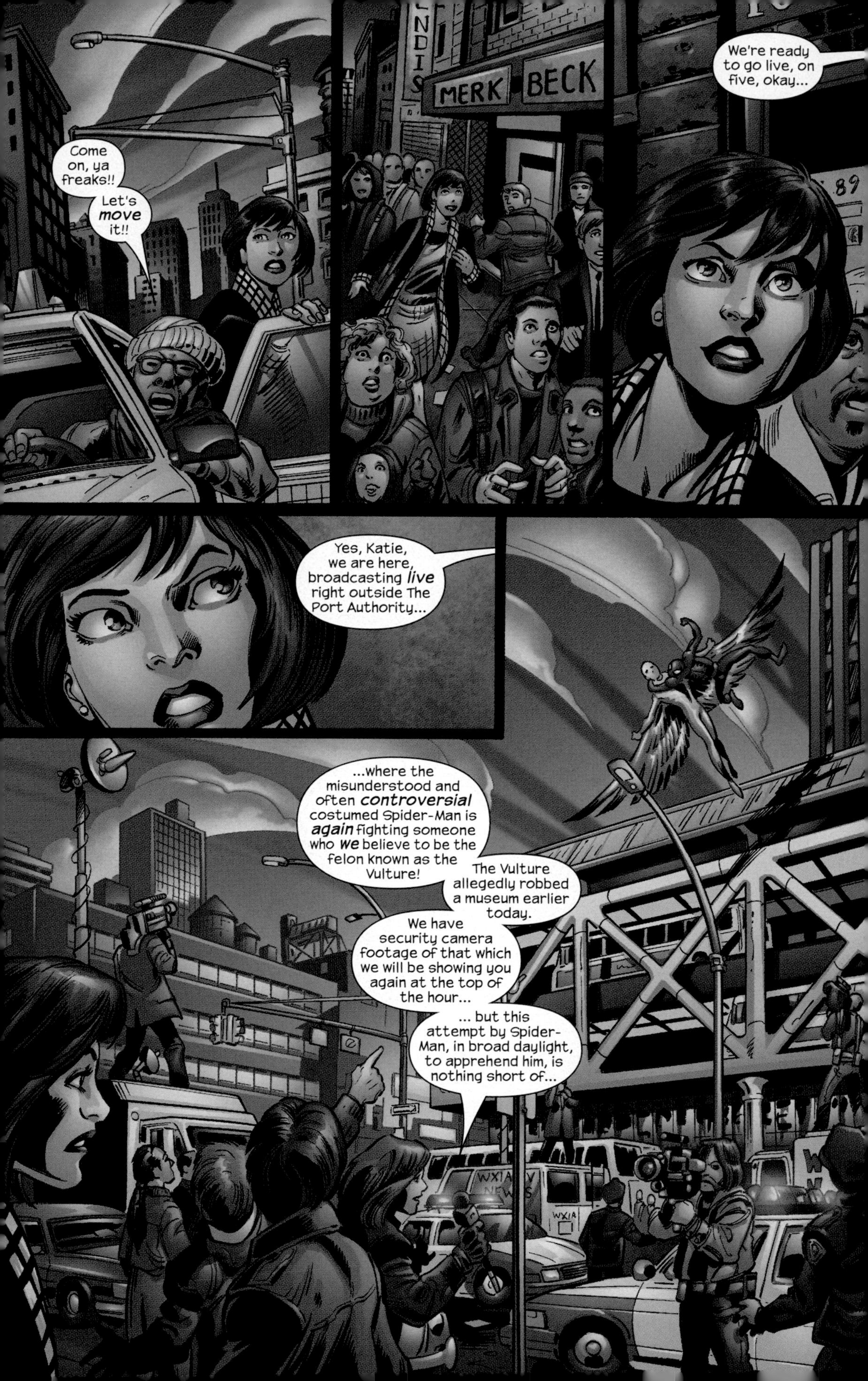
Come on, ya freaks!!
Let's *move* it!!
MERK
BECK
We're ready to go live, on five, okay...
Yes, Katie, we are here, broadcasting *live* right outside The Port Authority...
...where the misunderstood and often *controversial* costumed Spider-Man is *again* fighting someone who *we* believe to be the felon known as the Vulture!
The Vulture allegedly robbed a museum earlier today.
We have security camera footage of that which we will be showing you again at the top of the hour...
... but this attempt by Spider-Man, in broad daylight, to apprehend him, is nothing short of...
WXIA TV NEWS
WXIA

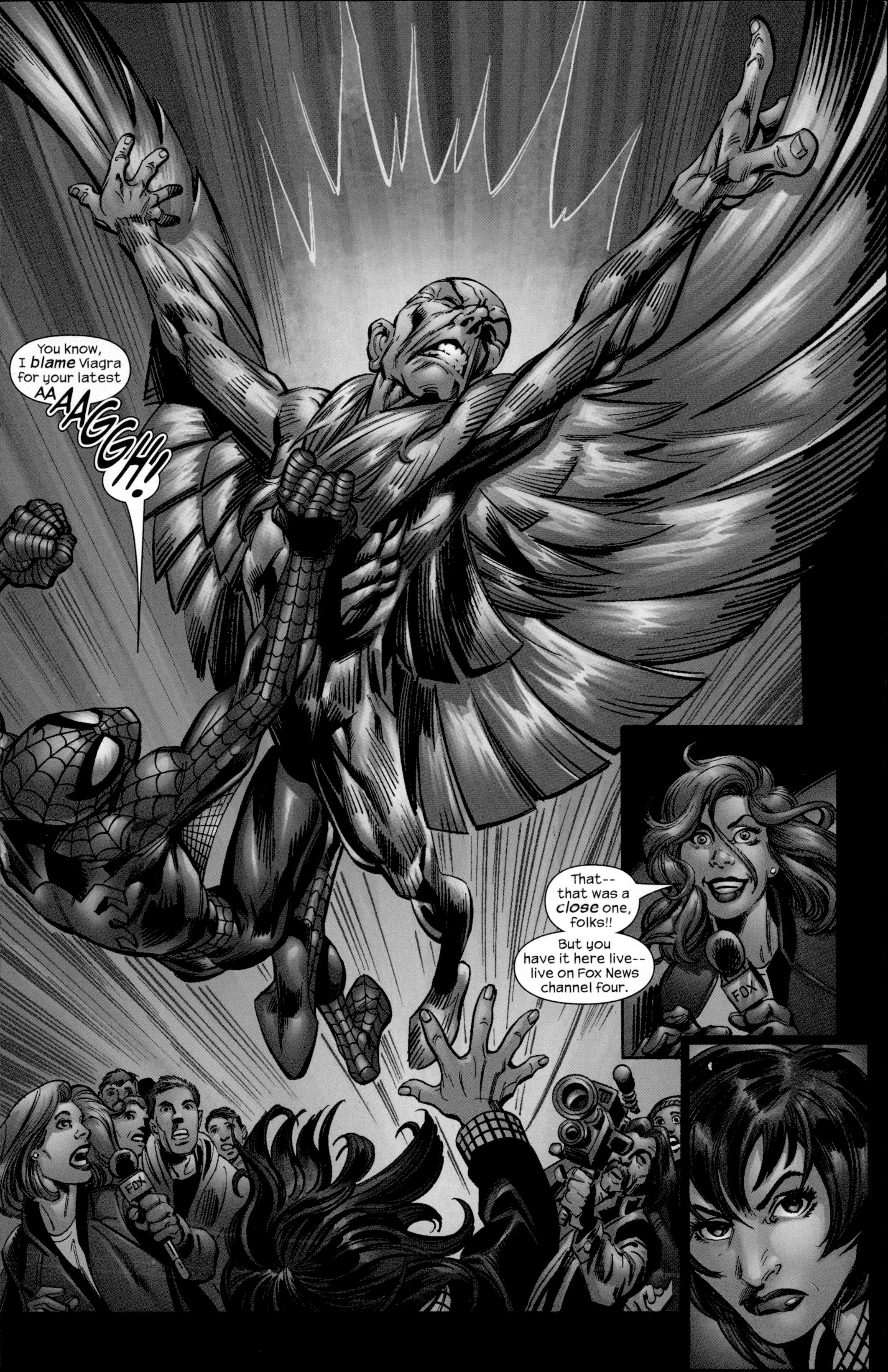
You know, I *blame* Viagra for your latest
AAAAGGH!!
That-- that was a *close* one, folks!!
But you have it here live-- live on Fox News channel four.
FOX
FOX

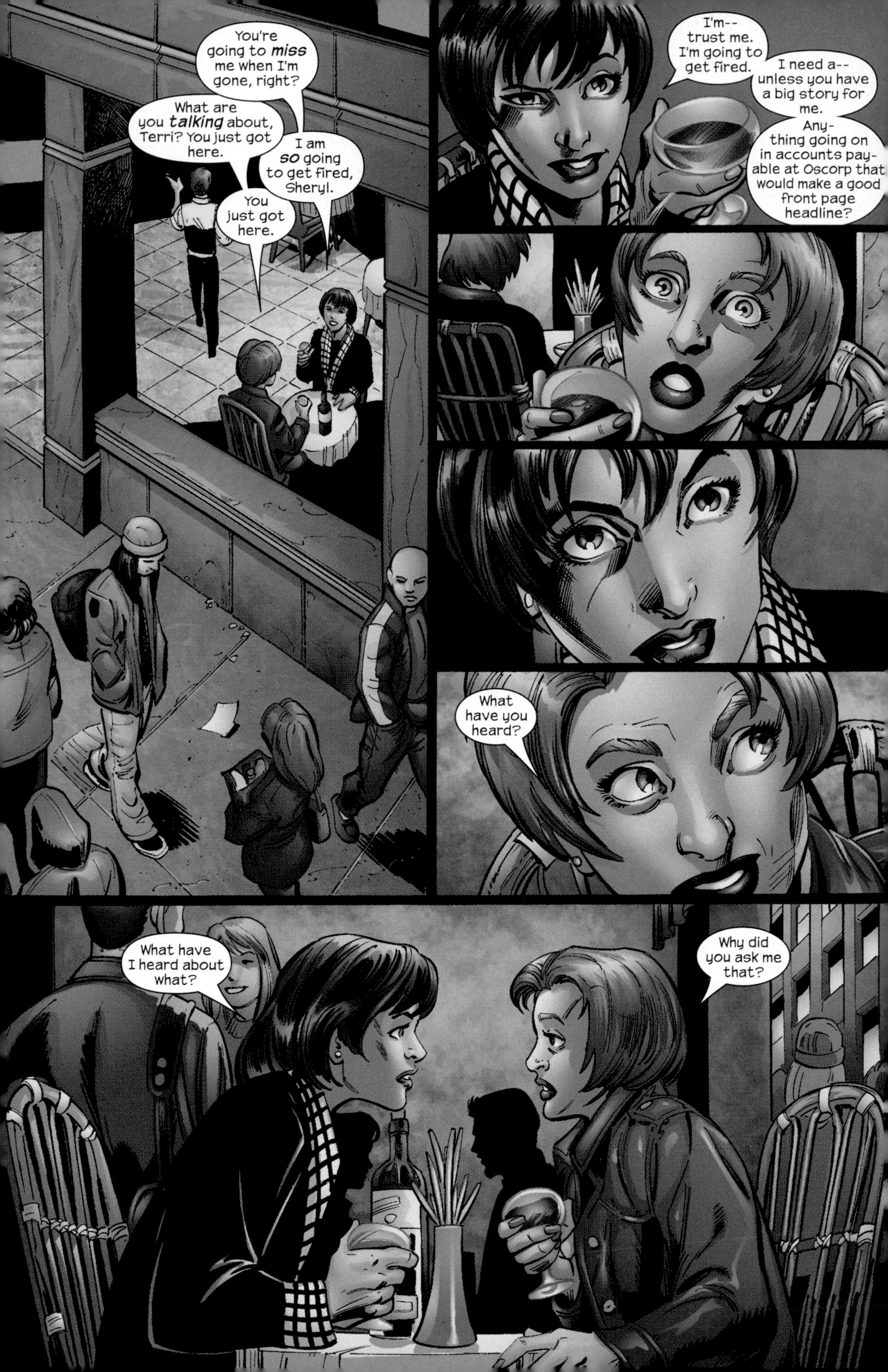
You're going to miss me when I'm gone, right?
What are you talking about, Terri? You just got here.
I am so going to get fired, Sheryl.
You just got here.
I'm-- trust me. I'm going to get fired.
I need a-- unless you have a big story for me.
Any-thing going on in accounts pay-able at Oscorp that would make a good front page headline?
What have you heard?
What have I heard about what?
Why did you ask me that?

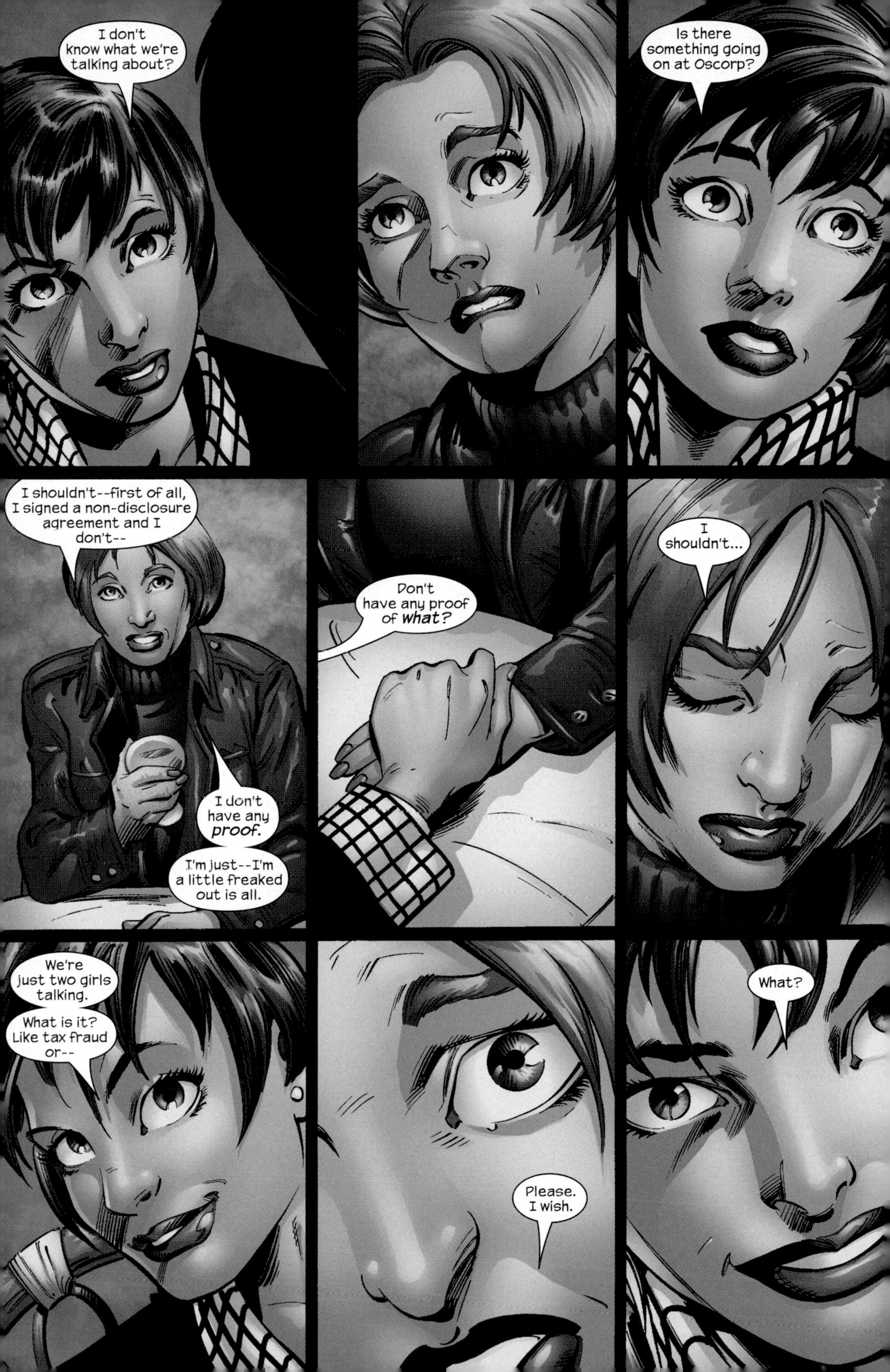
I don't know what we're talking about?
Is there something going on at Oscorp?
I shouldn't--first of all, I signed a non-disclosure agreement and I don't--
I don't have any *proof.*
I'm just--I'm a little freaked out is all.
Don't have any proof of *what?*
I shouldn't...
We're just two girls talking.
What is it? Like tax fraud or--
Please. I wish.
What?

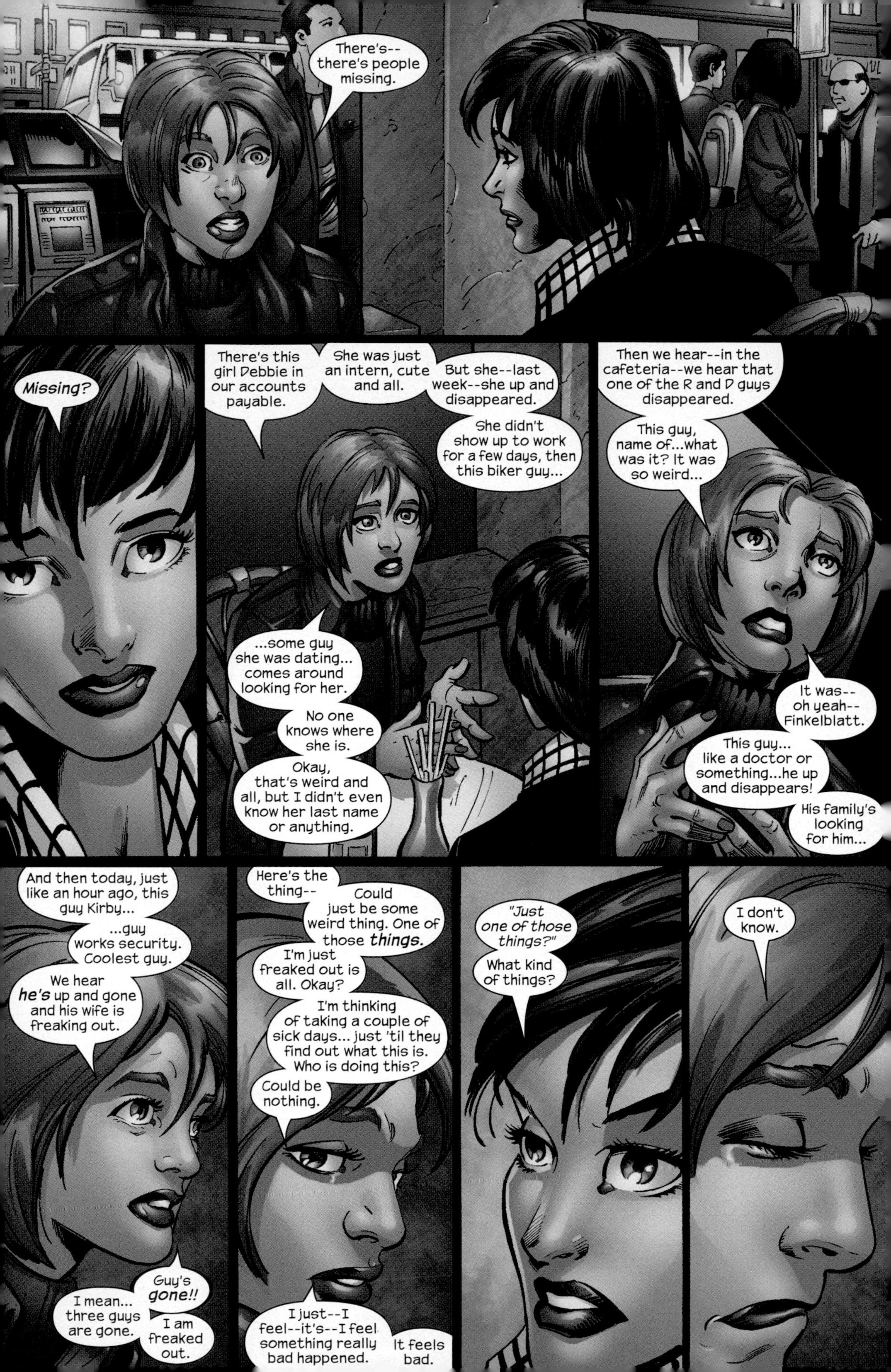
There's--
there's people
missing.
Missing?
There's this
girl Debbie in
our accounts
payable.
She was just
an intern, cute
and all.
But she--last
week--she up and
disappeared.
She didn't
show up to work
for a few days, then
this biker guy...
...some guy
she was dating...
comes around
looking for her.
No one
knows where
she is.
Okay,
that's weird and
all, but I didn't even
know her last name
or anything.
Then we hear--in the
cafeteria--we hear that
one of the R and D guys
disappeared.
This guy,
name of...what
was it? It was
so weird...
It was--
oh yeah--
Finkelblatt.
This guy...
like a doctor or
something...he up
and disappears!
His family's
looking
for him...
And then today, just
like an hour ago, this
guy Kirby...
...guy
works security.
Coolest guy.
We hear
he's up and gone
and his wife is
freaking out.
Guy's
gone!!
I mean...
three guys
are gone.
I am
freaked
out.
Here's the
thing--
Could
just be some
weird thing. One of
those *things.*
I'm just
freaked out is
all. Okay?
I'm thinking
of taking a couple of
sick days... just 'til they
find out what this is.
Who is doing this?
Could be
nothing.
I just--I
feel--it's--I feel
something really
bad happened.
It feels
bad.
"Just
one of those
things?"
What kind
of things?
I don't
know.

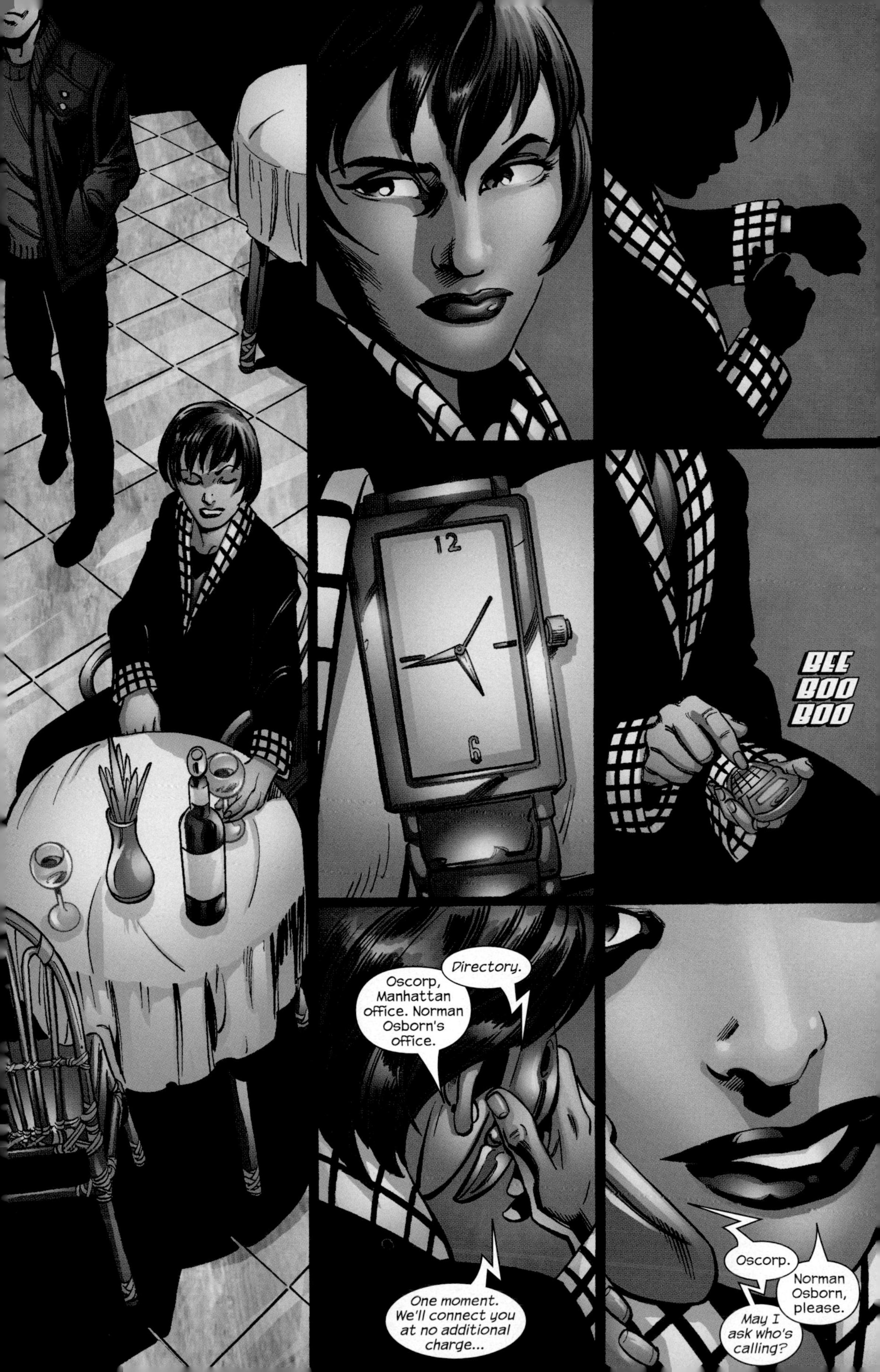
BEE
BOO
BOO
Directory.
Oscorp, Manhattan office. Norman Osborn's office.
One moment. We'll connect you at no additional charge...
Oscorp.
Norman Osborn, please.
May I ask who's calling?

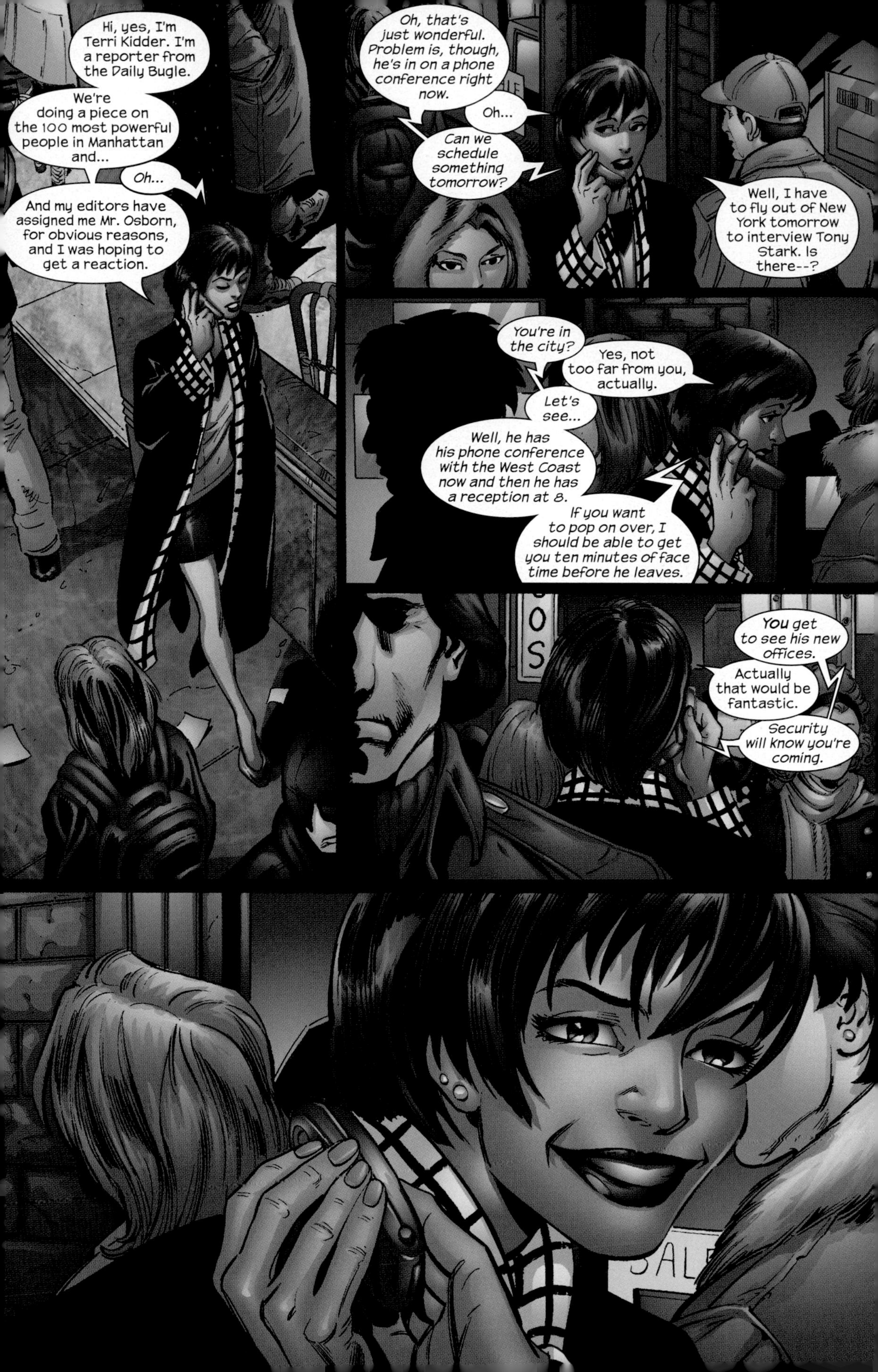
Hi, yes, I'm Terri Kidder. I'm a reporter from the Daily Bugle.
We're doing a piece on the 100 most powerful people in Manhattan and...
Oh...
And my editors have assigned me Mr. Osborn, for obvious reasons, and I was hoping to get a reaction.
Oh, that's just wonderful. Problem is, though, he's in on a phone conference right now.
Oh...
Can we schedule something tomorrow?
Well, I have to fly out of New York tomorrow to interview Tony Stark. Is there--?
You're in the city?
Yes, not too far from you, actually.
Let's see...
Well, he has his phone conference with the West Coast now and then he has a reception at 8.
If you want to pop on over, I should be able to get you ten minutes of face time before he leaves.
YOU get to see his new offices.
Actually that would be fantastic.
Security will know you're coming.

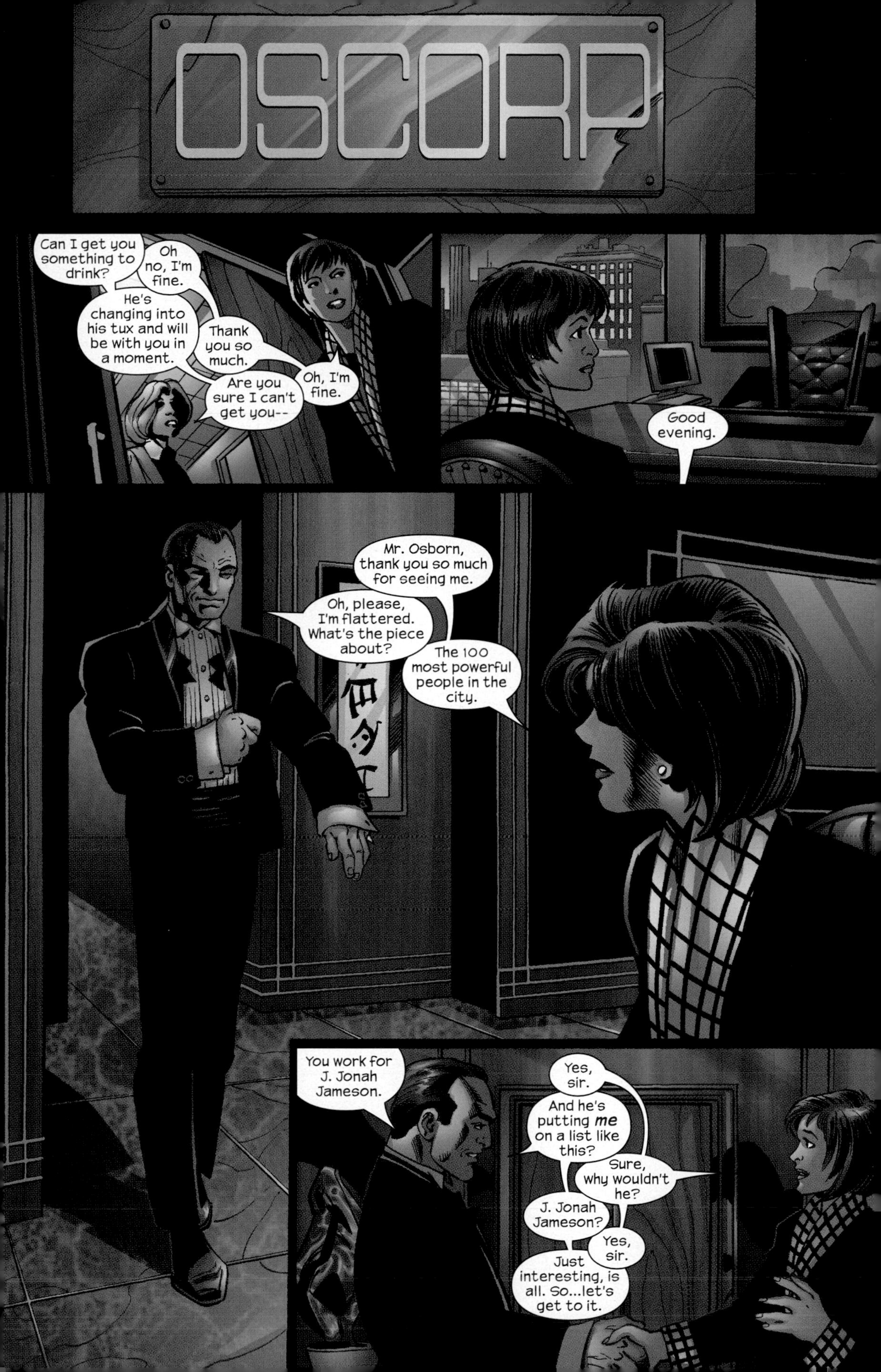
OSCORP
Can I get you something to drink?
Oh no, I'm fine.
He's changing into his tux and will be with you in a moment.
Thank you so much.
Are you sure I can't get you--
Oh, I'm fine.
Good evening.
Mr. Osborn, thank you so much for seeing me.
Oh, please, I'm flattered. What's the piece about?
The 100 most powerful people in the city.
You work for J. Jonah Jameson.
Yes, sir.
And he's putting *me* on a list like this?
Sure, why wouldn't he?
J. Jonah Jameson?
Yes, sir.
Just interesting, is all. So...let's get to it.

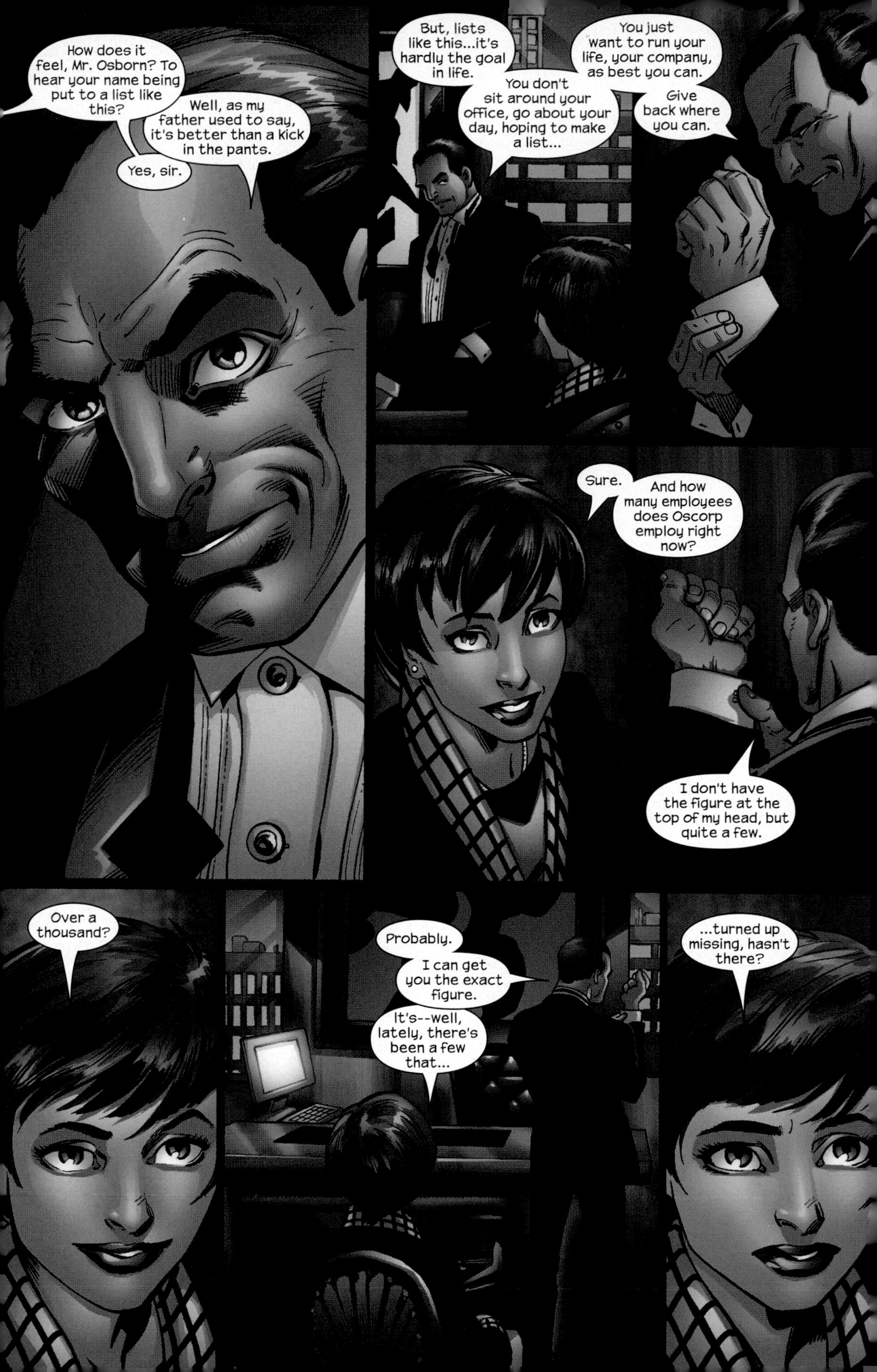
How does it feel, Mr. Osborn? To hear your name being put to a list like this?
Well, as my father used to say, it's better than a kick in the pants.
Yes, sir.
But, lists like this...it's hardly the goal in life.
You don't sit around your office, go about your day, hoping to make a list...
You just want to run your life, your company, as best you can.
Give back where you can.
Sure.
And how many employees does Oscorp employ right now?
I don't have the figure at the top of my head, but quite a few.
Over a thousand?
Probably.
I can get you the exact figure.
It's--well, lately, there's been a few that...
...turned up missing, hasn't there?

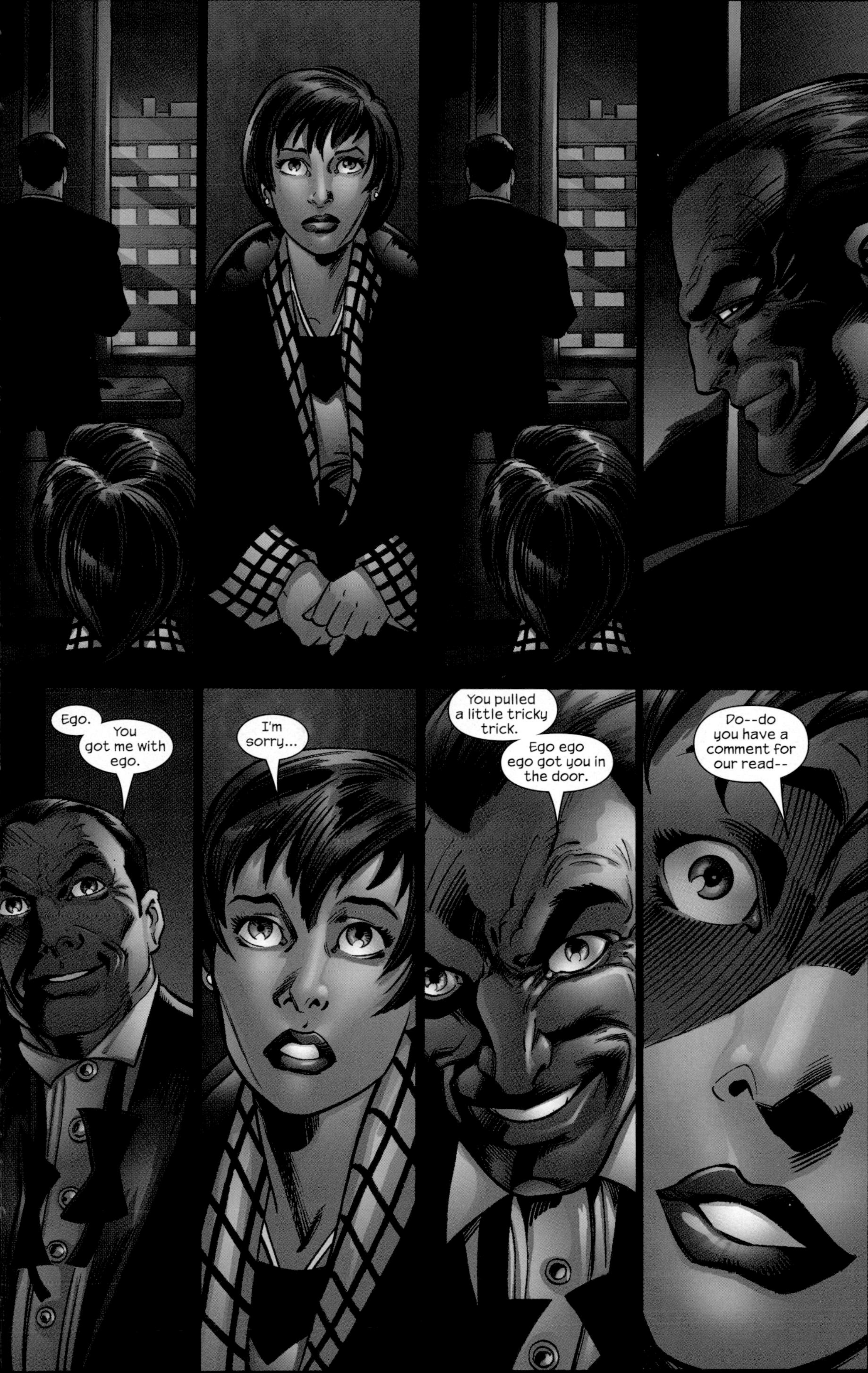
Ego.
You got me with ego.
I'm sorry...
You pulled a little tricky trick.
Ego ego ego got you in the door.
Do--do you have a comment for our read--

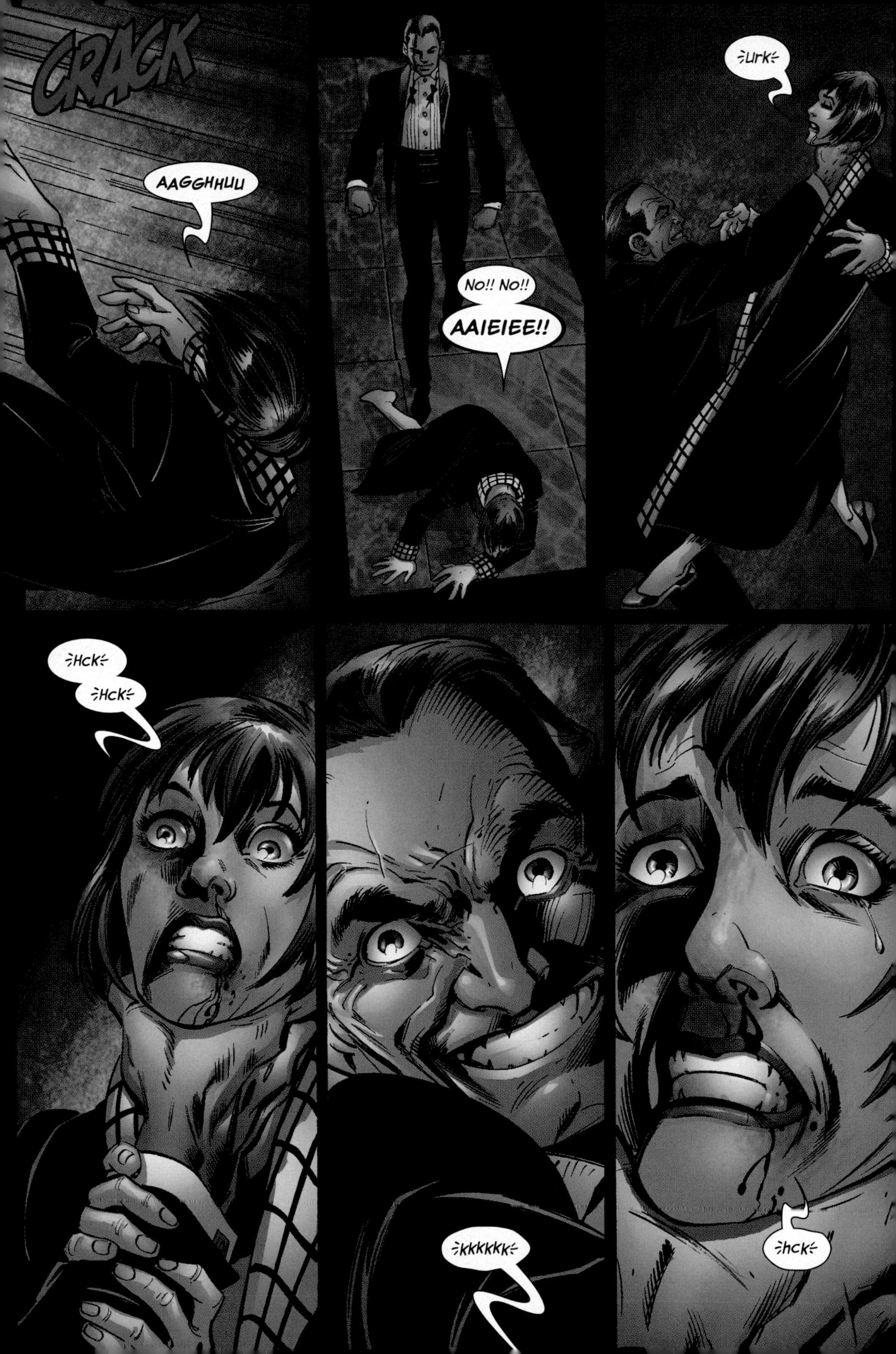
CRACK
AAGGHHUU
No!! No!!
AAIEIEE!!
urk
HCK
HCK
KKKKKK
hck

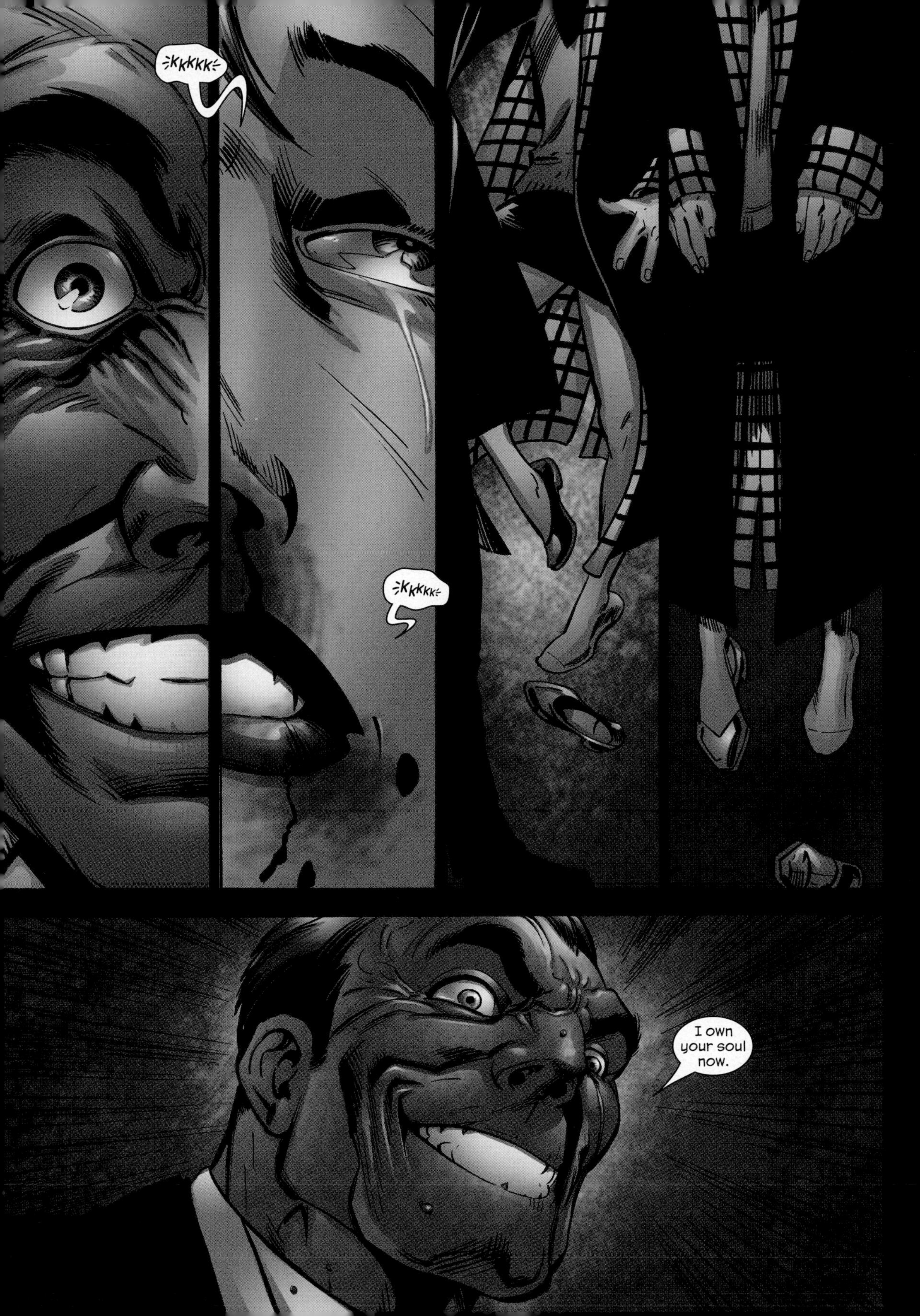
KKKKK
KKKKK
I own your soul now.

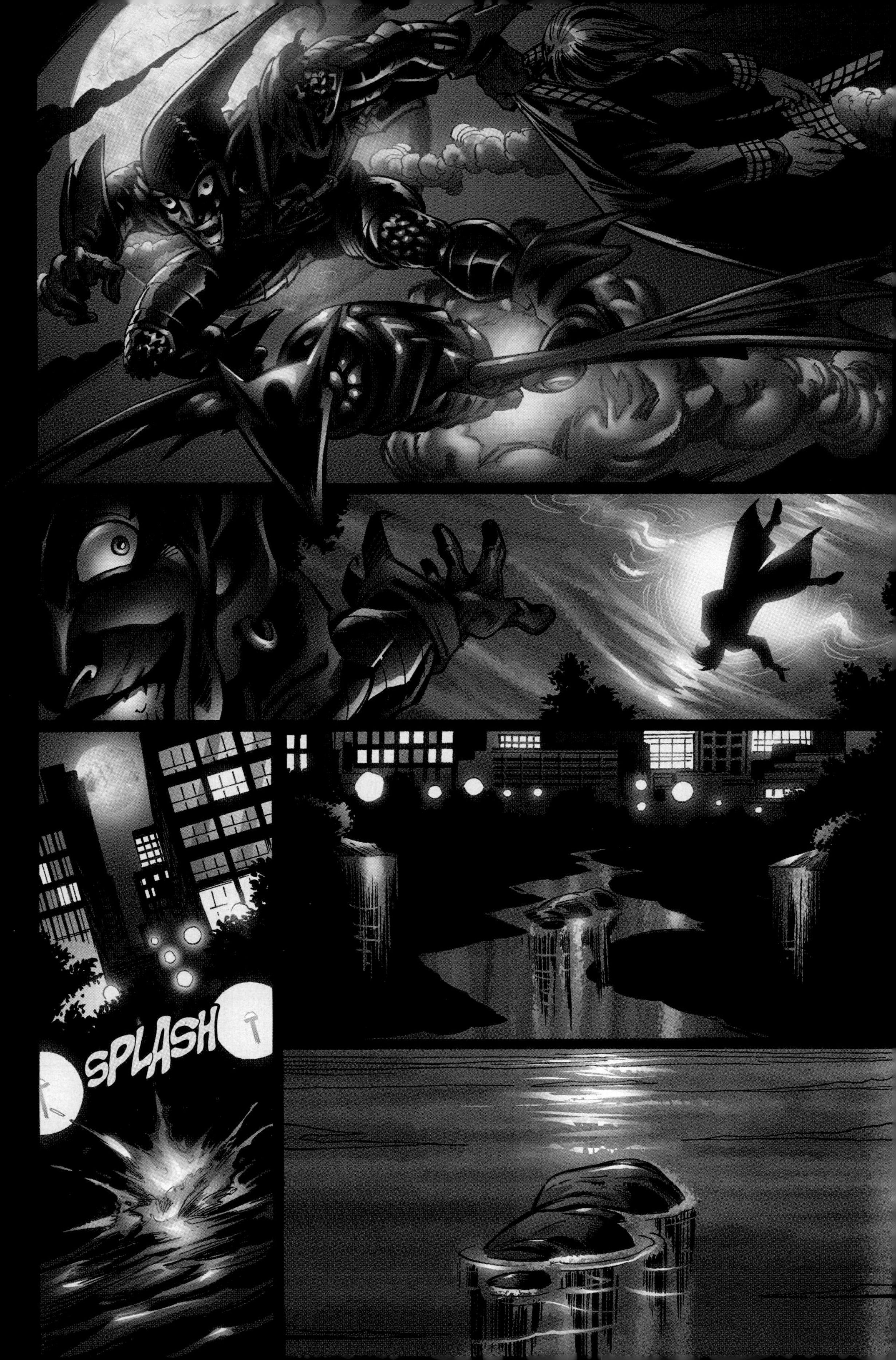
SPLASH

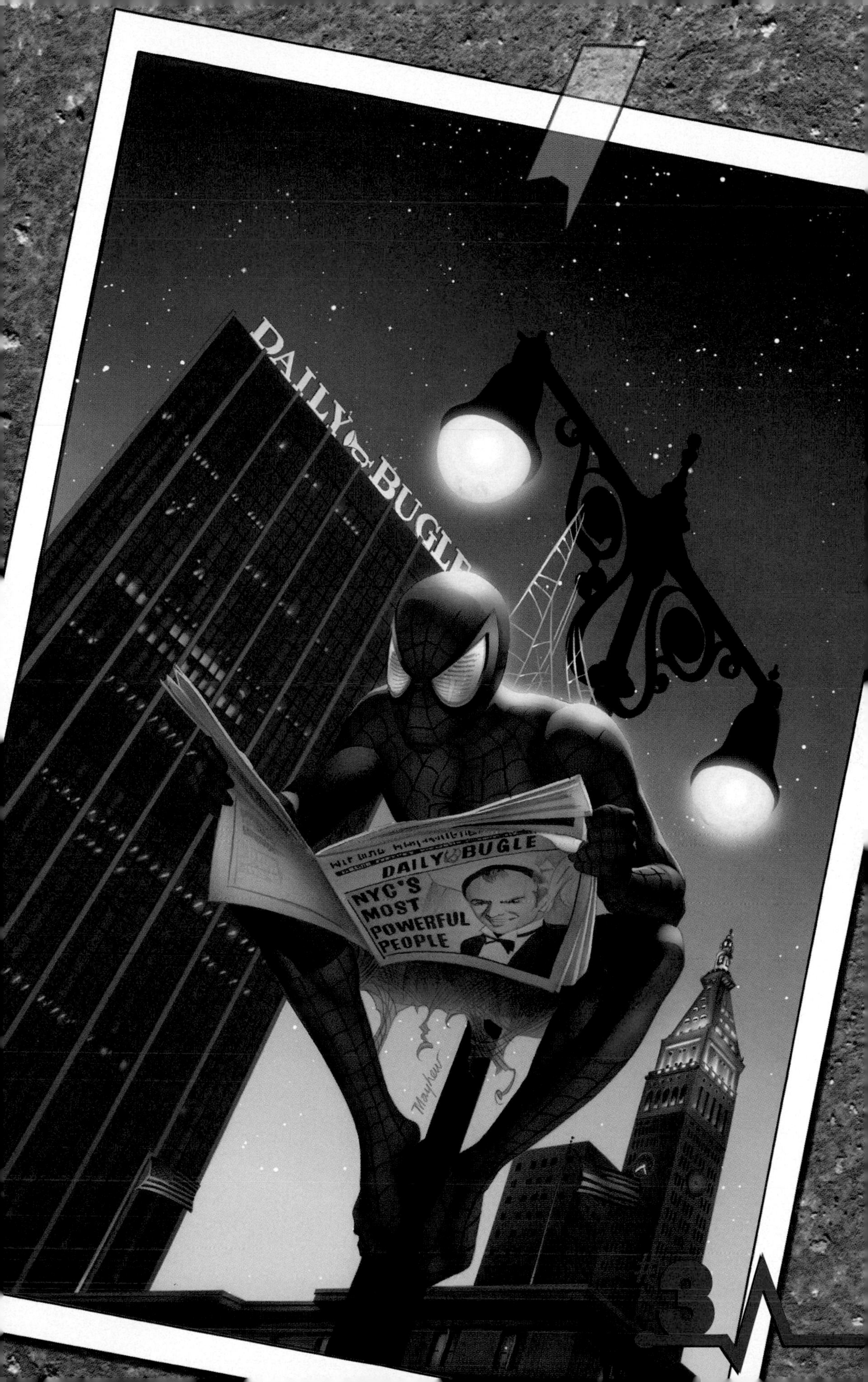
DAILY BUGLE
DAILY BUGLE
NYC'S MOST POWERFUL PEOPLE
Mayhew
3

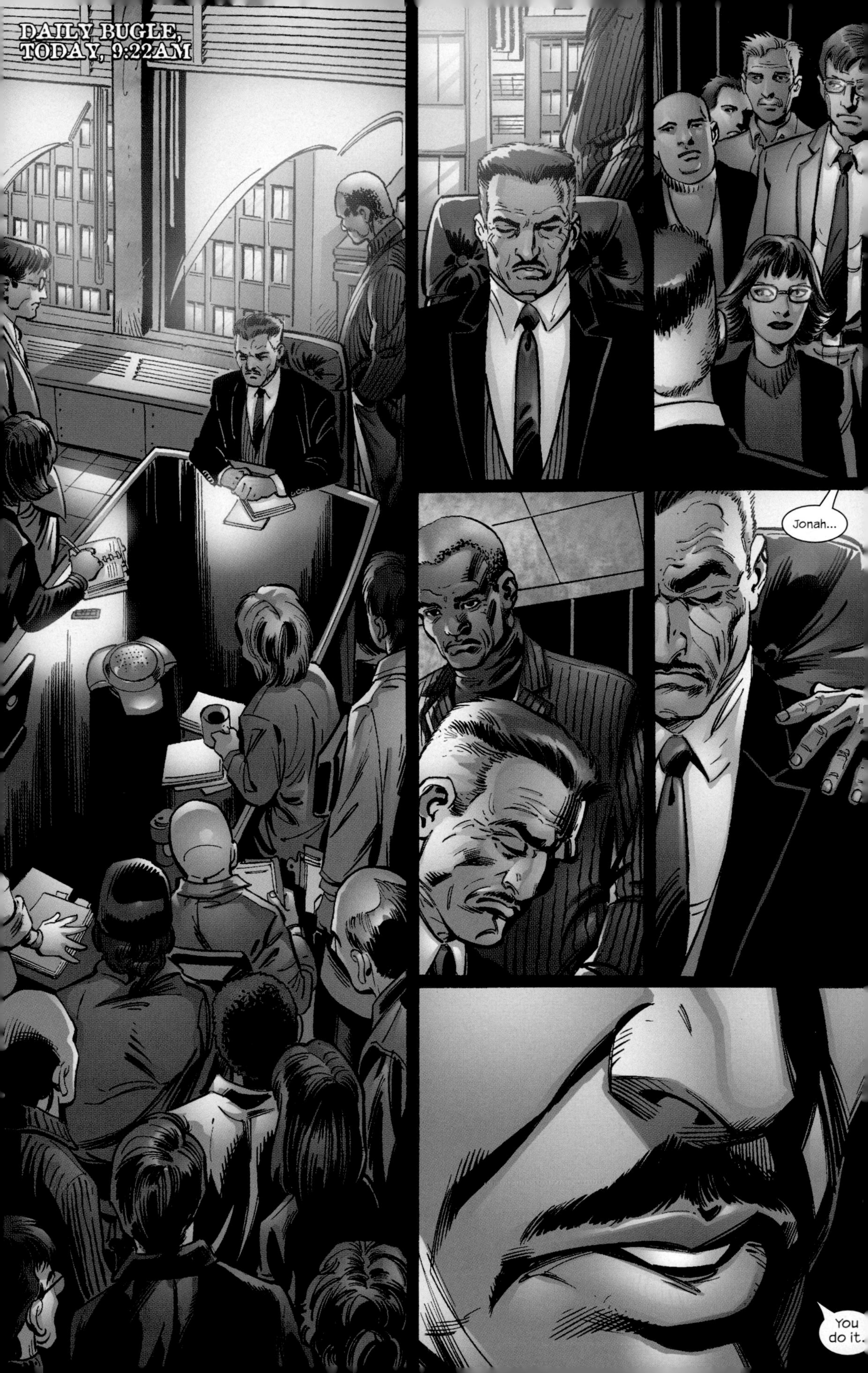
DAILY BUGLE, TODAY, 9:22AM
Jonah...
You do it.

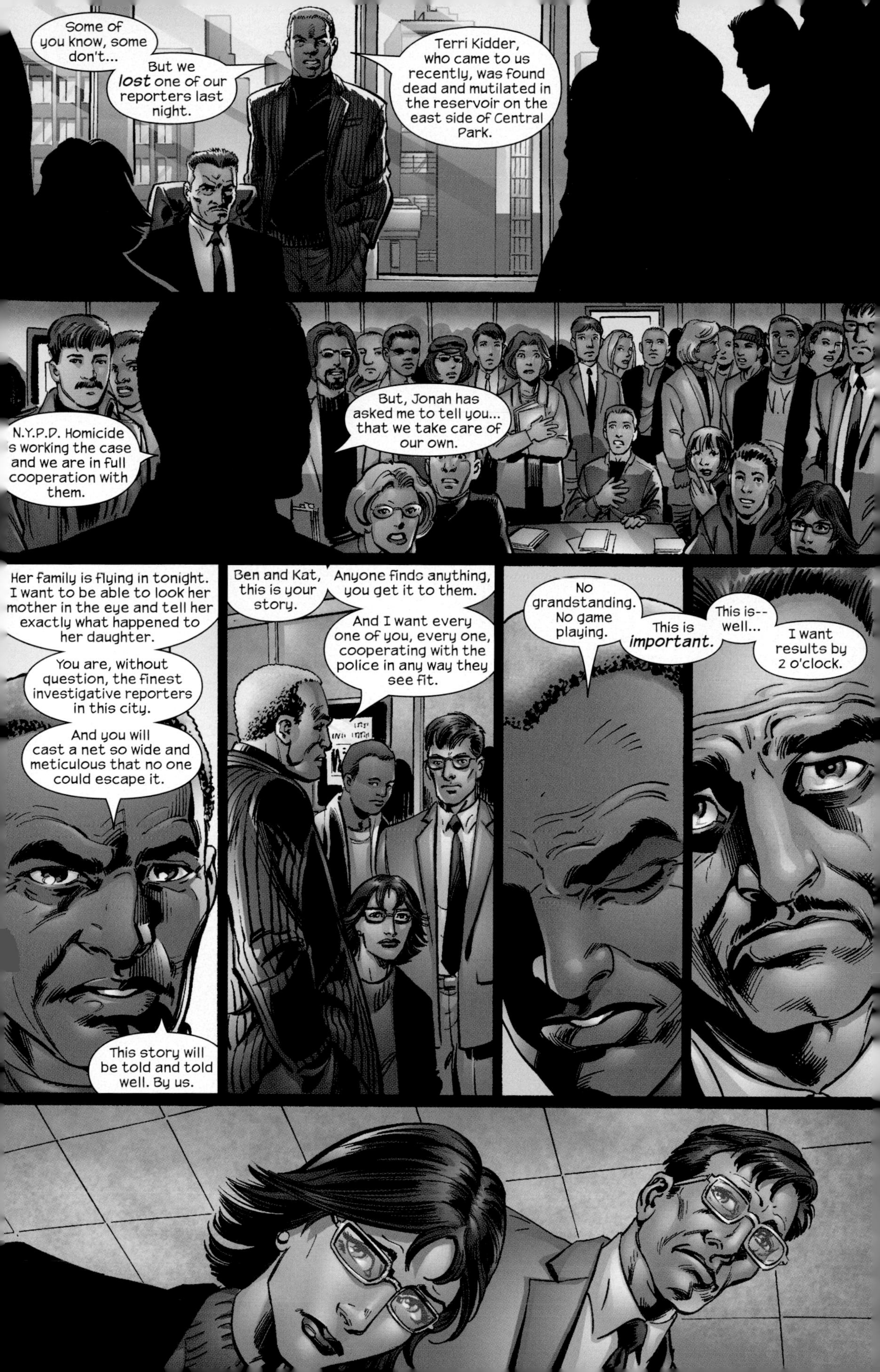
Some of you know, some don't...
But we *lost* one of our reporters last night.
Terri Kidder, who came to us recently, was found dead and mutilated in the reservoir on the east side of Central Park.
N.Y.P.D. Homicide s working the case and we are in full cooperation with them.
But, Jonah has asked me to tell you... that we take care of our own.
Her family is flying in tonight. I want to be able to look her mother in the eye and tell her exactly what happened to her daughter.
You are, without question, the finest investigative reporters in this city.
And you will cast a net so wide and meticulous that no one could escape it.
This story will be told and told well. By us.
Ben and Kat, this is your story.
Anyone finds anything, you get it to them.
And I want every one of you, every one, cooperating with the police in any way they see fit.
No grandstanding. No game playing.
This is *important.*
This is-- well...
I want results by 2 o'clock.

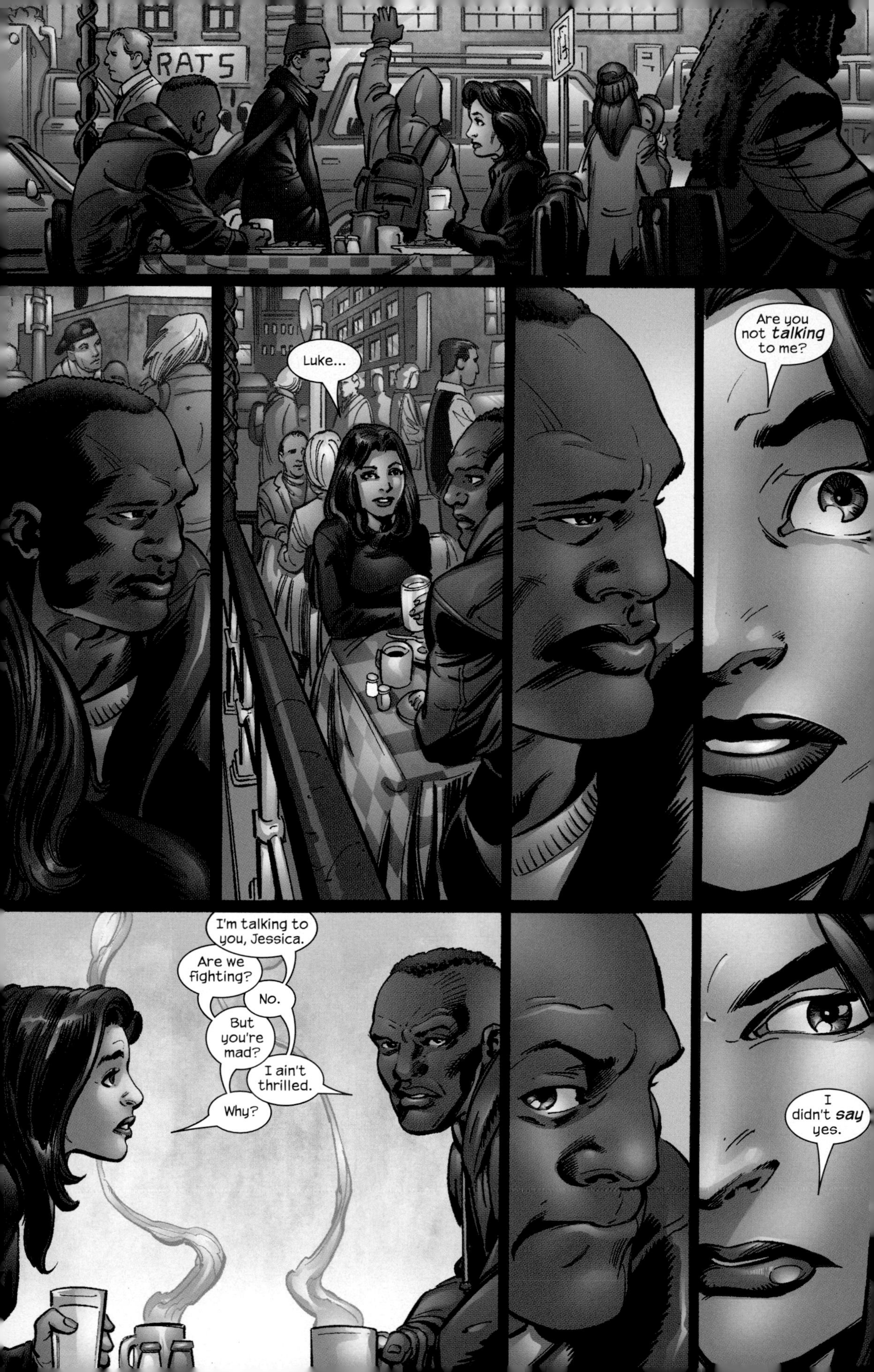
RATS
Luke...
Are you not talking to me?
I'm talking to you, Jessica.
Are we fighting?
No.
But you're mad?
I ain't thrilled.
Why?
I didn't say yes.

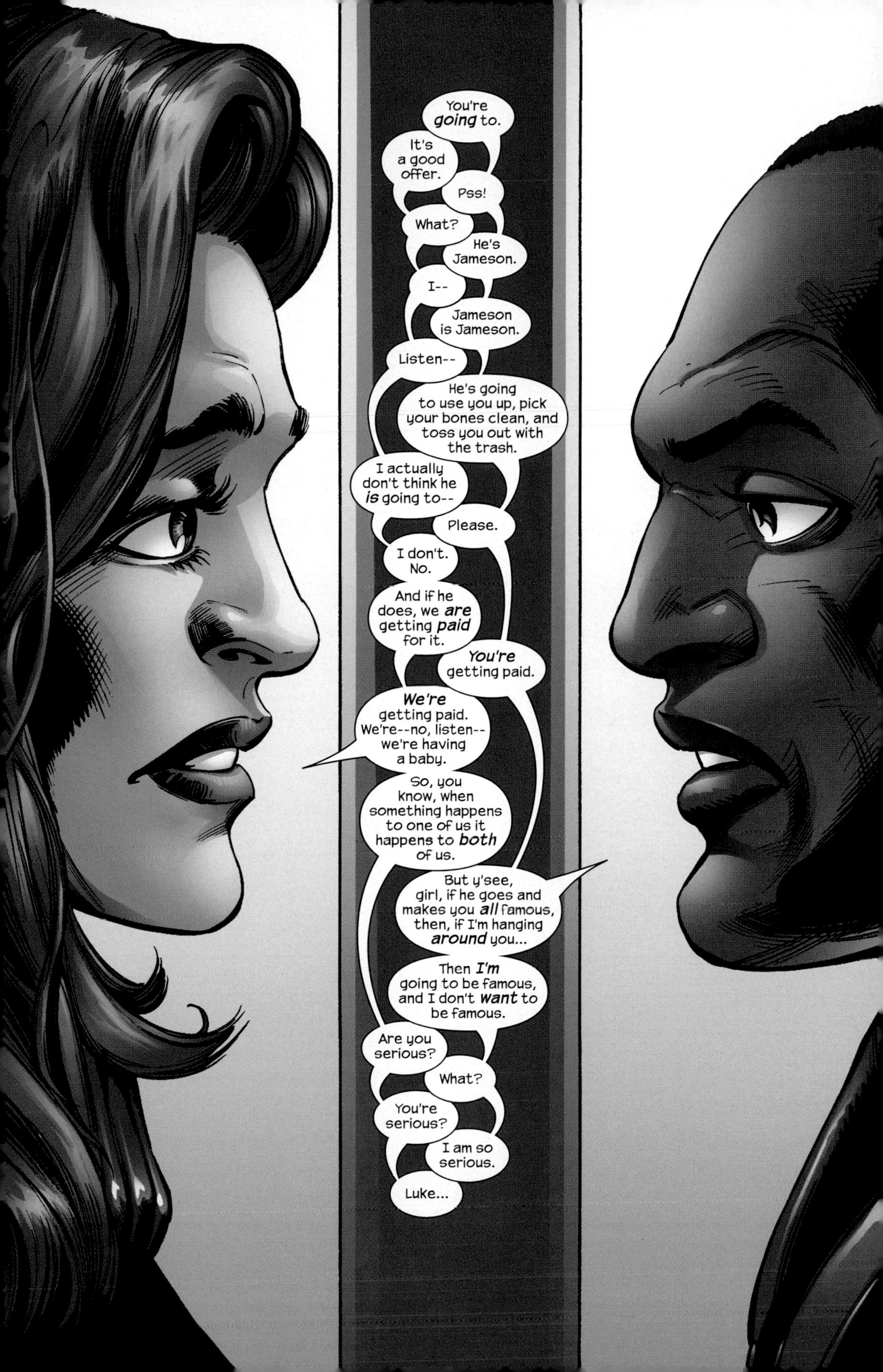
You're *going* to.
It's a good offer.
Pss!
What?
He's Jameson.
I--
Jameson is Jameson.
Listen--
He's going to use you up, pick your bones clean, and toss you out with the trash.
I actually don't think he *is* going to--
Please.
I don't. No.
And if he does, we *are* getting *paid* for it.
You're getting paid.
We're getting paid. We're--no, listen-- we're having a baby.
So, you know, when something happens to one of us it happens to *both* of us.
But y'see, girl, if he goes and makes you *all* famous, then, if I'm hanging *around* you...
Then *I'm* going to be famous, and I don't *want* to be famous.
Are you serious?
What?
You're serious?
I am so serious.
Luke...

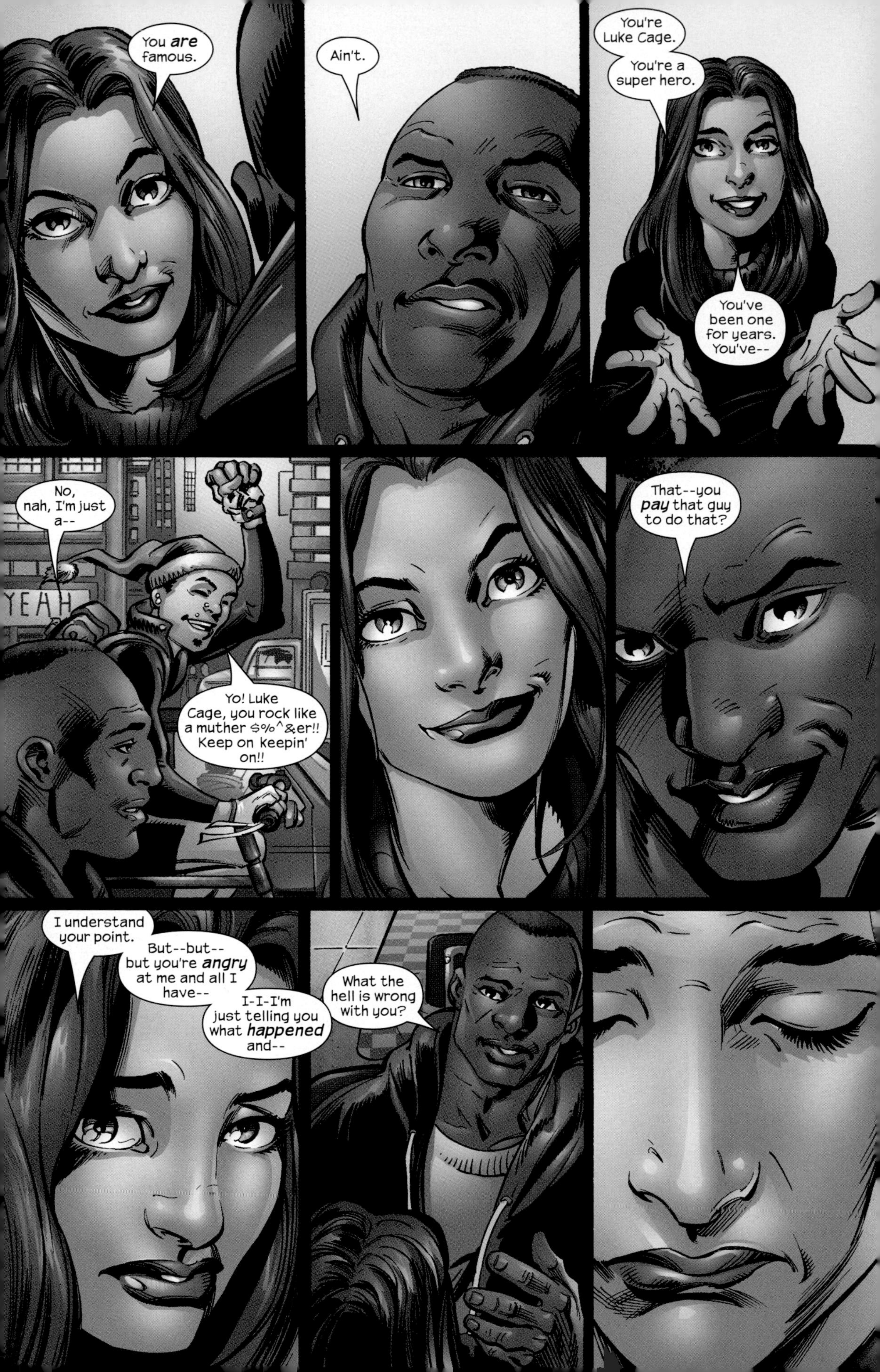
You **are** famous.
Ain't.
You're Luke Cage.
You're a super hero.
You've been one for years. You've--
No, nah, I'm just a--
YEAH
Yo! Luke Cage, you rock like a muther $%^&er!! Keep on keepin' on!!
That--you **pay** that guy to do that?
I understand your point.
But--but--but you're **angry** at me and all I have--
I-I-I'm just telling you what **happened** and--
What the hell is wrong with you?

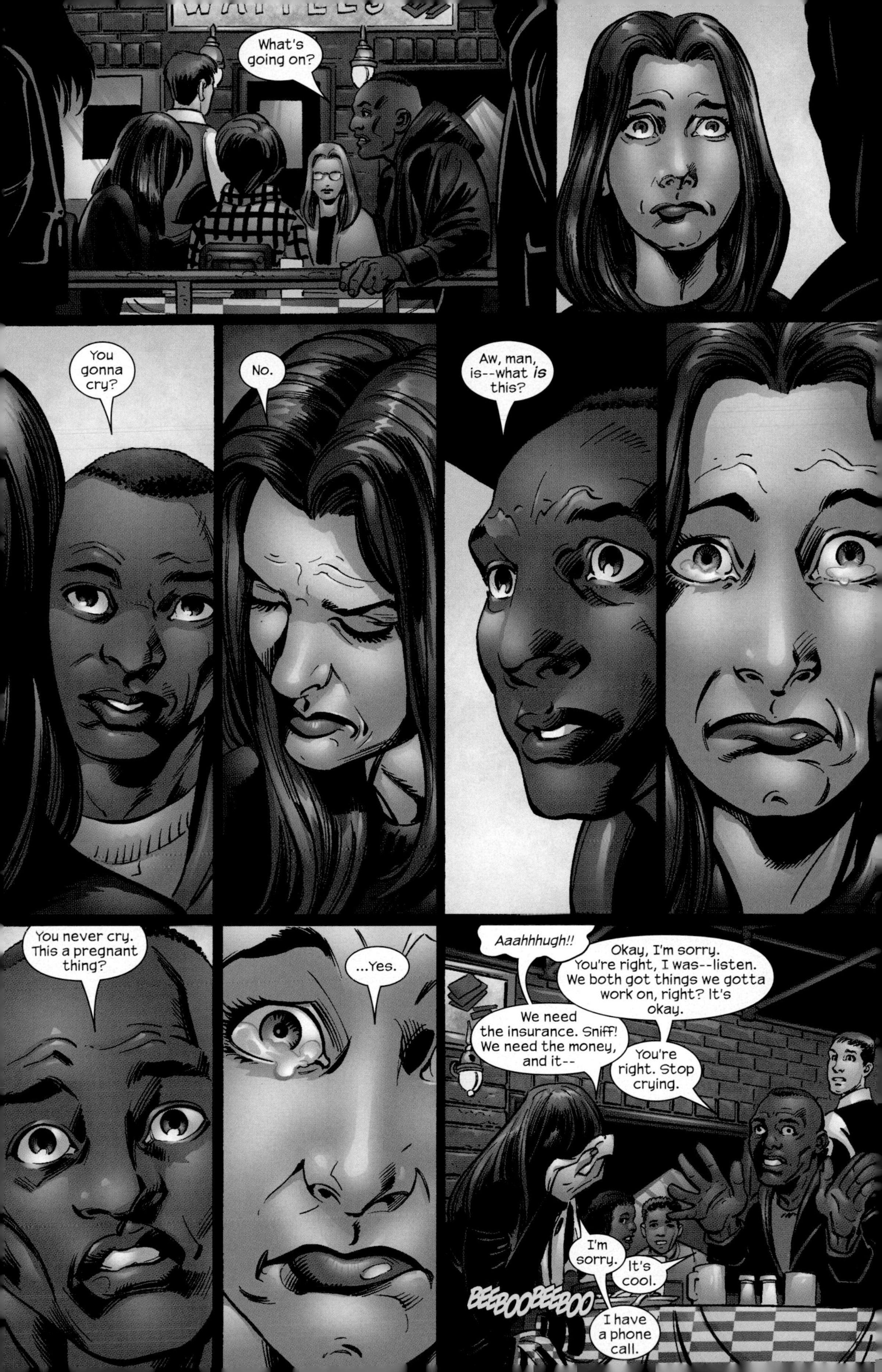
What's going on?
You gonna cry?
No.
Aw, man, is--what *is* this?
You never cry. This a pregnant thing?
...Yes.
Aaahhhugh!!
We need the insurance. Sniff! We need the money, and it--
Okay, I'm sorry. You're right, I was--listen. We both got things we gotta work on, right? It's okay.
You're right. Stop crying.
I'm sorry.
It's cool.
BEEBOOBEEBOO
I have a phone call.

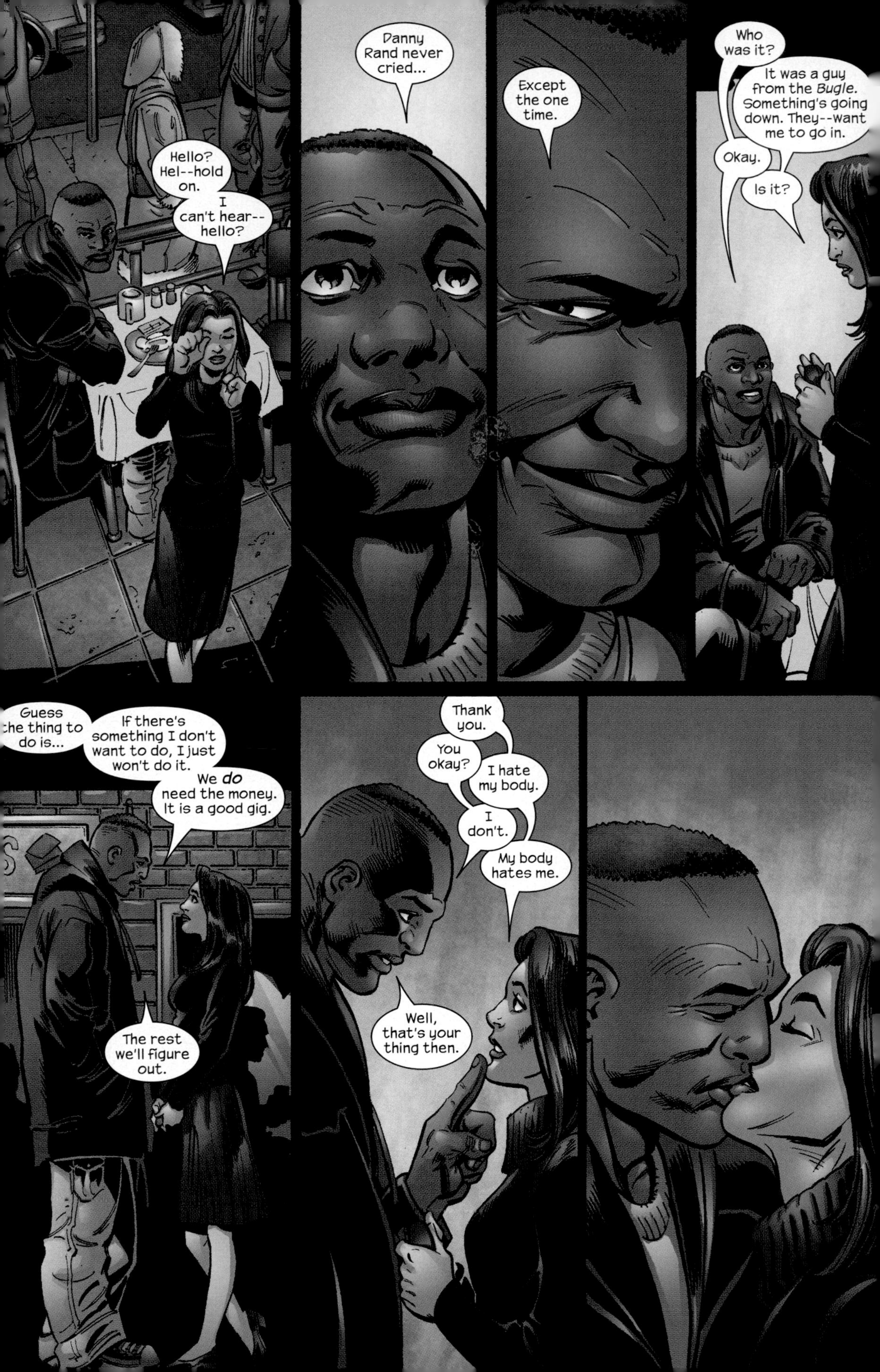
Hello? Hel--hold on.
I can't hear-- hello?
Danny Rand never cried...
Except the one time.
Who was it?
It was a guy from the Bugle. Something's going down. They--want me to go in.
Okay.
Is it?
Guess the thing to do is...
If there's something I don't want to do, I just won't do it.
We do need the money. It is a good gig.
The rest we'll figure out.
Thank you.
You okay?
I hate my body.
I don't.
My body hates me.
Well, that's your thing then.

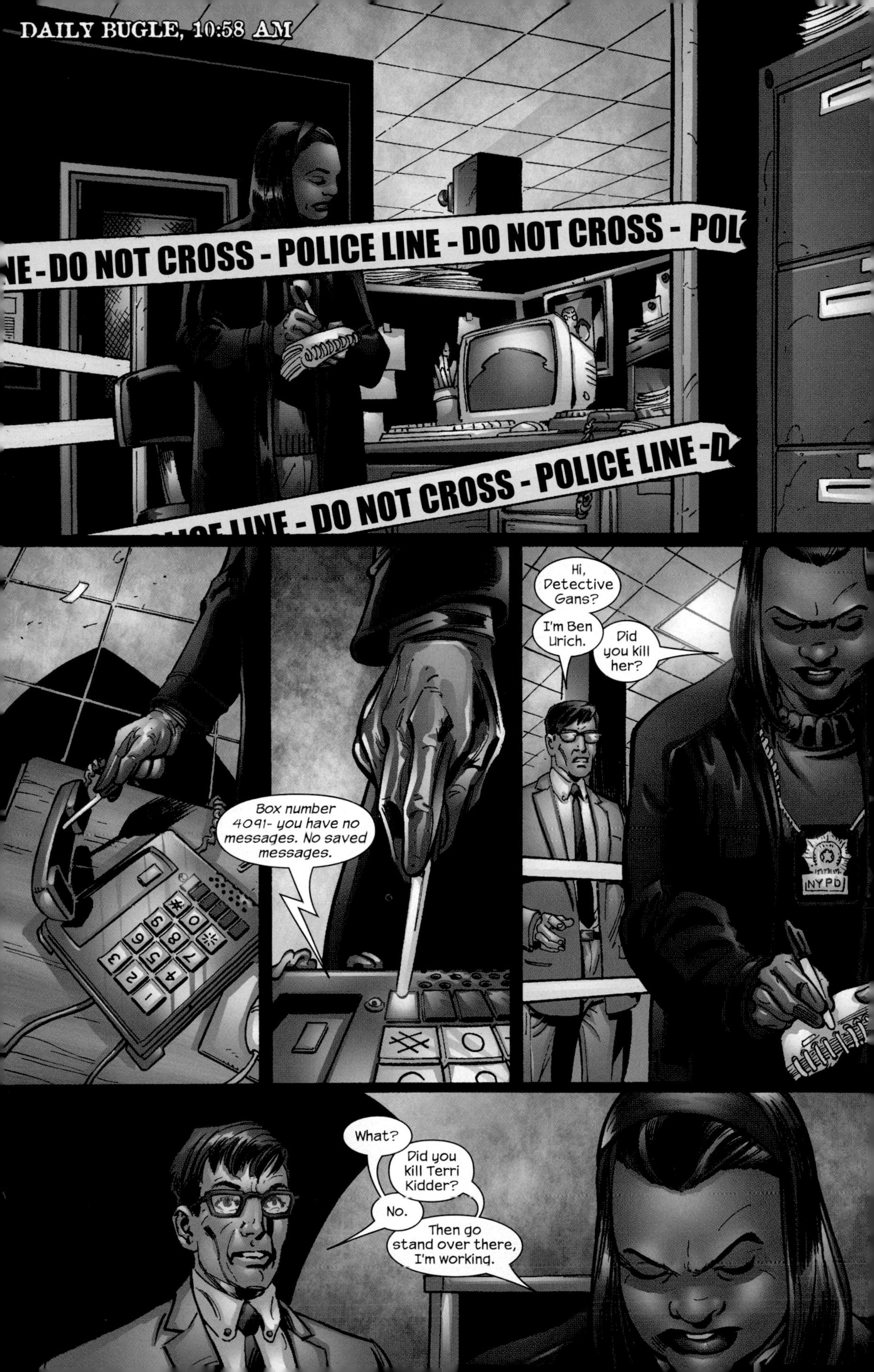
DAILY BUGLE, 10:58 AM
NE - DO NOT CROSS - POLICE LINE - DO NOT CROSS - POL
POLICE LINE - DO NOT CROSS - POLICE LINE - D
Box number 4091- you have no messages. No saved messages.
Hi, Detective Gans?
I'm Ben Urich.
Did you kill her?
What?
Did you kill Terri Kidder?
No.
Then go stand over there, I'm working.

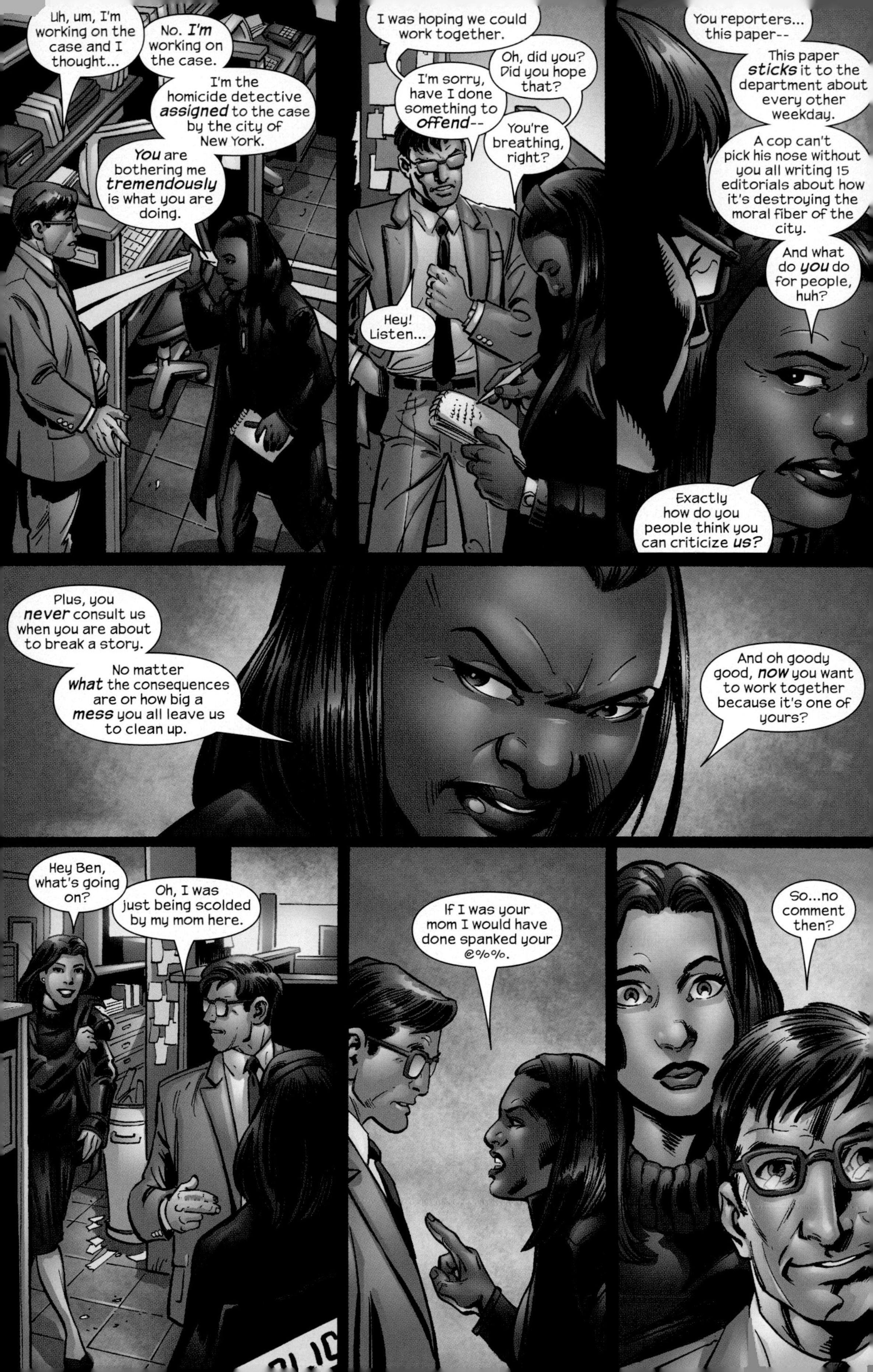

Uh, um, I'm working on the case and I thought...
No. I'm working on the case.
I'm the homicide detective assigned to the case by the city of New York.
You are bothering me tremendously is what you are doing.
I was hoping we could work together.
Oh, did you? Did you hope that?
I'm sorry, have I done something to offend--
You're breathing, right?
Hey! Listen...
You reporters... this paper--
This paper sticks it to the department about every other weekday.
A cop can't pick his nose without you all writing 15 editorials about how it's destroying the moral fiber of the city.
And what do you do for people, huh?
Exactly how do you people think you can criticize us?
Plus, you never consult us when you are about to break a story.
No matter what the consequences are or how big a mess you all leave us to clean up.
And oh goody good, now you want to work together because it's one of yours?
Hey Ben, what's going on?
Oh, I was just being scolded by my mom here.
If I was your mom I would have done spanked your @%%.
So...no comment then?

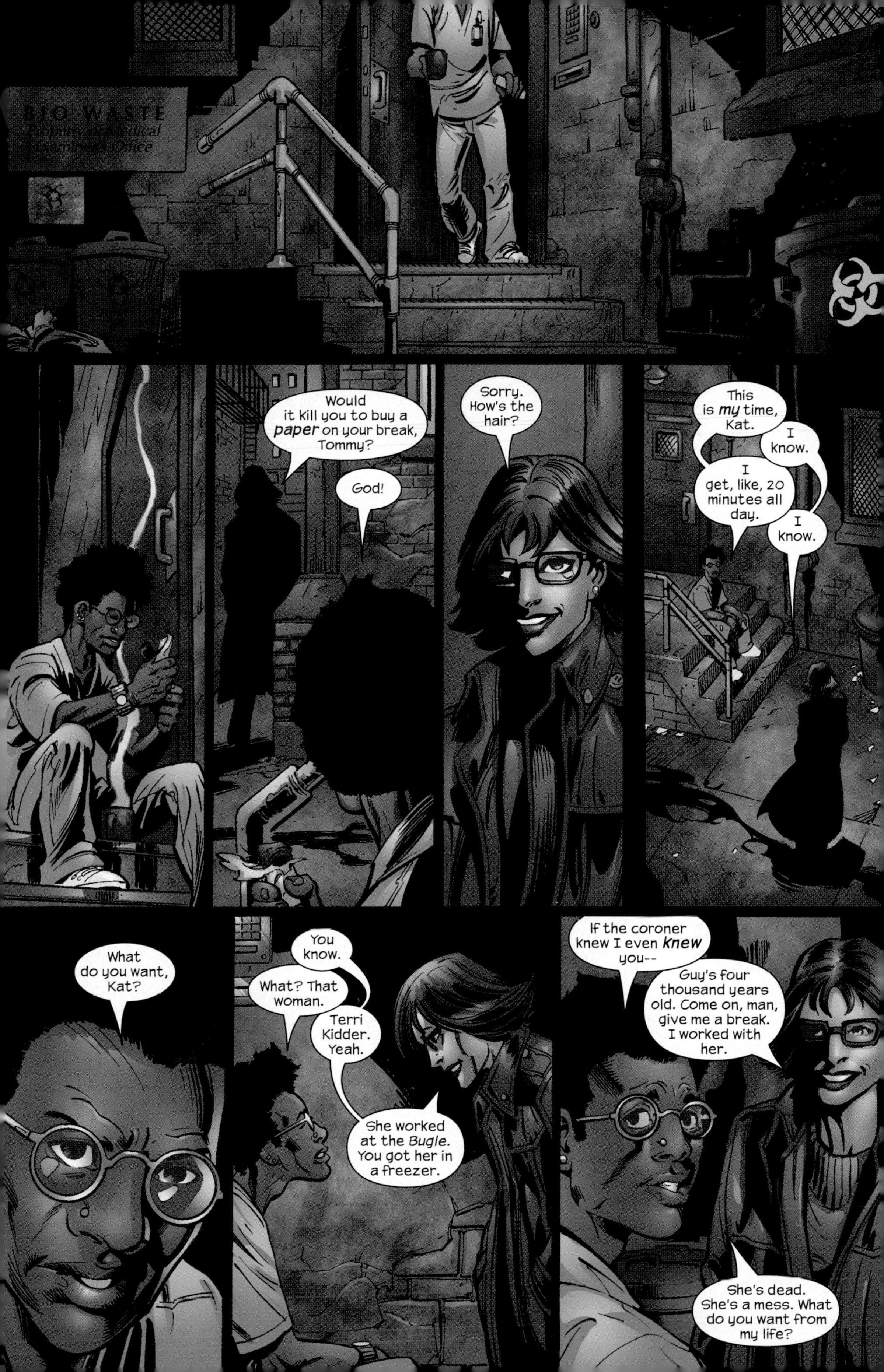

BIO WASTE
Would it kill you to buy a *paper* on your break, Tommy?
God!
Sorry. How's the hair?
This is *my* time, Kat.
I know.
I get, like, 20 minutes all day.
I know.
What do you want, Kat?
You know.
What? That woman.
Terri Kidder. Yeah.
She worked at the *Bugle*. You got her in a freezer.
If the coroner knew I even *knew* you--
Guy's four thousand years old. Come on, man, give me a break. I worked with her.
She's dead. She's a mess. What do you want from my life?

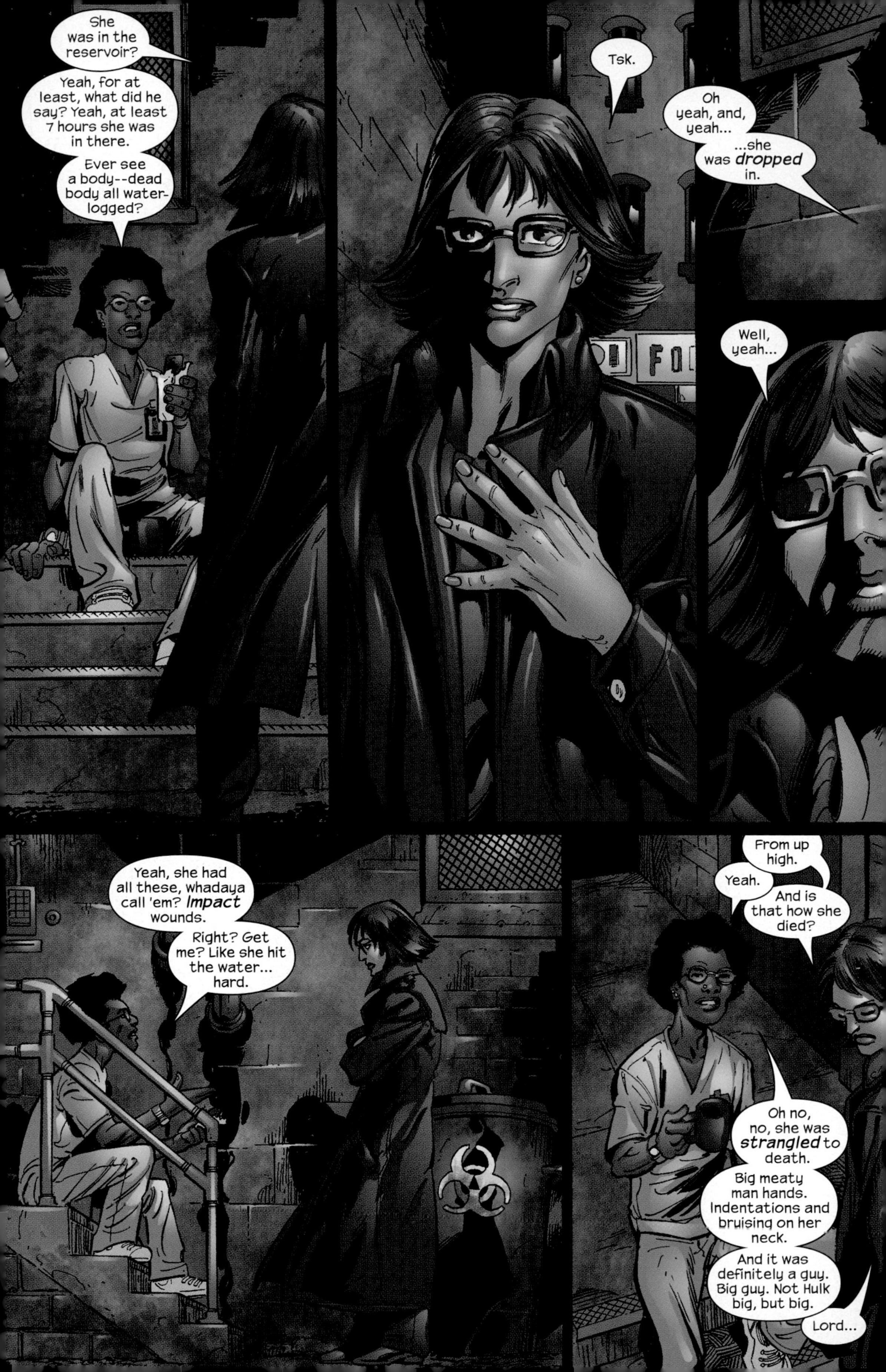
She was in the reservoir?
Yeah, for at least, what did he say? Yeah, at least 7 hours she was in there.
Ever see a body--dead body all water-logged?
Tsk.
Oh yeah, and, yeah...
...she was *dropped* in.
Well, yeah...
Yeah, she had all these, whadaya call 'em? *Impact* wounds.
Right? Get me? Like she hit the water... hard.
From up high.
Yeah.
And is that how she died?
Oh no, no, she was *strangled* to death.
Big meaty man hands. Indentations and bruising on her neck.
And it was definitely a guy. Big guy. Not Hulk big, but big.
Lord...

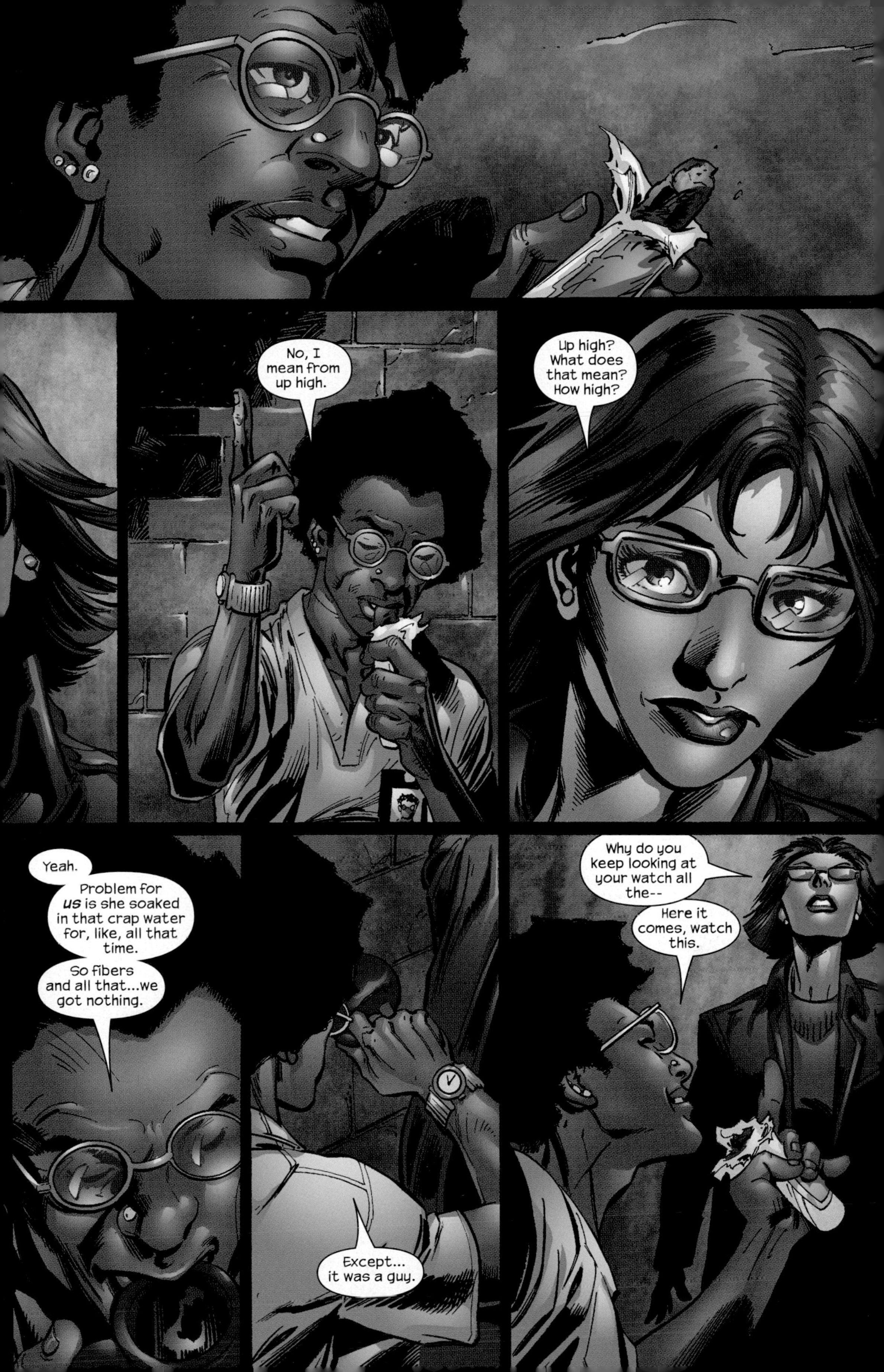
No, I mean from up high.
Up high? What does that mean? How high?
Yeah.
Problem for us is she soaked in that crap water for, like, all that time.
So fibers and all that...we got nothing.
Except... it was a guy.
Why do you keep looking at your watch all the--
Here it comes, watch this.

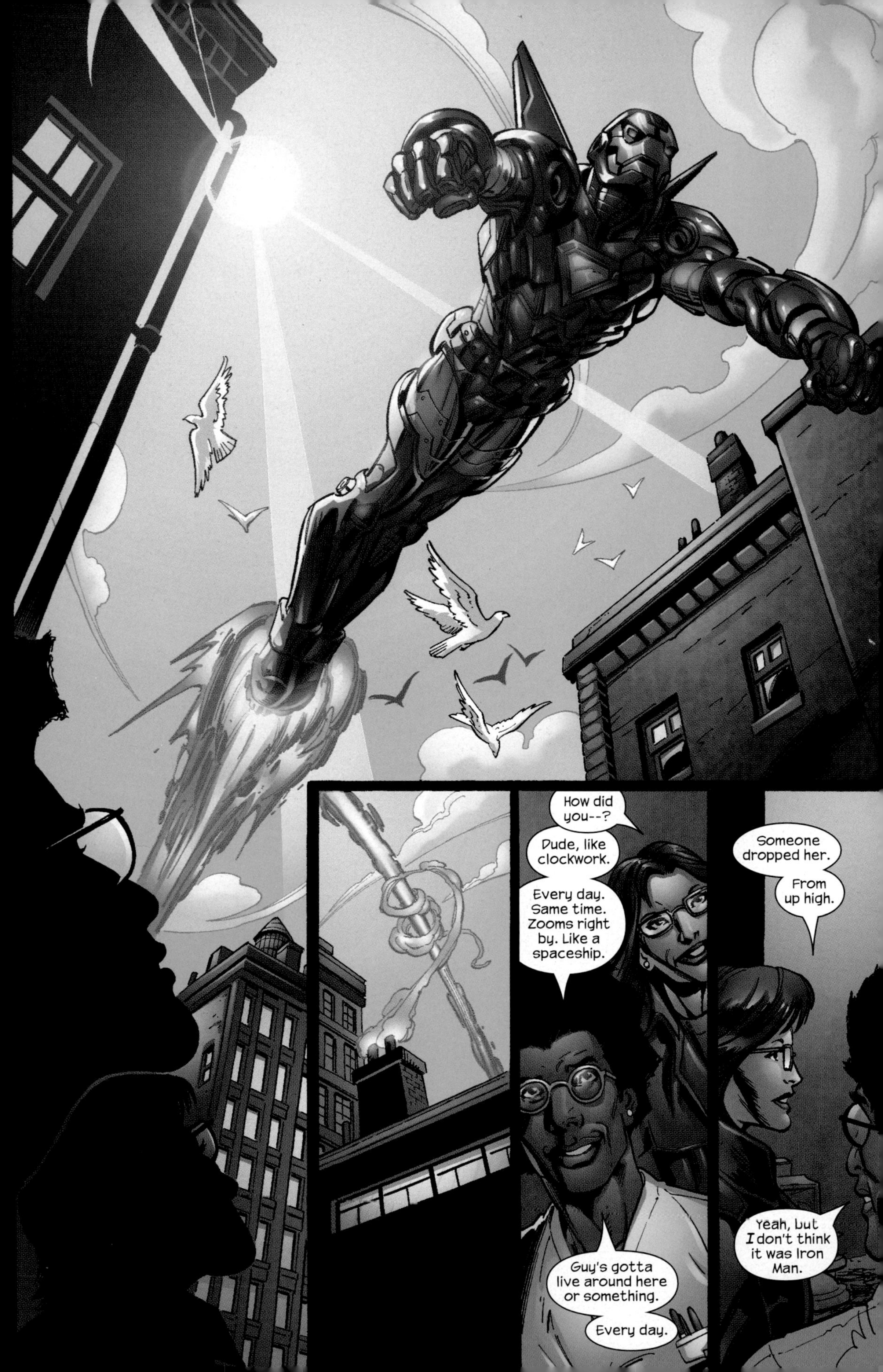
How did you--?
Dude, like clockwork.
Every day. Same time. Zooms right by. Like a spaceship.
Guy's gotta live around here or something.
Every day.
Someone dropped her.
From up high.
Yeah, but I don't think it was Iron Man.

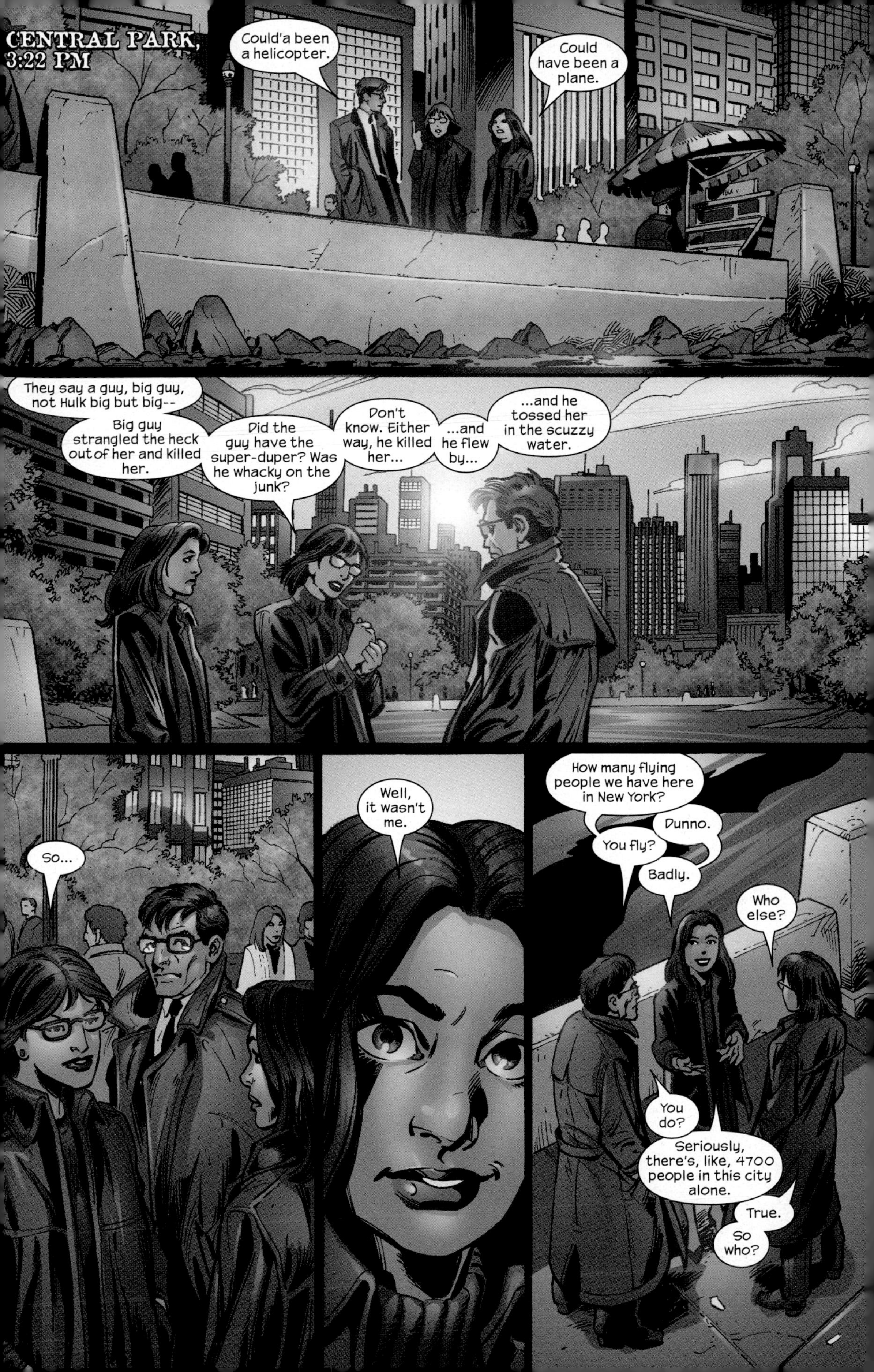
CENTRAL PARK, 3:22 PM
Could'a been a helicopter.
Could have been a plane.
They say a guy, big guy, not Hulk big but big--
Big guy strangled the heck out of her and killed her.
Did the guy have the super-duper? Was he whacky on the junk?
Don't know. Either way, he killed her...
...and he flew by...
...and he tossed her in the scuzzy water.
So...
Well, it wasn't me.
How many flying people we have here in New York?
Dunno.
You fly?
Badly.
Who else?
You do?
Seriously, there's, like, 4700 people in this city alone.
True.
So who?

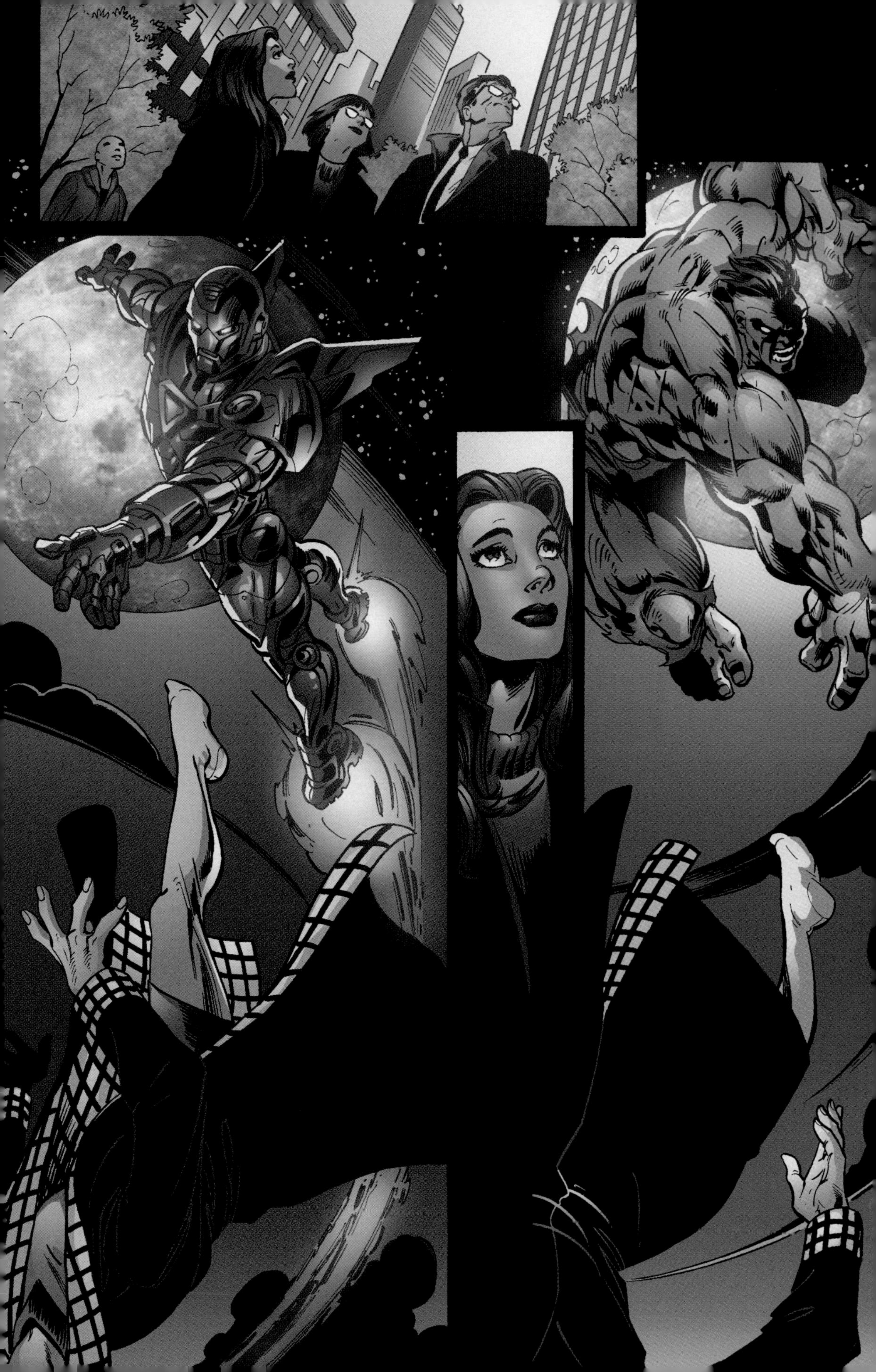

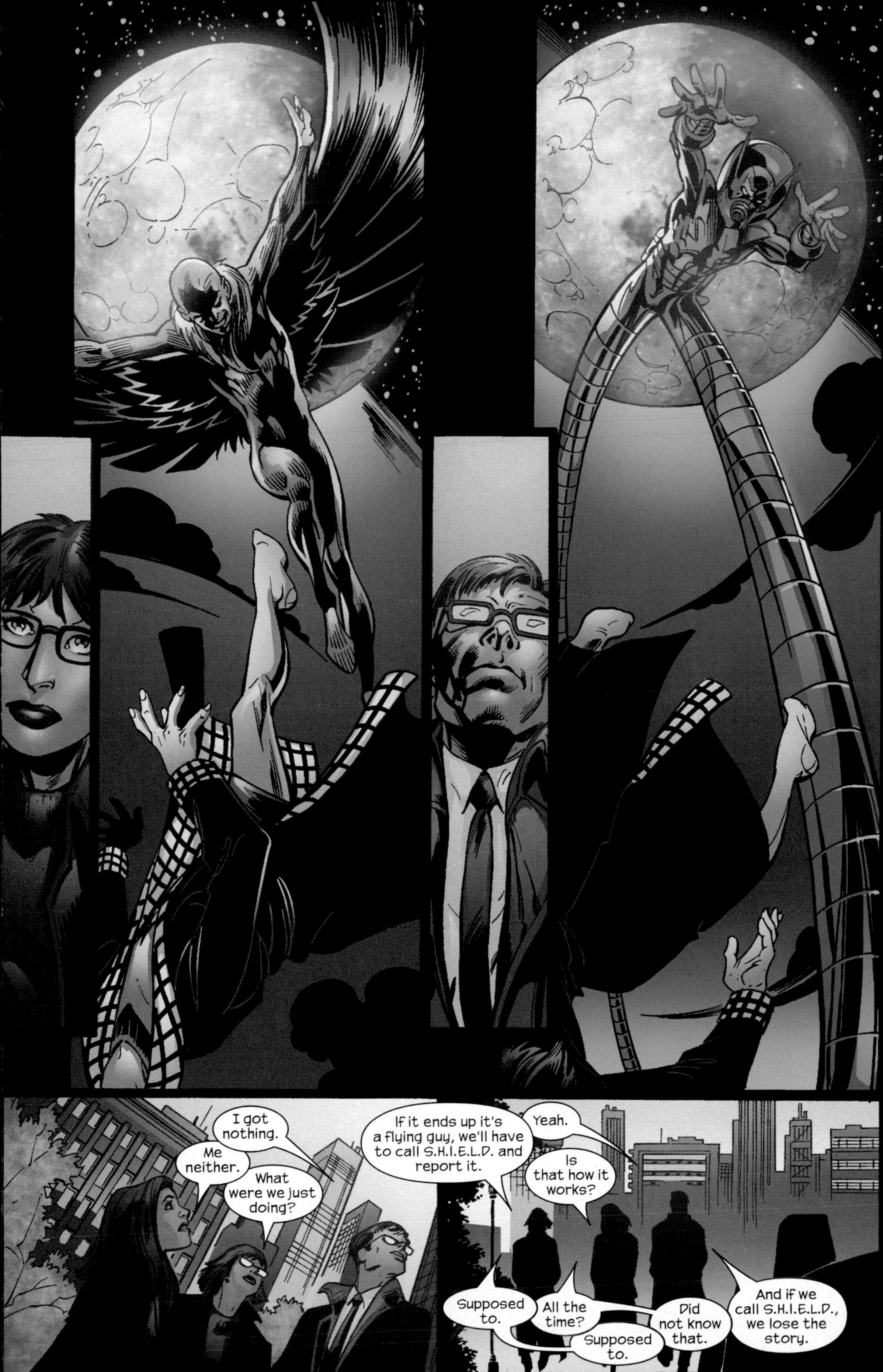

Me neither.
I got nothing.
What were we just doing?
If it ends up it's a flying guy, we'll have to call S.H.I.E.L.D. and report it.
Yeah.
Is that how it works?
Supposed to.
All the time?
Supposed to.
Did not know that.
And if we call S.H.I.E.L.D., we lose the story.

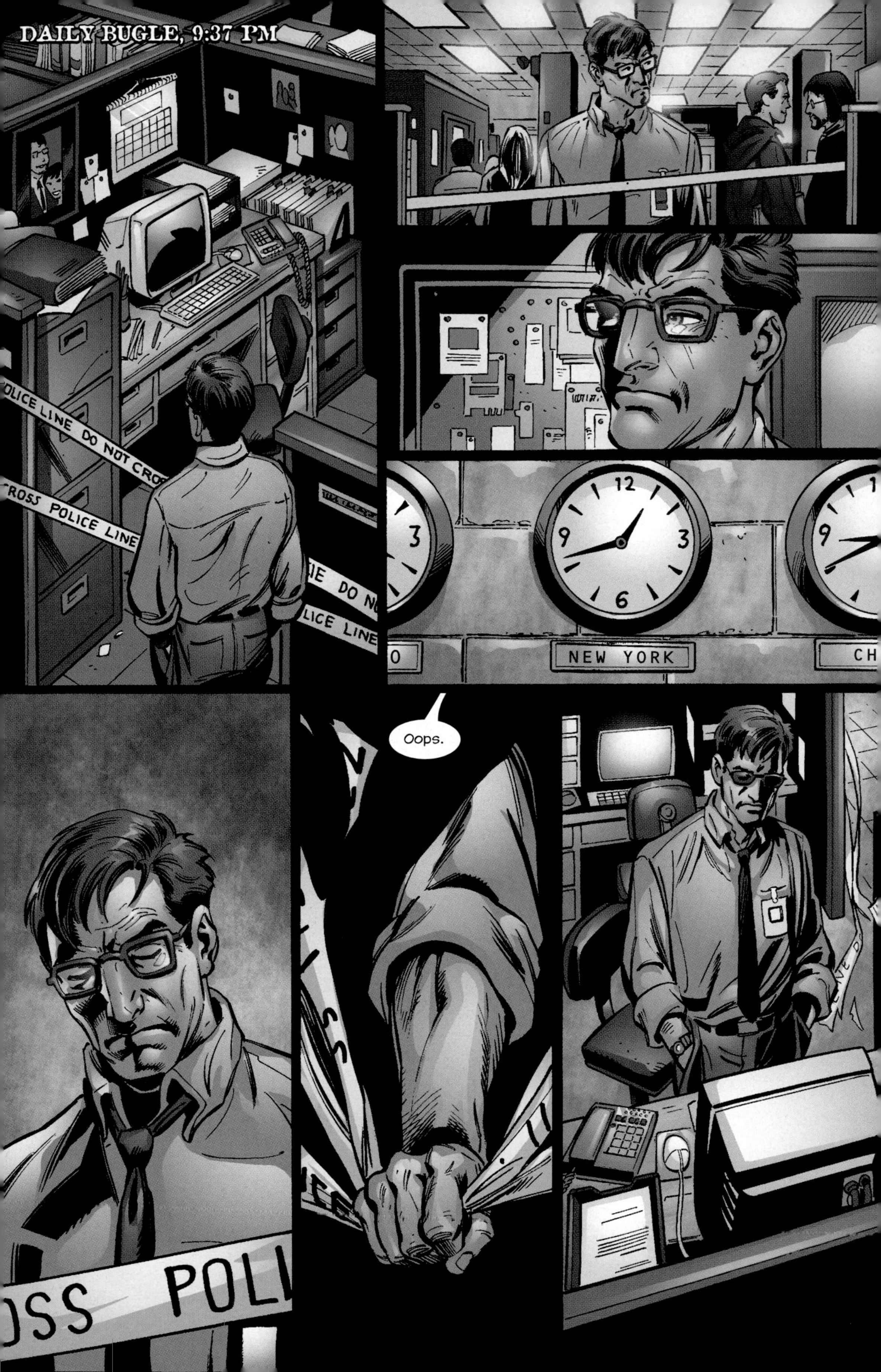
DAILY BUGLE, 9:37 PM
POLICE LINE DO NOT CROSS
CROSS POLICE LINE
NEW YORK
Oops.
OSS POLI

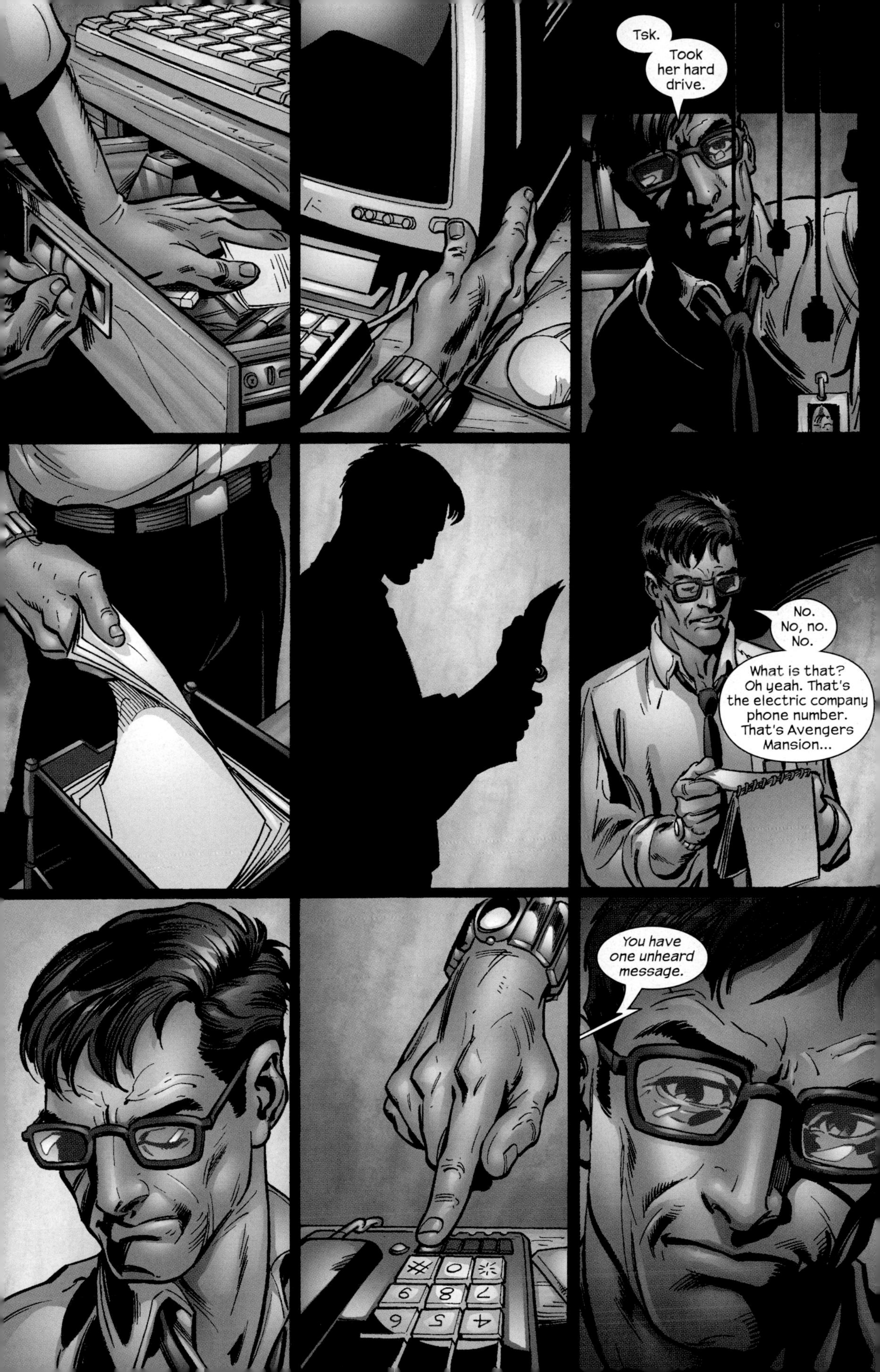
Tsk.
Took her hard drive.
No. No, no. No.
What is that? Oh yeah. That's the electric company phone number. That's Avengers Mansion...
You have one unheard message.

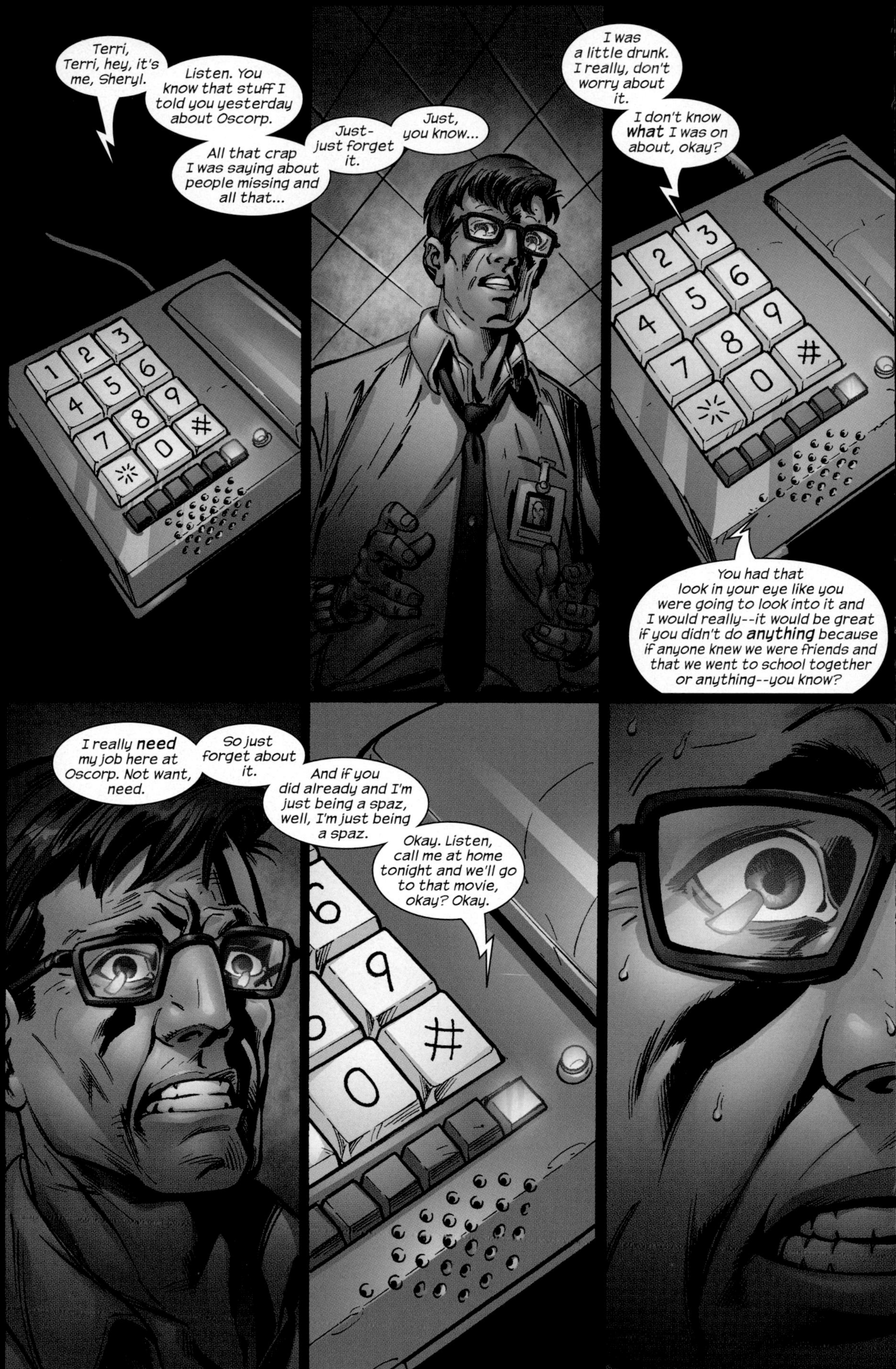

Terri, Terri, hey, it's me, Sheryl.
Listen. You know that stuff I told you yesterday about Oscorp.
All that crap I was saying about people missing and all that...
Just- just forget it.
Just, you know...
I was a little drunk. I really, don't worry about it.
I don't know **what** I was on about, okay?
You had that look in your eye like you were going to look into it and I would really--it would be great if you didn't do **anything** because if anyone knew we were friends and that we went to school together or anything--you know?
I really **need** my job here at Oscorp. Not want, need.
So just forget about it.
And if you did already and I'm just being a spaz, well, I'm just being a spaz.
Okay. Listen, call me at home tonight and we'll go to that movie, okay? Okay.

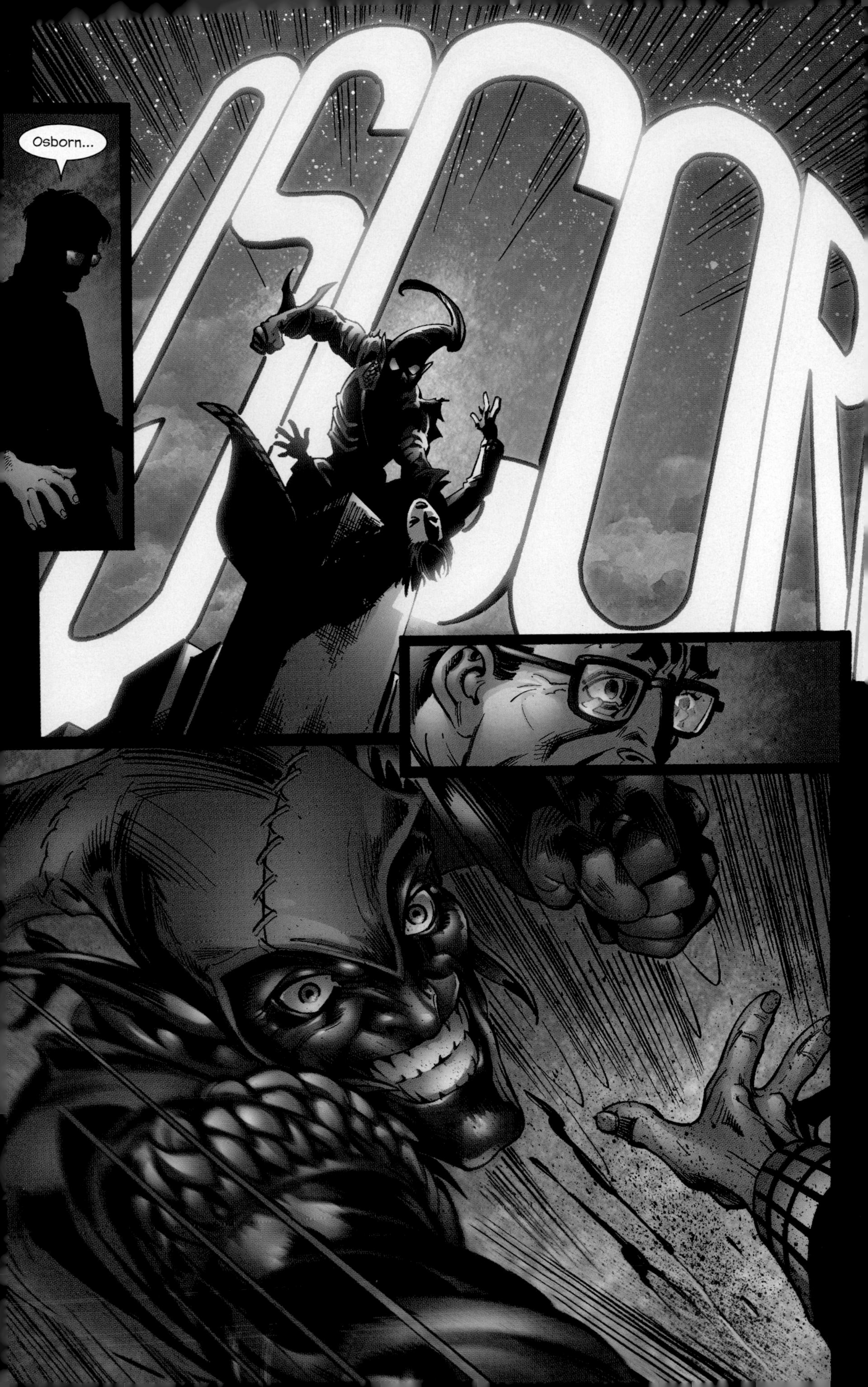
Osborn...

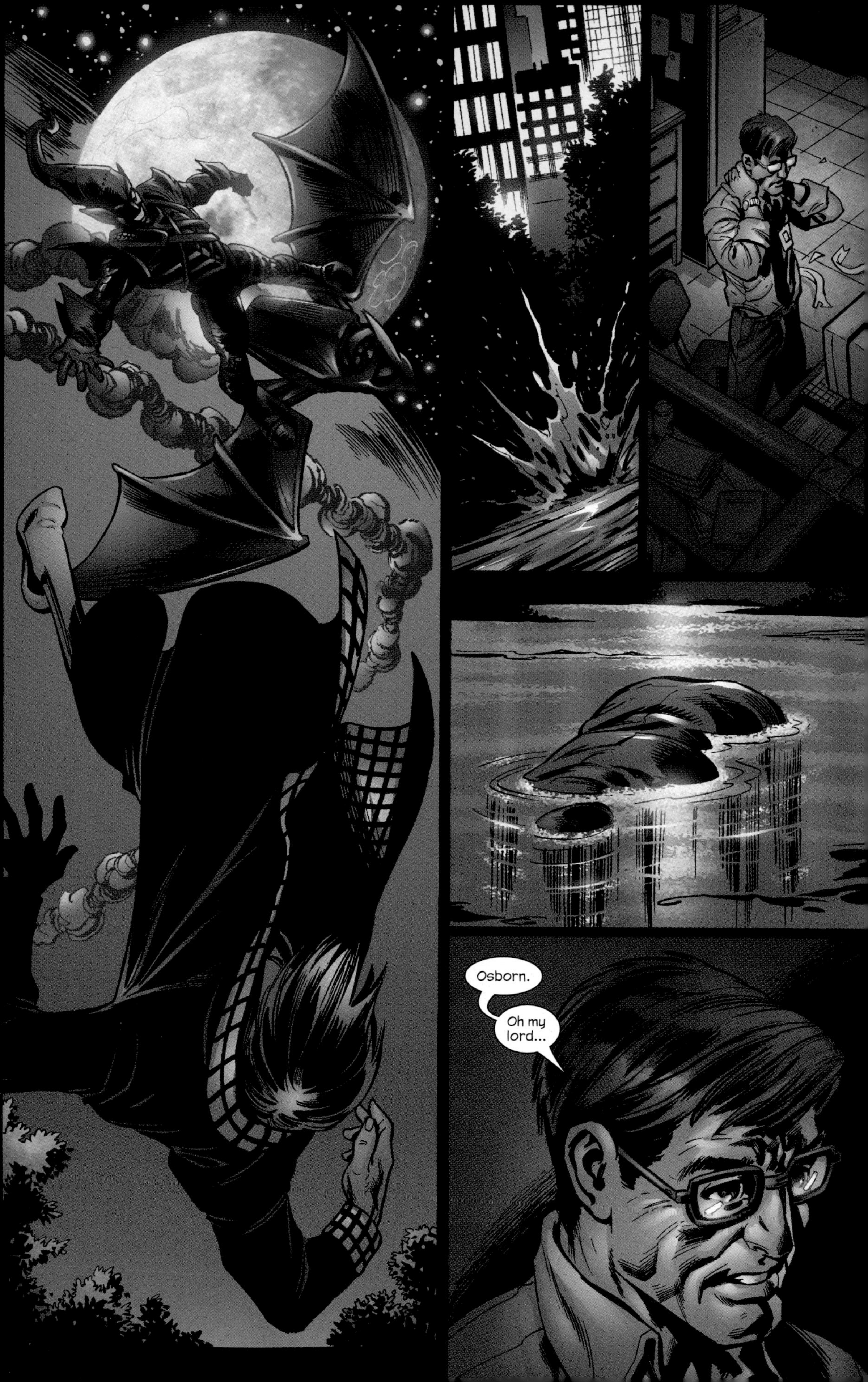
Osborn.
Oh my lord...

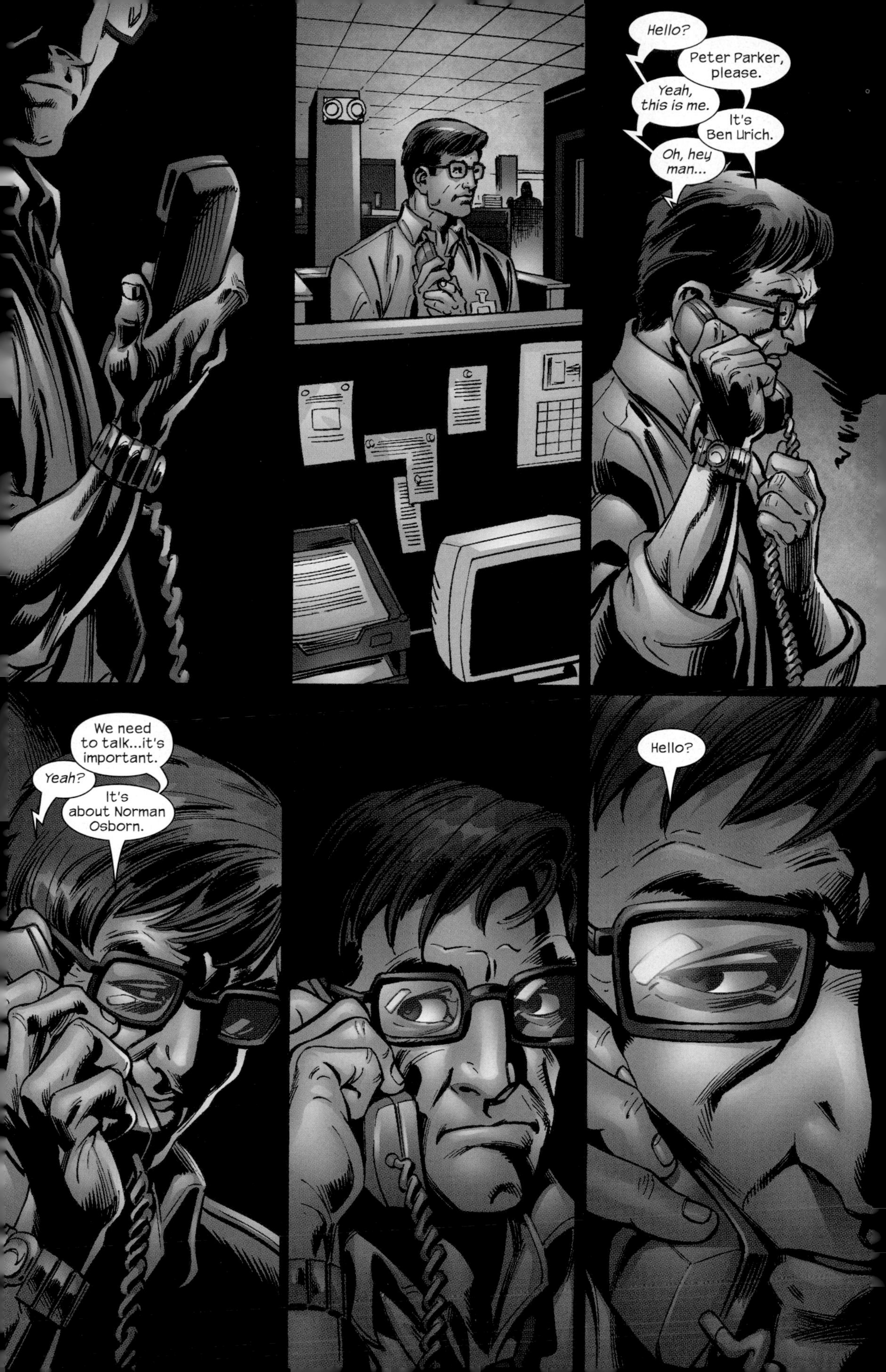
Hello?
Peter Parker, please.
Yeah, this is me.
It's Ben Urich.
Oh, hey man...
We need to talk...it's important.
Yeah?
It's about Norman Osborn.
Hello?

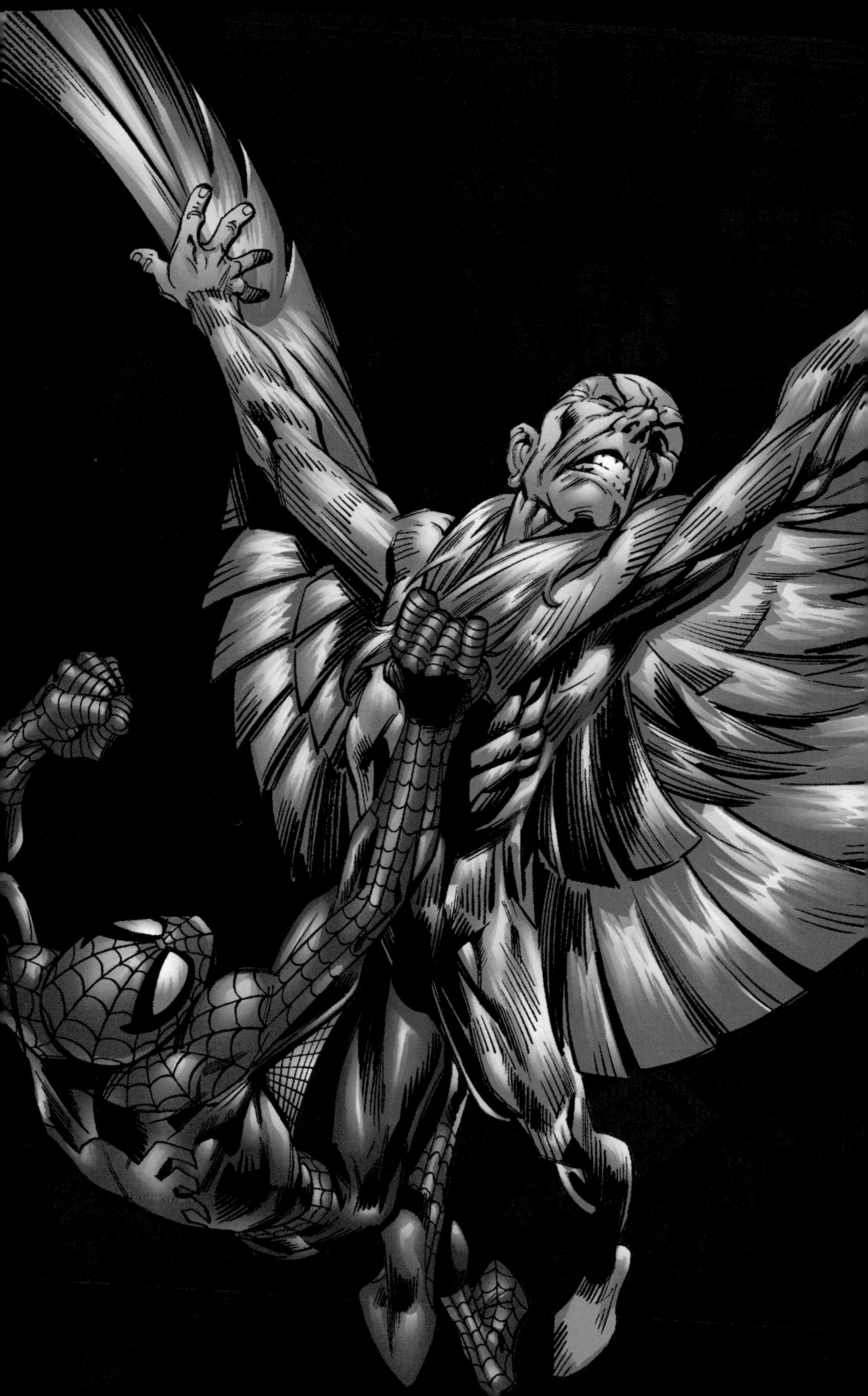

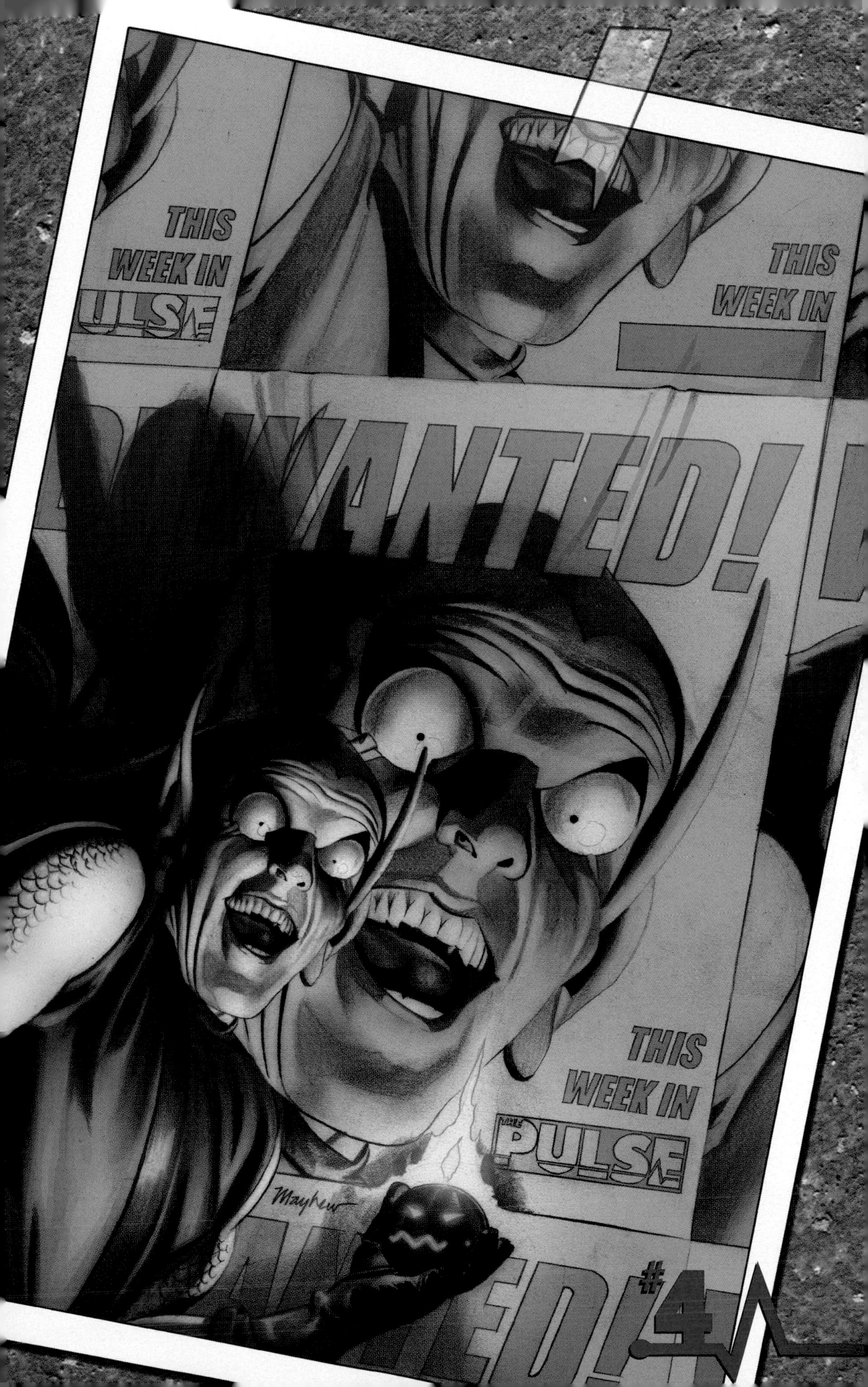
THIS
WEEK IN
ULSE
THIS
WEEK IN
WANTED!
THIS
WEEK IN
THE PULSE
Mayhew
#4

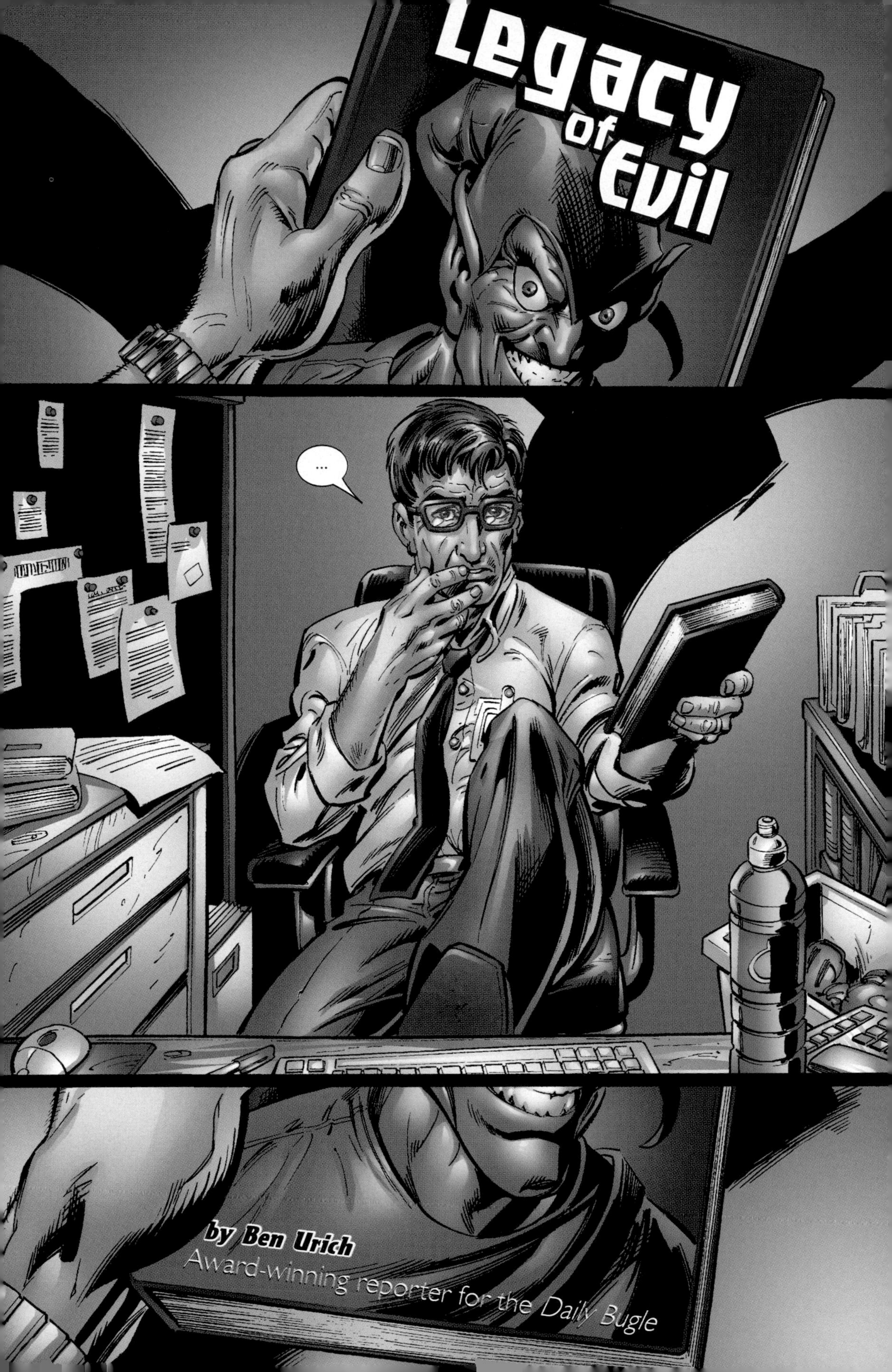
Legacy of Evil
...
by Ben Urich
Award-winning reporter for the Daily Bugle

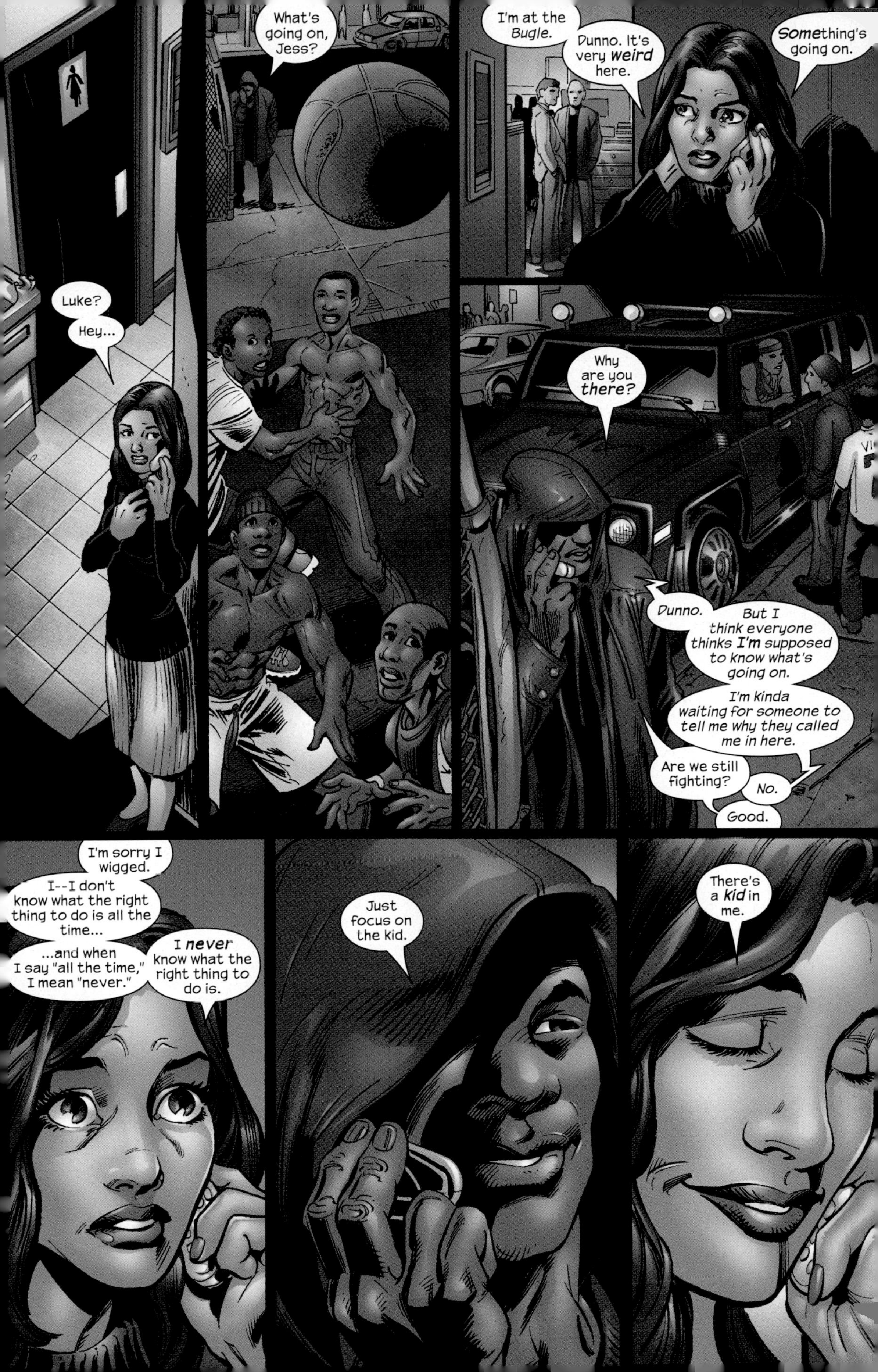

Luke?
Hey...
What's going on, Jess?
I'm at the *Bugle*.
Dunno. It's very **weird** here.
Something's going on.
Why are you **there**?
Dunno.
But I think everyone thinks **I'm** supposed to know what's going on.
I'm kinda waiting for someone to tell me why they called me in here.
Are we still fighting?
No.
Good.
I'm sorry I wigged.
I--I don't know what the right thing to do is all the time...
...and when I say "all the time," I mean "never."
I **never** know what the right thing to do is.
Just focus on the kid.
There's a **kid** in me.

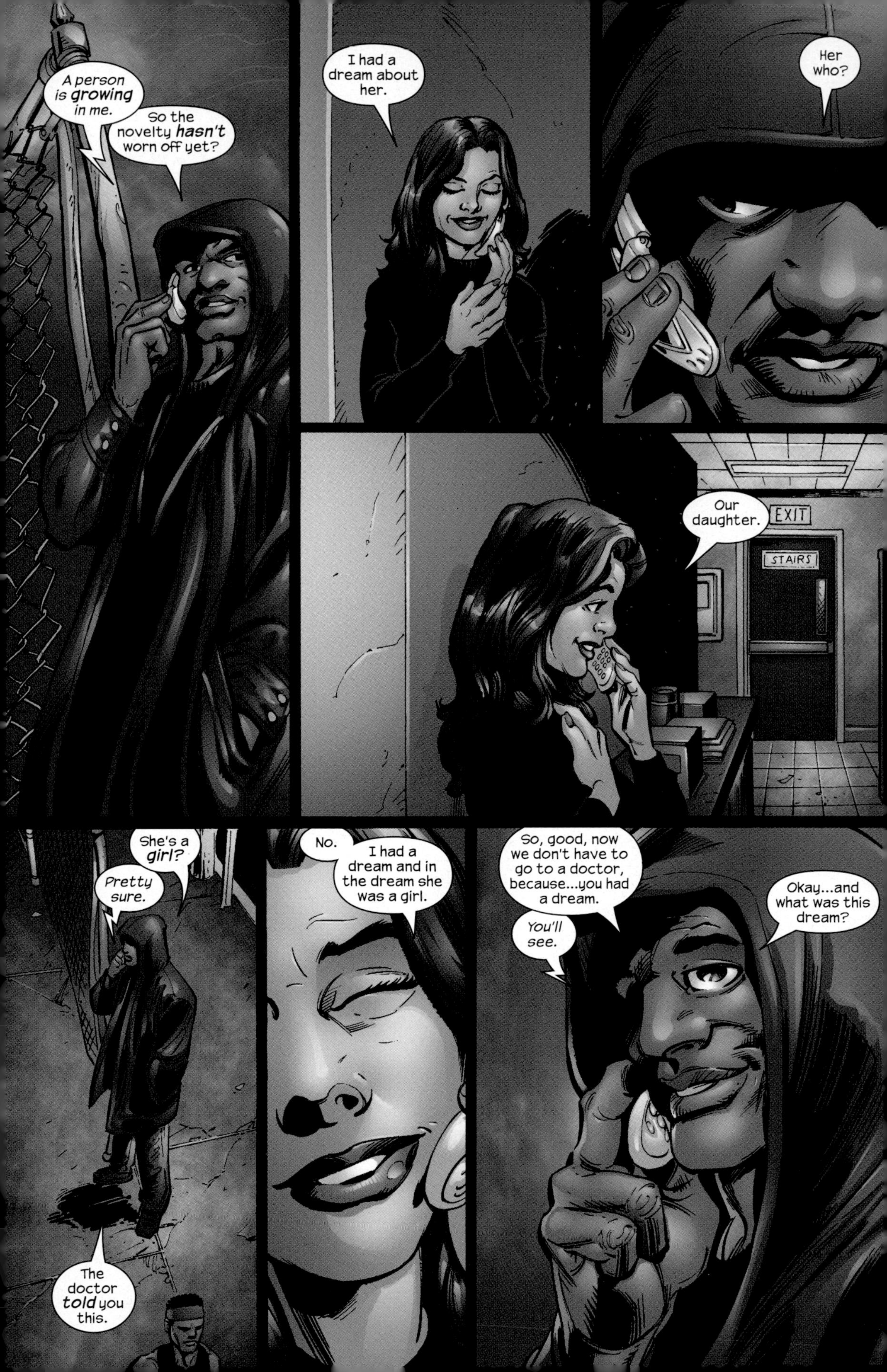
A person is growing in me.
So the novelty hasn't worn off yet?
I had a dream about her.
Her who?
Our daughter.
EXIT
STAIRS
She's a girl?
Pretty sure.
The doctor told you this.
No.
I had a dream and in the dream she was a girl.
So, good, now we don't have to go to a doctor, because...you had a dream.
You'll see.
Okay...and what was this dream?

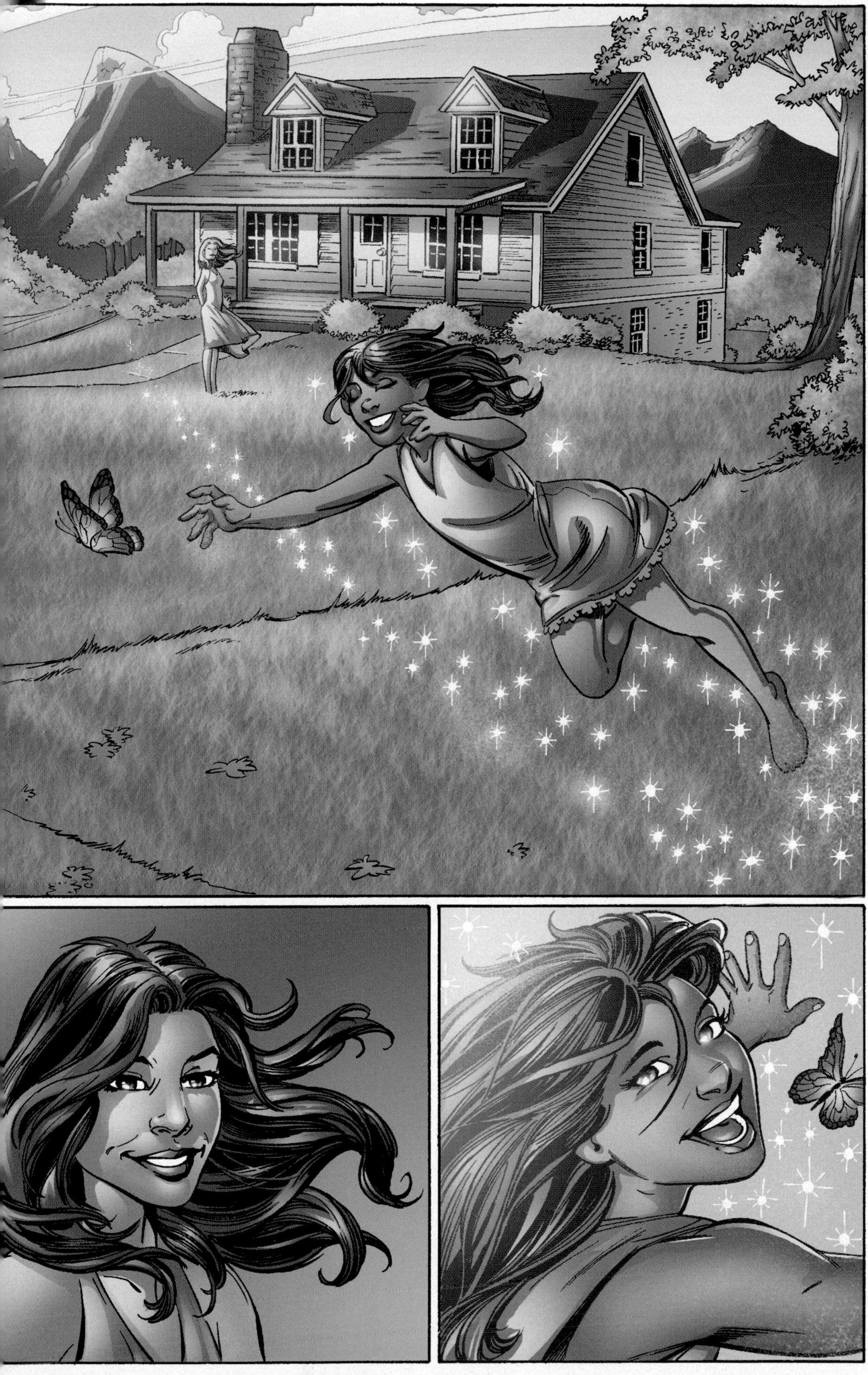

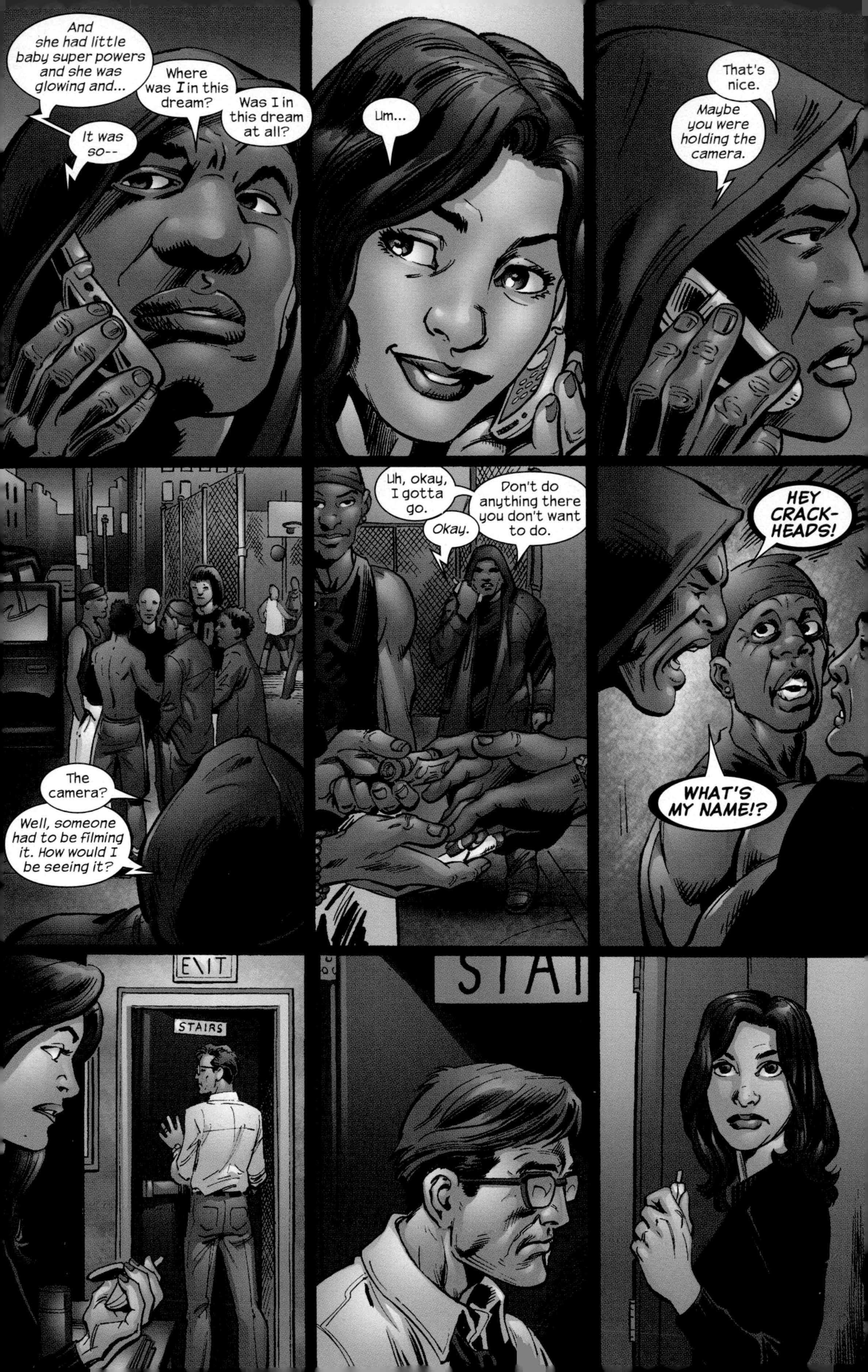

And she had little baby super powers and she was glowing and...
Where was I in this dream?
Was I in this dream at all?
It was so--
Um...
That's nice.
Maybe you were holding the camera.
The camera?
Well, someone had to be filming it. How would I be seeing it?
Uh, okay, I gotta go.
Okay.
Don't do anything there you don't want to do.
HEY CRACK-HEADS!
WHAT'S MY NAME!?
EXIT
STAIRS
STAI

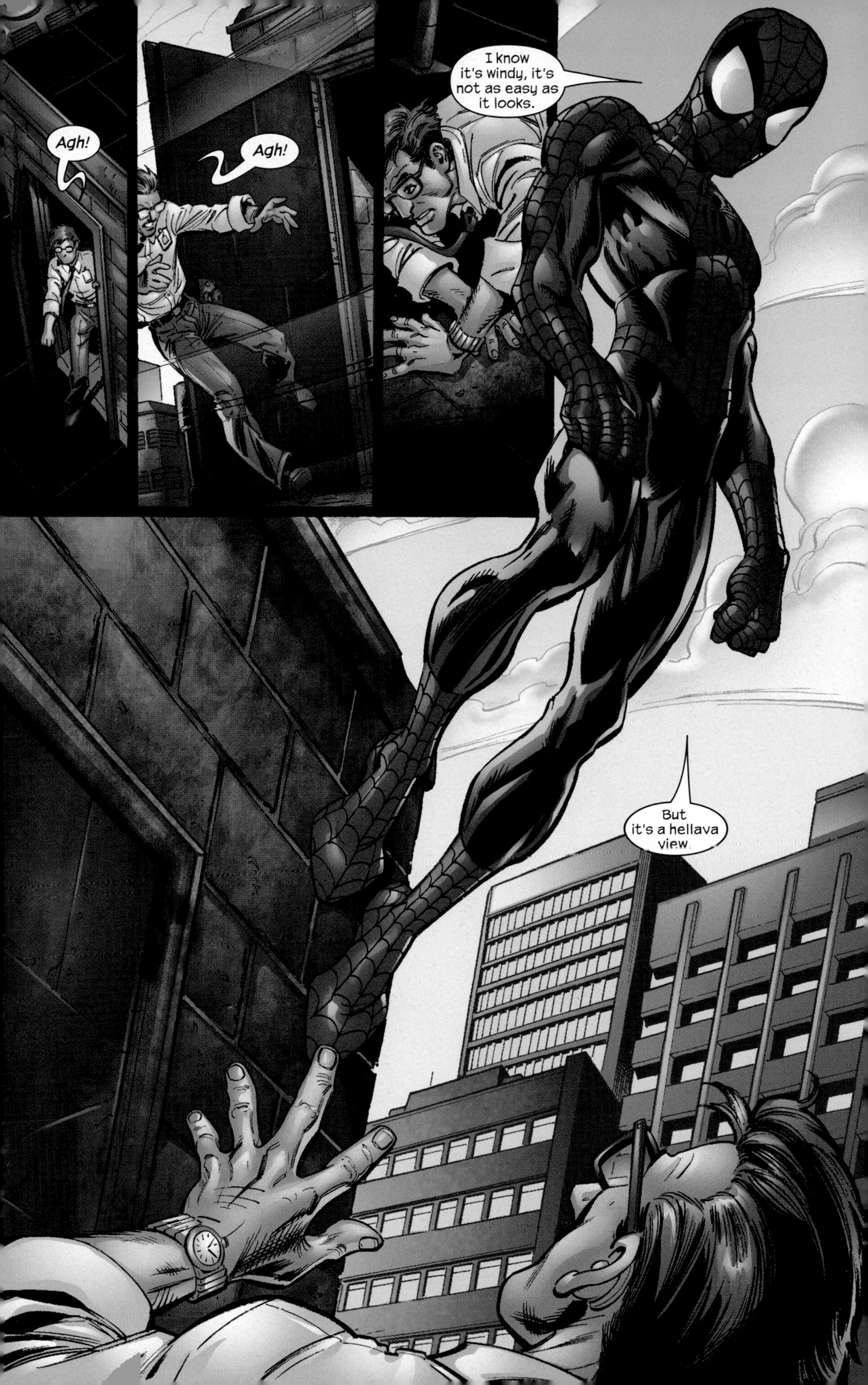
Agh!
Agh!
I know it's windy, it's not as easy as it looks.
But it's a hellava view.

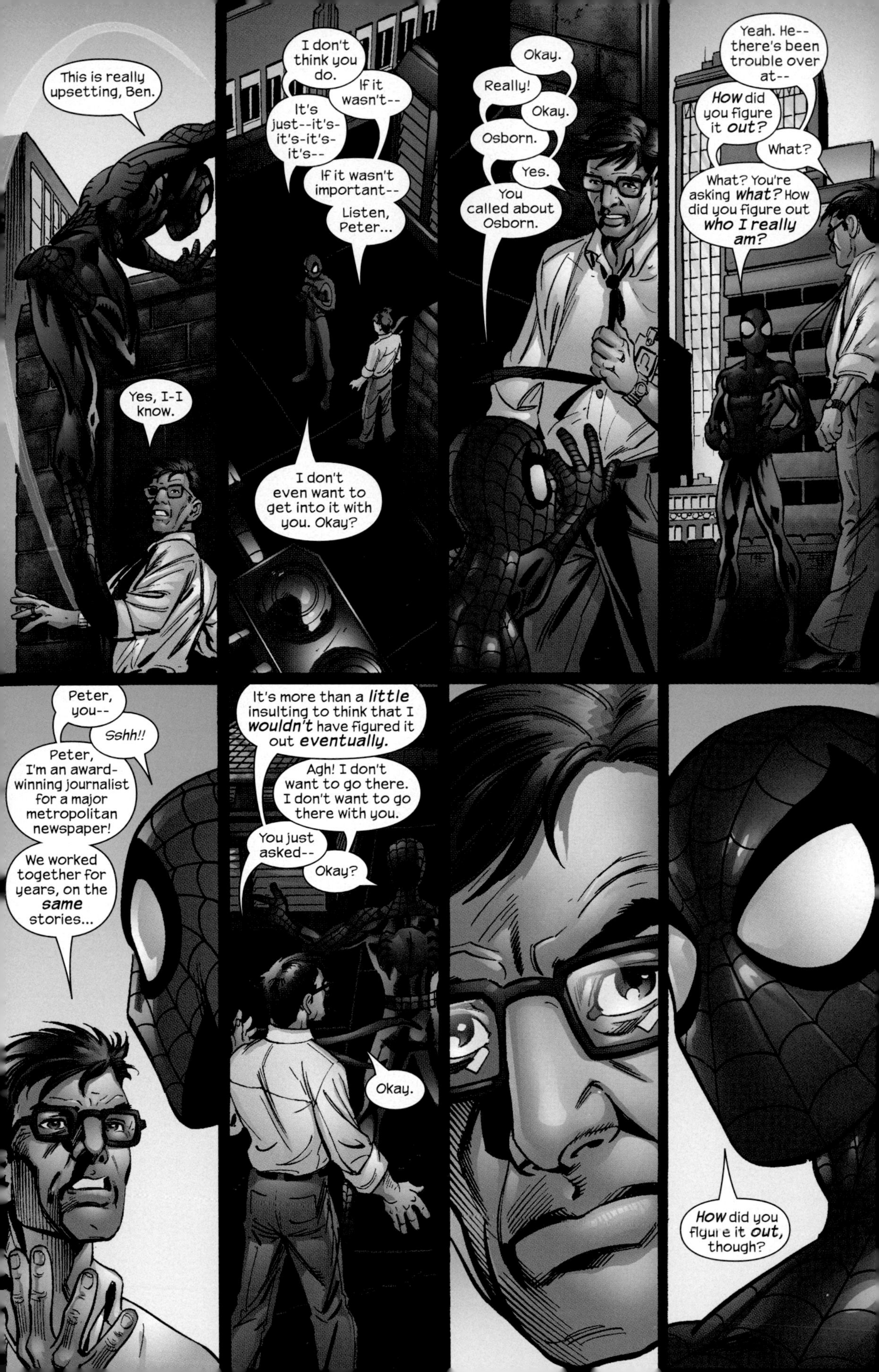

This is really upsetting, Ben.
Yes, I-I know.
I don't think you do.
If it wasn't--
It's just--it's-it's-it's-it's--
If it wasn't important--
Listen, Peter...
I don't even want to get into it with you. Okay?
Okay.
Really!
Okay.
Osborn.
Yes.
You called about Osborn.
Yeah. He--there's been trouble over at--
HOW did you figure it OUT?
What?
What? You're asking WHAT? How did you figure out WHO I REALLY AM?
Peter, you--
Sshh!!
Peter, I'm an award-winning journalist for a major metropolitan newspaper!
We worked together for years, on the SAME stories...
It's more than a LITTLE insulting to think that I WOULDN'T have figured it out EVENTUALLY.
Agh! I don't want to go there. I don't want to go there with you.
You just asked--
Okay?
Okay.
HOW did you figure it OUT, though?

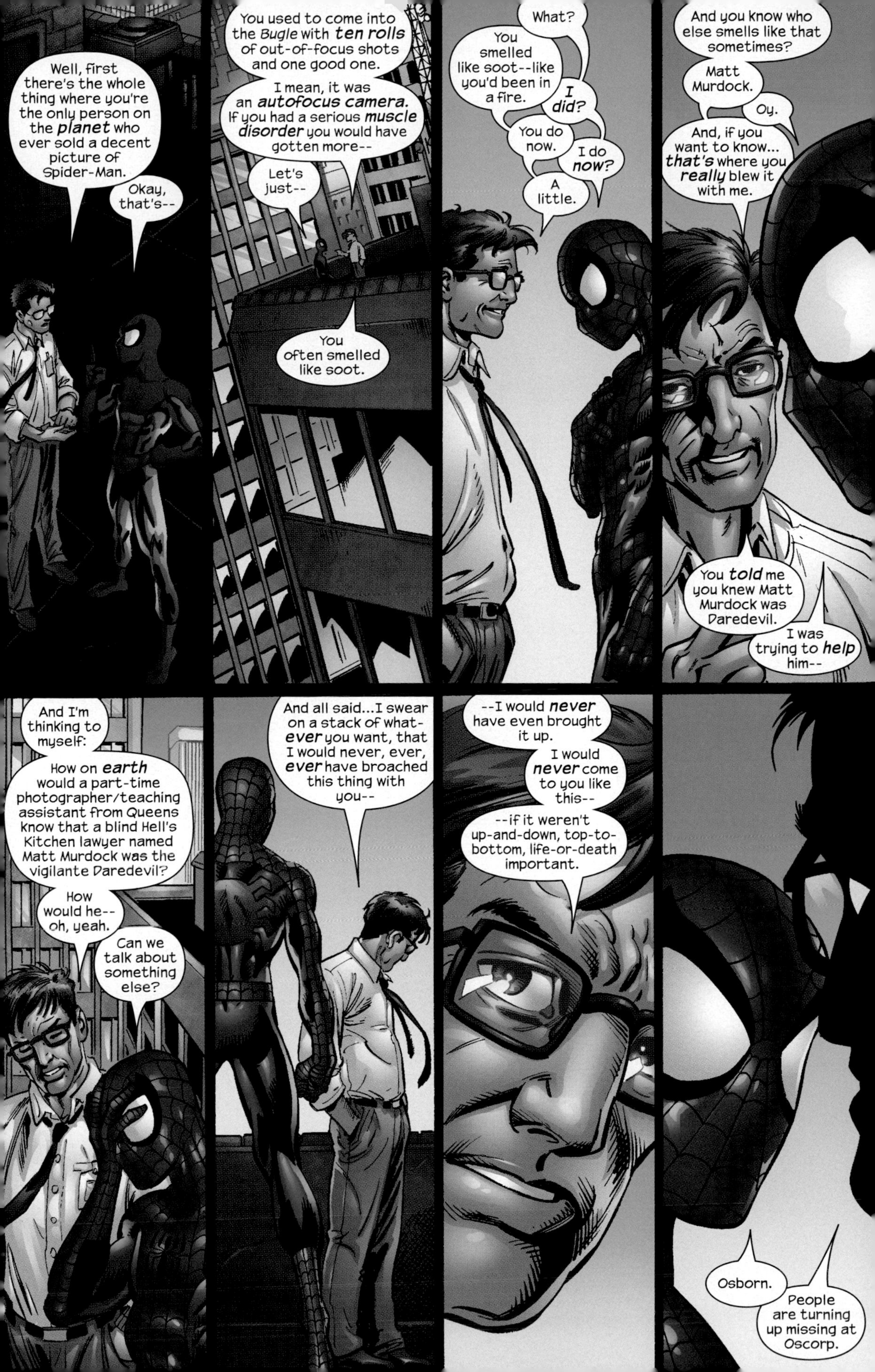
Well, first there's the whole thing where you're the only person on the planet who ever sold a decent picture of Spider-Man.
Okay, that's--
You used to come into the Bugle with ten rolls of out-of-focus shots and one good one.
I mean, it was an autofocus camera. If you had a serious muscle disorder you would have gotten more--
Let's just--
You often smelled like soot.
What?
You smelled like soot--like you'd been in a fire.
I did?
You do now.
I do now?
A little.
And you know who else smells like that sometimes?
Matt Murdock.
Oy.
And, if you want to know... that's where you really blew it with me.
You told me you knew Matt Murdock was Daredevil.
I was trying to help him--
And I'm thinking to myself:
How on earth would a part-time photographer/teaching assistant from Queens know that a blind Hell's Kitchen lawyer named Matt Murdock was the vigilante Daredevil?
How would he-- oh, yeah.
Can we talk about something else?
And all said...I swear on a stack of what-ever you want, that I would never, ever, ever have broached this thing with you--
--I would never have even brought it up.
I would never come to you like this--
--if it weren't up-and-down, top-to-bottom, life-or-death important.
Osborn.
People are turning up missing at Oscorp.

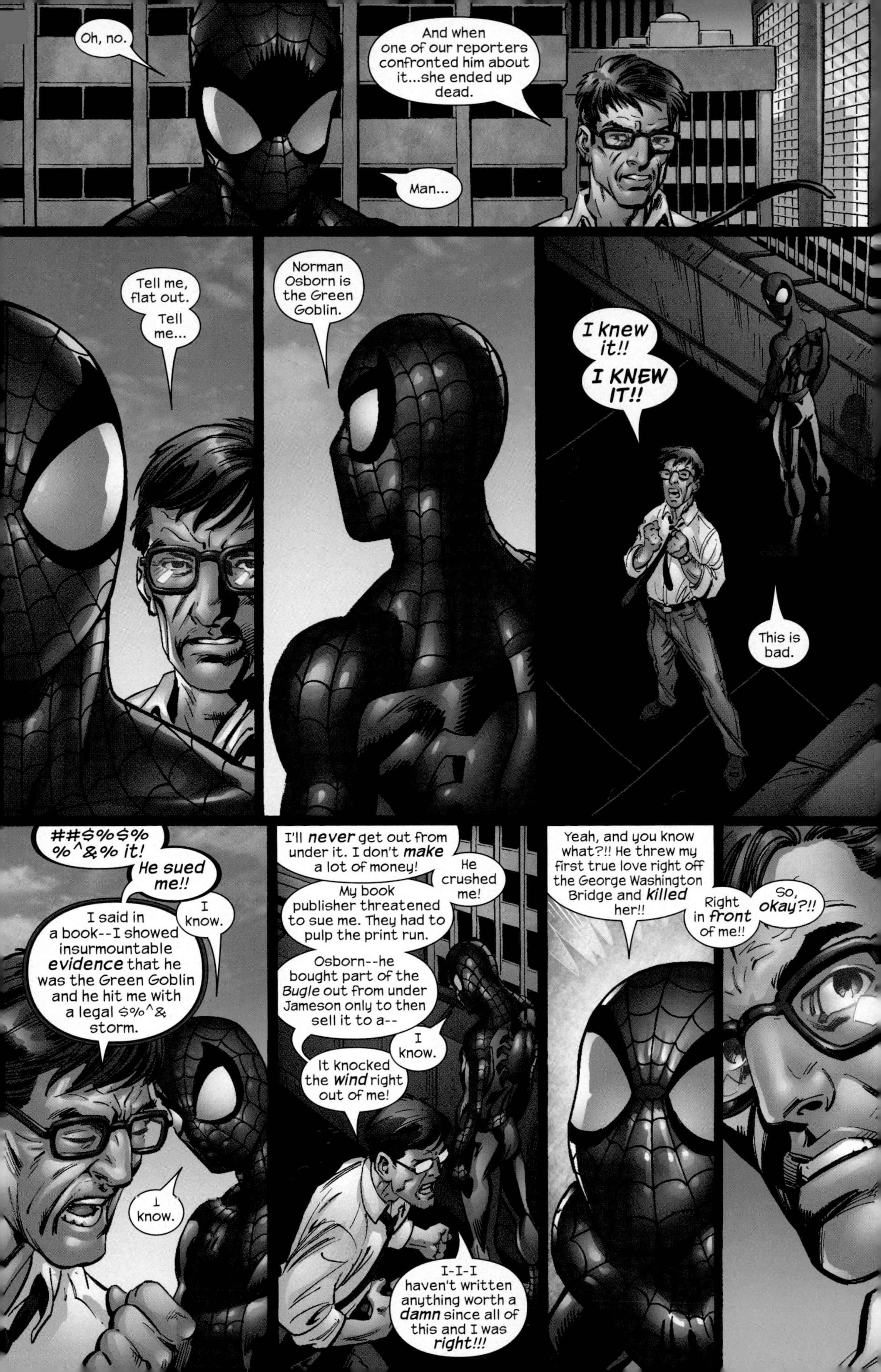
Oh, no.
And when one of our reporters confronted him about it...she ended up dead.
Man...
Tell me, flat out.
Tell me...
Norman Osborn is the Green Goblin.
I knew it!!
I KNEW IT!!
This is bad.
##$%$% %^&% it!
He sued me!!
I said in a book--I showed insurmountable evidence that he was the Green Goblin and he hit me with a legal $%^& storm.
I know.
I know.
I'll never get out from under it. I don't make a lot of money!
He crushed me!
My book publisher threatened to sue me. They had to pulp the print run.
Osborn--he bought part of the Bugle out from under Jameson only to then sell it to a--
I know.
It knocked the wind right out of me!
I-I-I haven't written anything worth a damn since all of this and I was right!!!
Yeah, and you know what?!! He threw my first true love right off the George Washington Bridge and killed her!!
Right in front of me!!
So, okay?!!

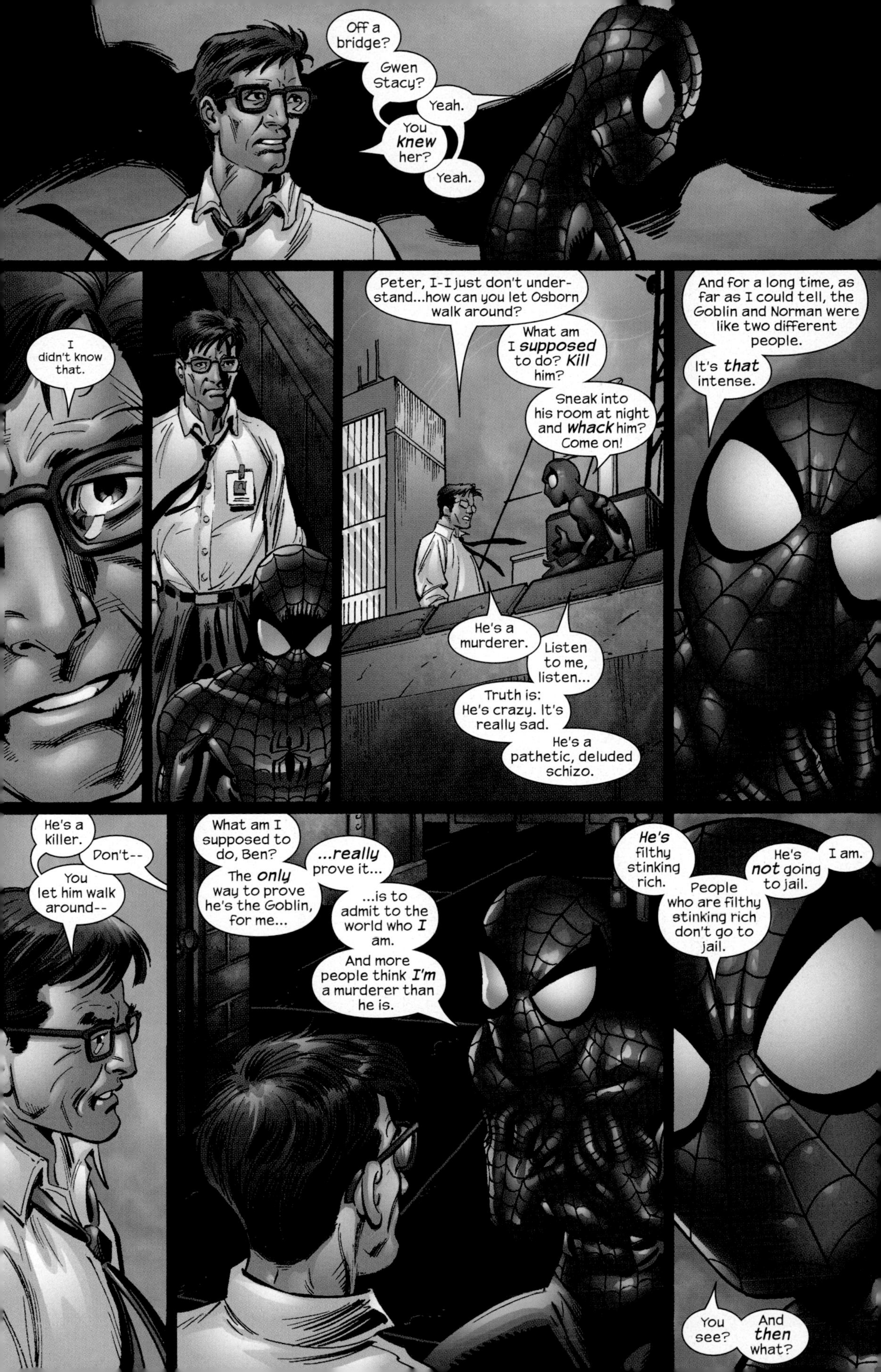

Off a bridge?
Gwen Stacy?
Yeah.
You *knew* her?
Yeah.
I didn't know that.
Peter, I-I just don't under-stand...how can you let Osborn walk around?
What am I *supposed* to do? *Kill* him?
Sneak into his room at night and *whack* him? Come on!
He's a murderer.
Listen to me, listen...
Truth is: He's crazy. It's really sad.
He's a pathetic, deluded schizo.
And for a long time, as far as I could tell, the Goblin and Norman were like two different people.
It's *that* intense.
He's a killer.
Don't--
You let him walk around--
What am I supposed to do, Ben?
The *only* way to prove he's the Goblin, for me...
...really prove it...
...is to admit to the world who *I* am.
And more people think *I'm* a murderer than he is.
He's filthy stinking rich.
People who are filthy stinking rich don't go to jail.
He's *not* going to jail.
I am.
You see?
And *then* what?

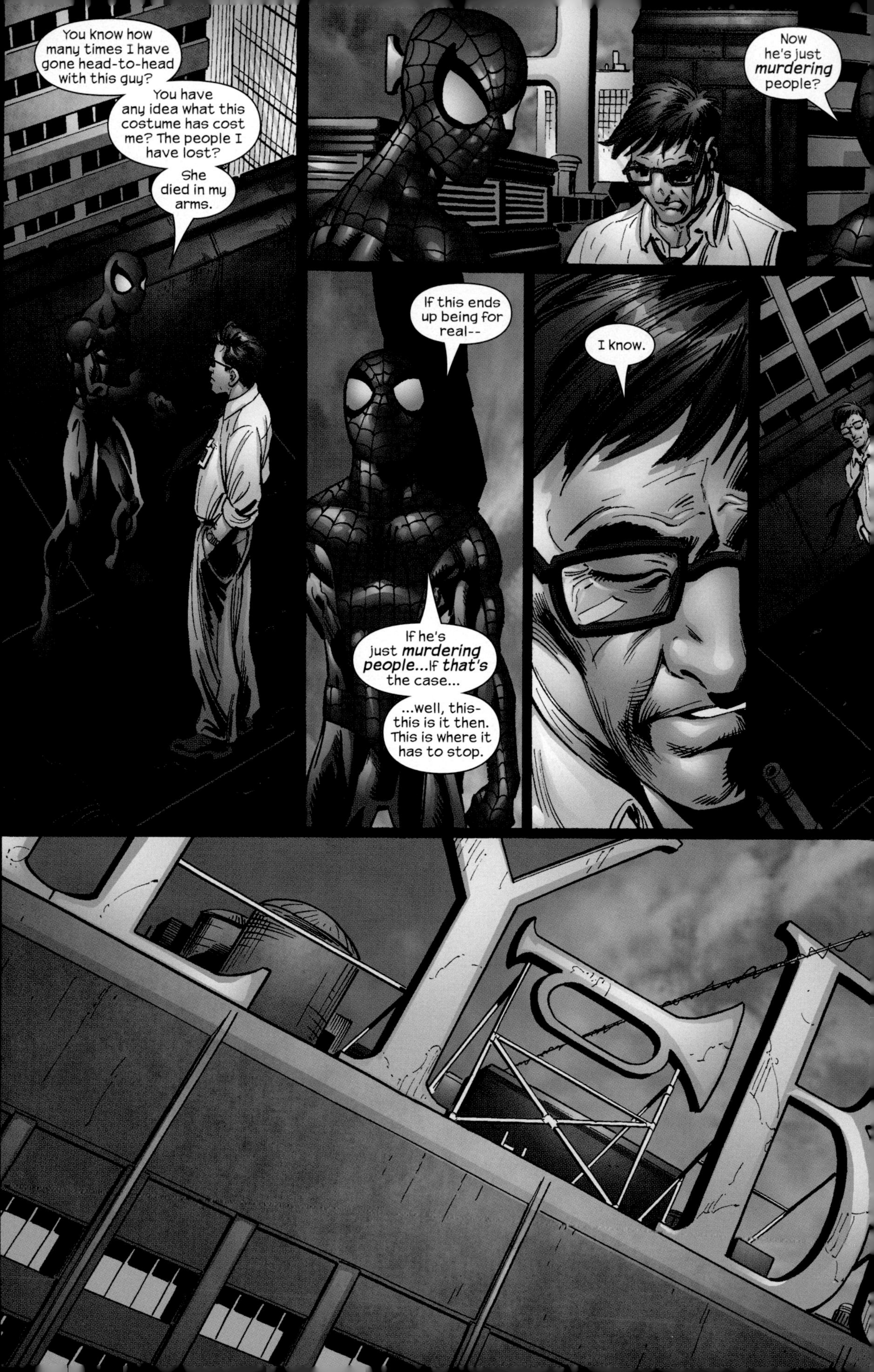
You know how many times I have gone head-to-head with this guy?
You have any idea what this costume has cost me? The people I have lost?
She died in my arms.
Now he's just *murdering* people?
If this ends up being for real--
If he's just *murdering people*...If *that's* the case...
...well, this- this is it then. This is where it has to stop.
I know.

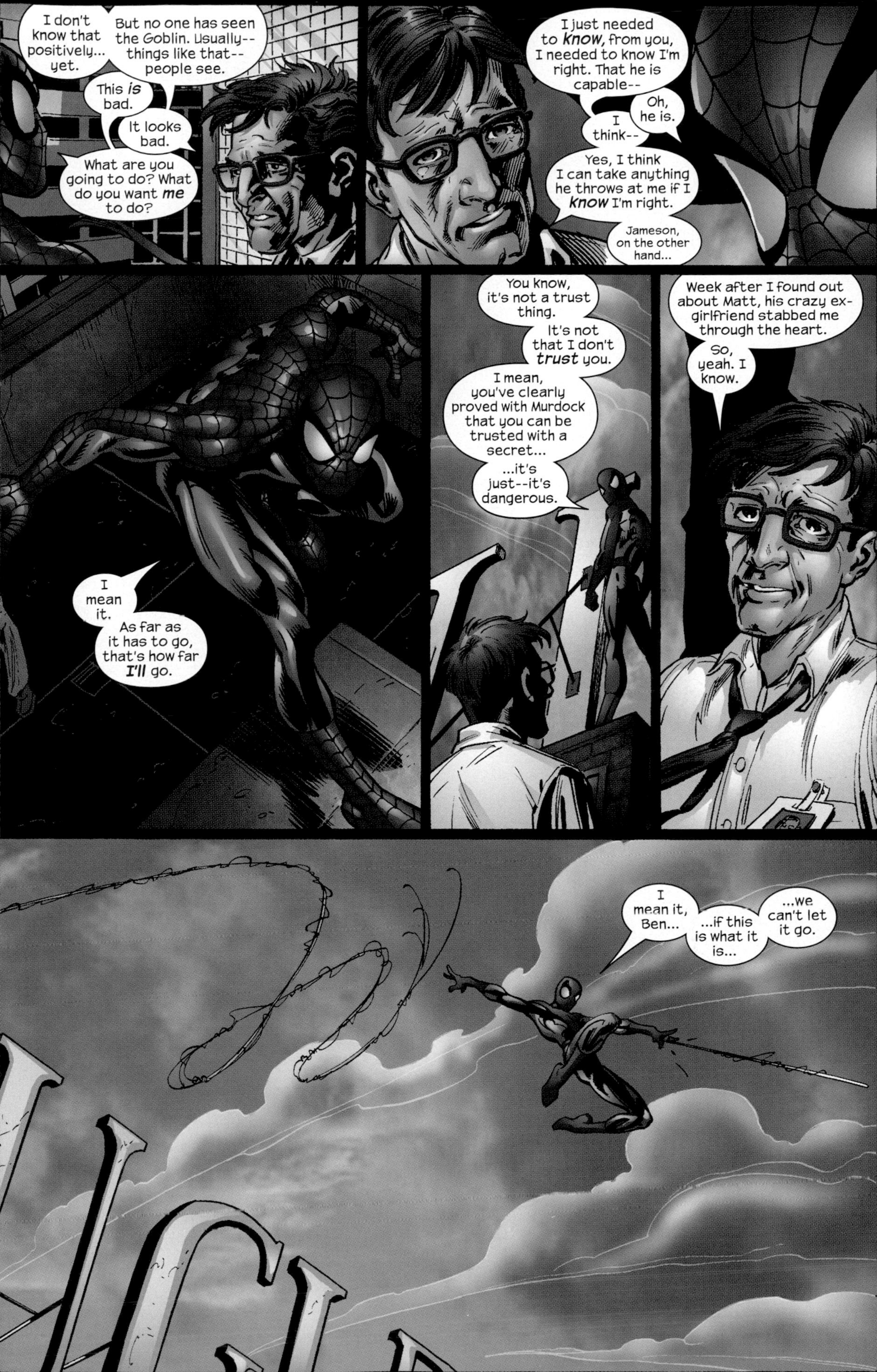
I don't know that positively... yet.
But no one has seen the Goblin. Usually-- things like that-- people see.
This *is* bad.
It looks bad.
What are you going to do? What do you want *me* to do?
I just needed to *know,* from you, I needed to know I'm right. That he is capable--
Oh, he is.
I think--
Yes, I think I can take anything he throws at me if I *know* I'm right.
Jameson, on the other hand...
I mean it.
As far as it has to go, that's how far *I'll* go.
You know, it's not a trust thing.
It's not that I don't *trust* you.
I mean, you've clearly proved with Murdock that you can be trusted with a secret...
...it's just--it's dangerous.
Week after I found out about Matt, his crazy ex-girlfriend stabbed me through the heart.
So, yeah. I know.
I mean it, Ben...
...if this is what it is...
...we can't let it go.

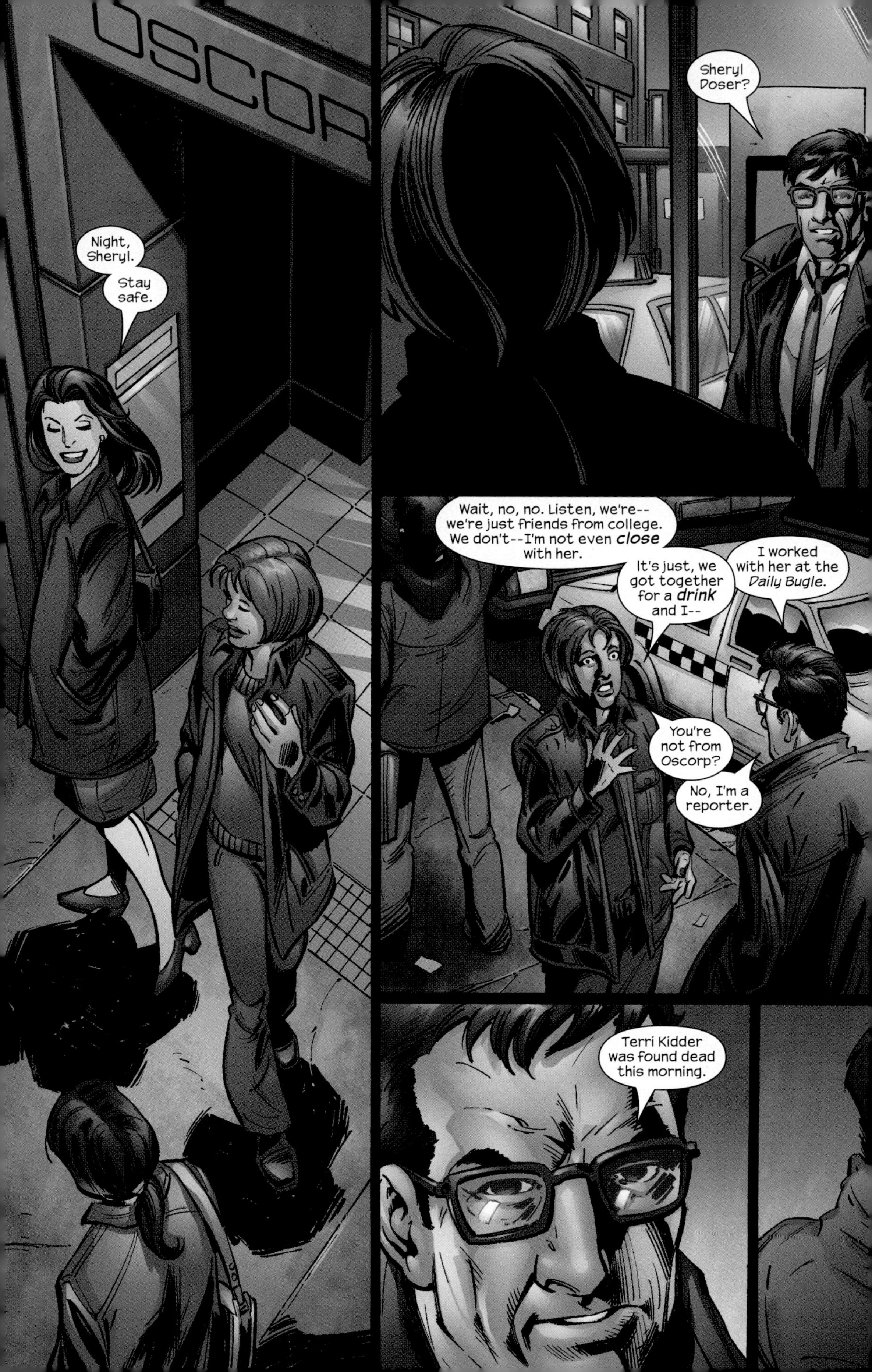
OSCORP
Sheryl Doser?
Night, Sheryl.
Stay safe.
Wait, no, no. Listen, we're-- we're just friends from college. We don't--I'm not even *close* with her.
It's just, we got together for a *drink* and I--
I worked with her at the *Daily Bugle*.
You're not from Oscorp?
No, I'm a reporter.
Terri Kidder was found dead this morning.

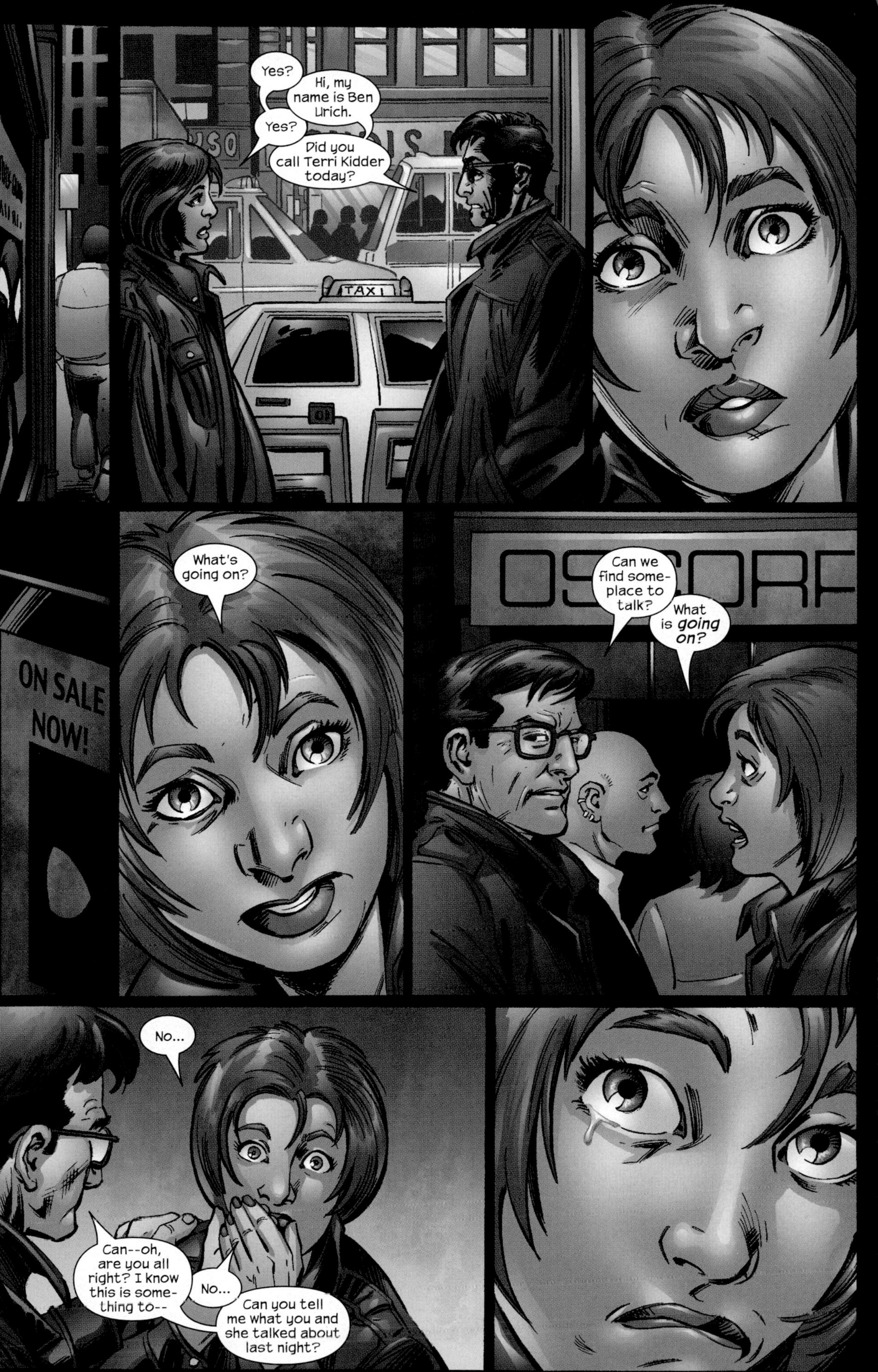
Yes?
Hi, my name is Ben Urich.
Yes?
Did you call Terri Kidder today?
What's going on?
ON SALE NOW!
OSCORP
Can we find some-place to talk?
What is *going on?*
No...
Can--oh, are you all right? I know this is some-thing to--
No...
Can you tell me what you and she talked about last night?

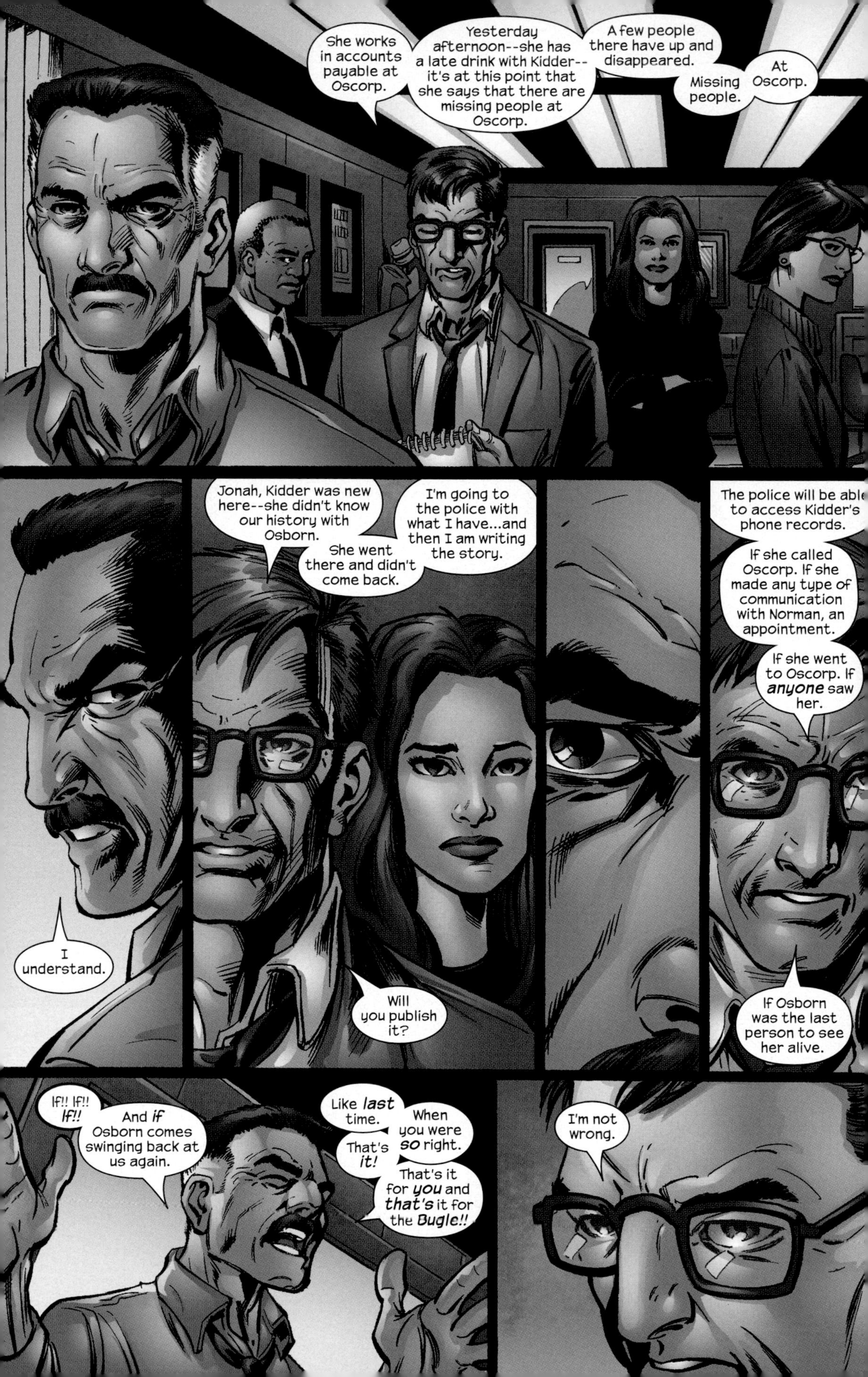
She works in accounts payable at Oscorp.
Yesterday afternoon--she has a late drink with Kidder--it's at this point that she says that there are missing people at Oscorp.
A few people there have up and disappeared.
Missing people.
At Oscorp.
I understand.
Jonah, Kidder was new here--she didn't know our history with Osborn.
She went there and didn't come back.
I'm going to the police with what I have...and then I am writing the story.
Will you publish it?
The police will be able to access Kidder's phone records.
If she called Oscorp. If she made any type of communication with Norman, an appointment.
If she went to Oscorp. If *anyone* saw her.
If Osborn was the last person to see her alive.
If!! If!! *If!!*
And *if* Osborn comes swinging back at us again.
Like *last* time.
When you were *so* right.
That's *it!*
That's it for *you* and *that's* it for the *Bugle!!*
I'm not wrong.

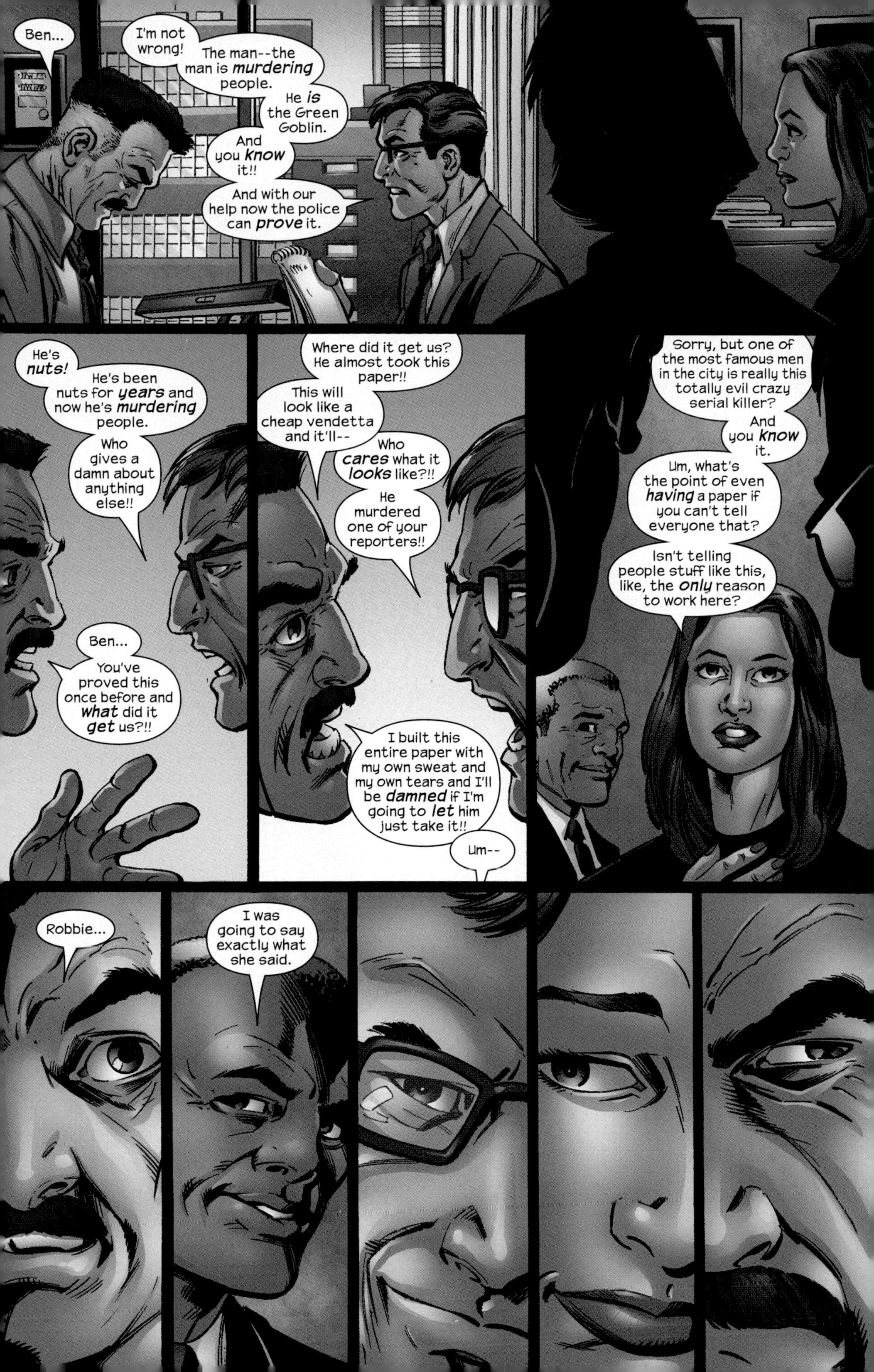

Ben...
I'm not wrong!
The man--the man is murdering people.
He is the Green Goblin.
And you know it!!
And with our help now the police can prove it.
He's nuts!
He's been nuts for years and now he's murdering people.
Who gives a damn about anything else!!
Ben...
You've proved this once before and what did it get us?!!
Where did it get us? He almost took this paper!!
This will look like a cheap vendetta and it'll--
Who cares what it looks like?!!
He murdered one of your reporters!!
I built this entire paper with my own sweat and my own tears and I'll be damned if I'm going to let him just take it!!
Um--
Sorry, but one of the most famous men in the city is really this totally evil crazy serial killer?
And you know it.
Um, what's the point of even having a paper if you can't tell everyone that?
Isn't telling people stuff like this, like, the only reason to work here?
Robbie...
I was going to say exactly what she said.

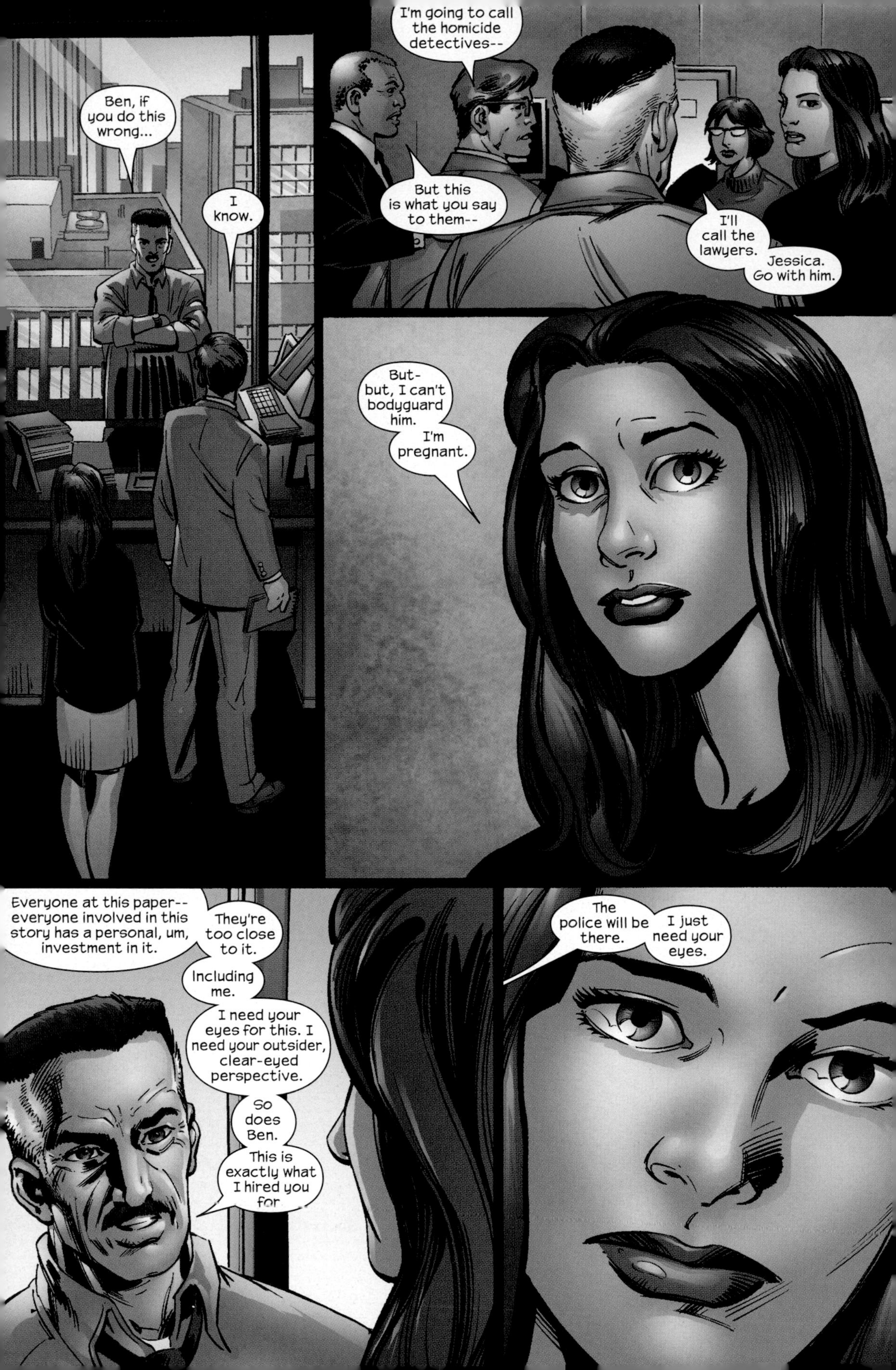

Ben, if you do this wrong...
I know.
I'm going to call the homicide detectives--
But this is what you say to them--
I'll call the lawyers.
Jessica. Go with him.
But- but, I can't bodyguard him.
I'm pregnant.
Everyone at this paper-- everyone involved in this story has a personal, um, investment in it.
They're too close to it.
Including me.
I need your eyes for this. I need your outsider, clear-eyed perspective.
So does Ben.
This is exactly what I hired you for.
The police will be there.
I just need your eyes.

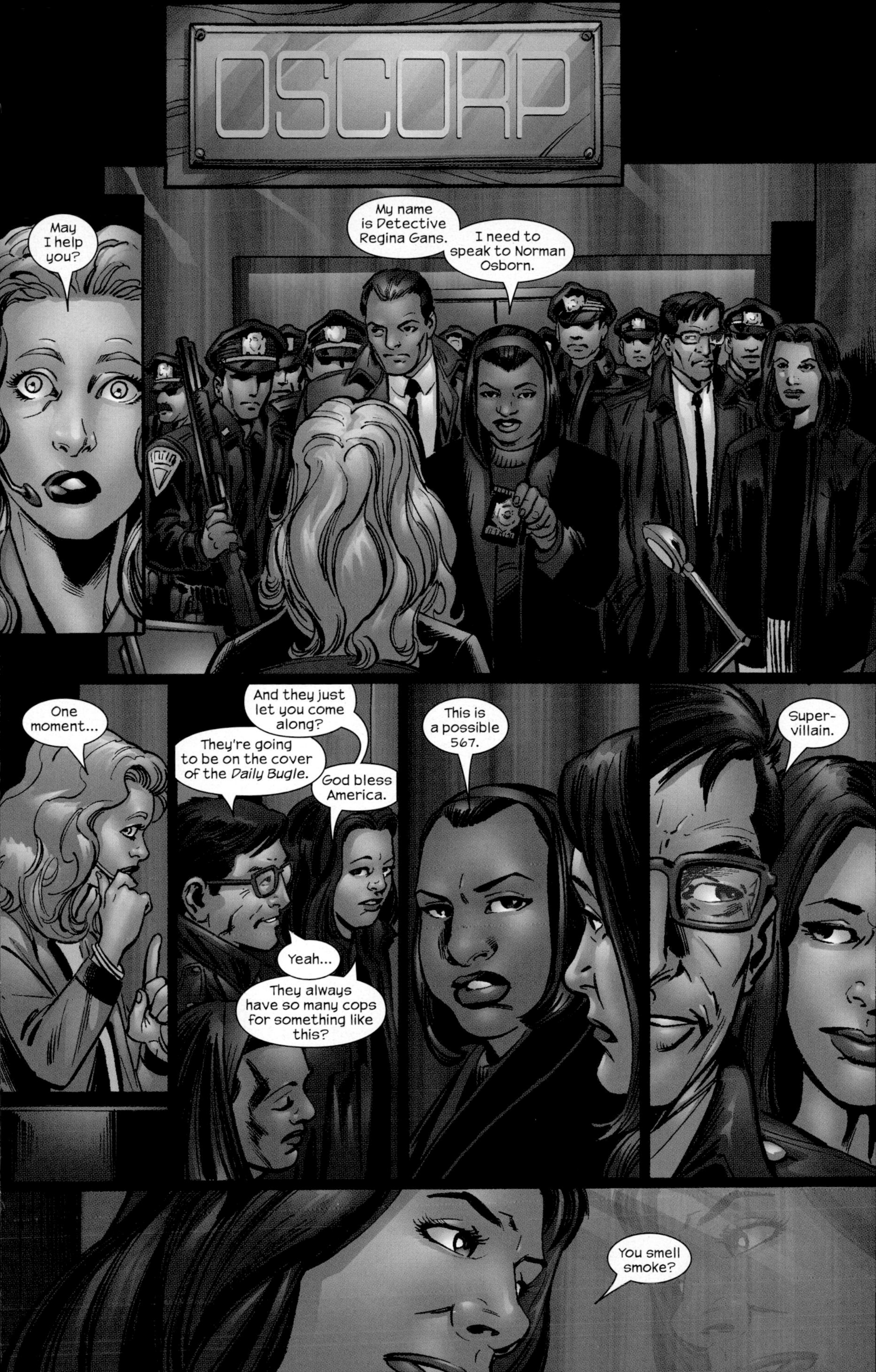
OSCORP
May I help you?
My name is Detective Regina Gans.
I need to speak to Norman Osborn.
One moment...
And they just let you come along?
They're going to be on the cover of the *Daily Bugle*.
God bless America.
Yeah...
They always have so many cops for something like this?
This is a possible 567.
Super-villain.
You smell smoke?

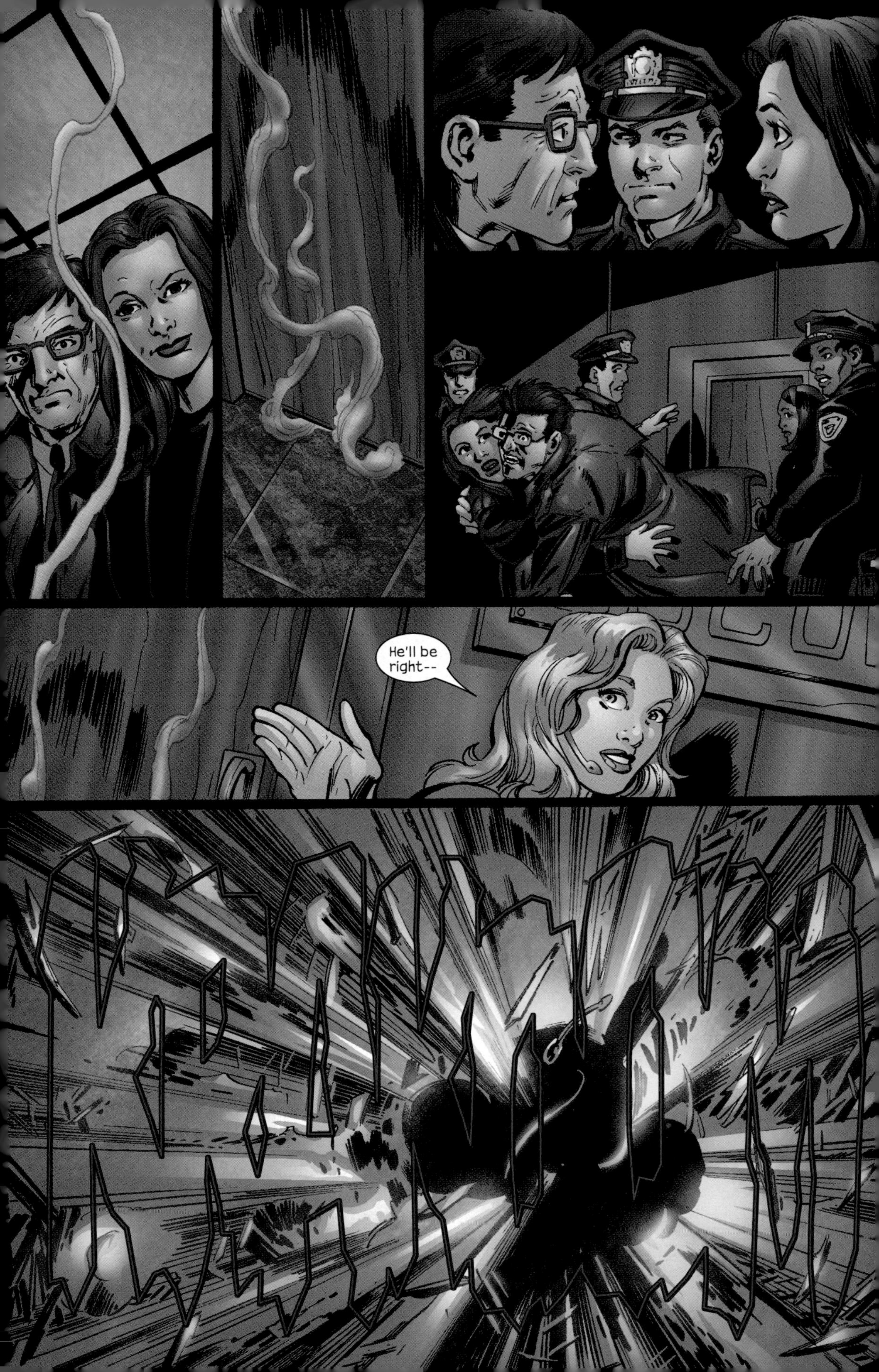
He'll be right--

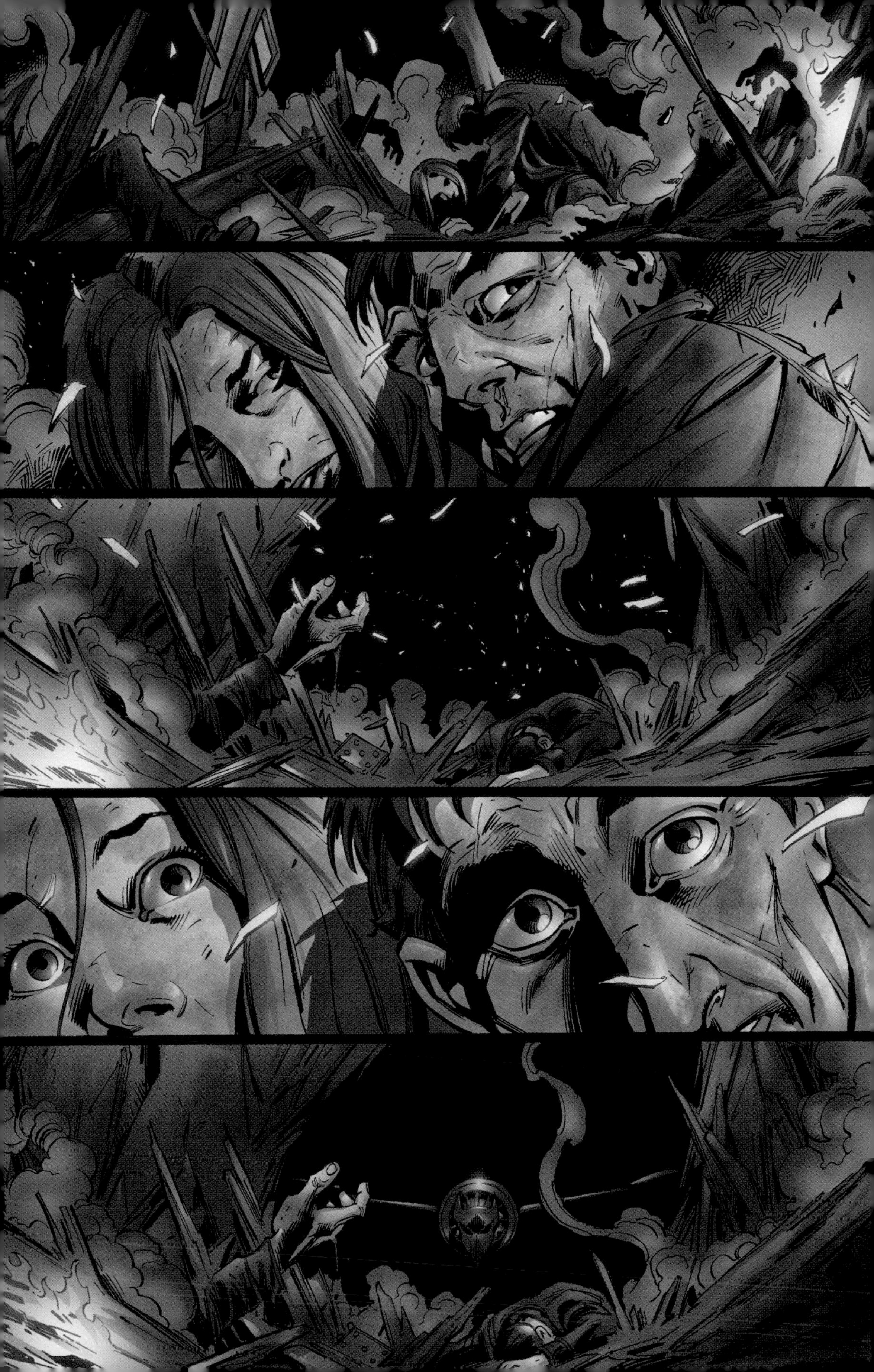

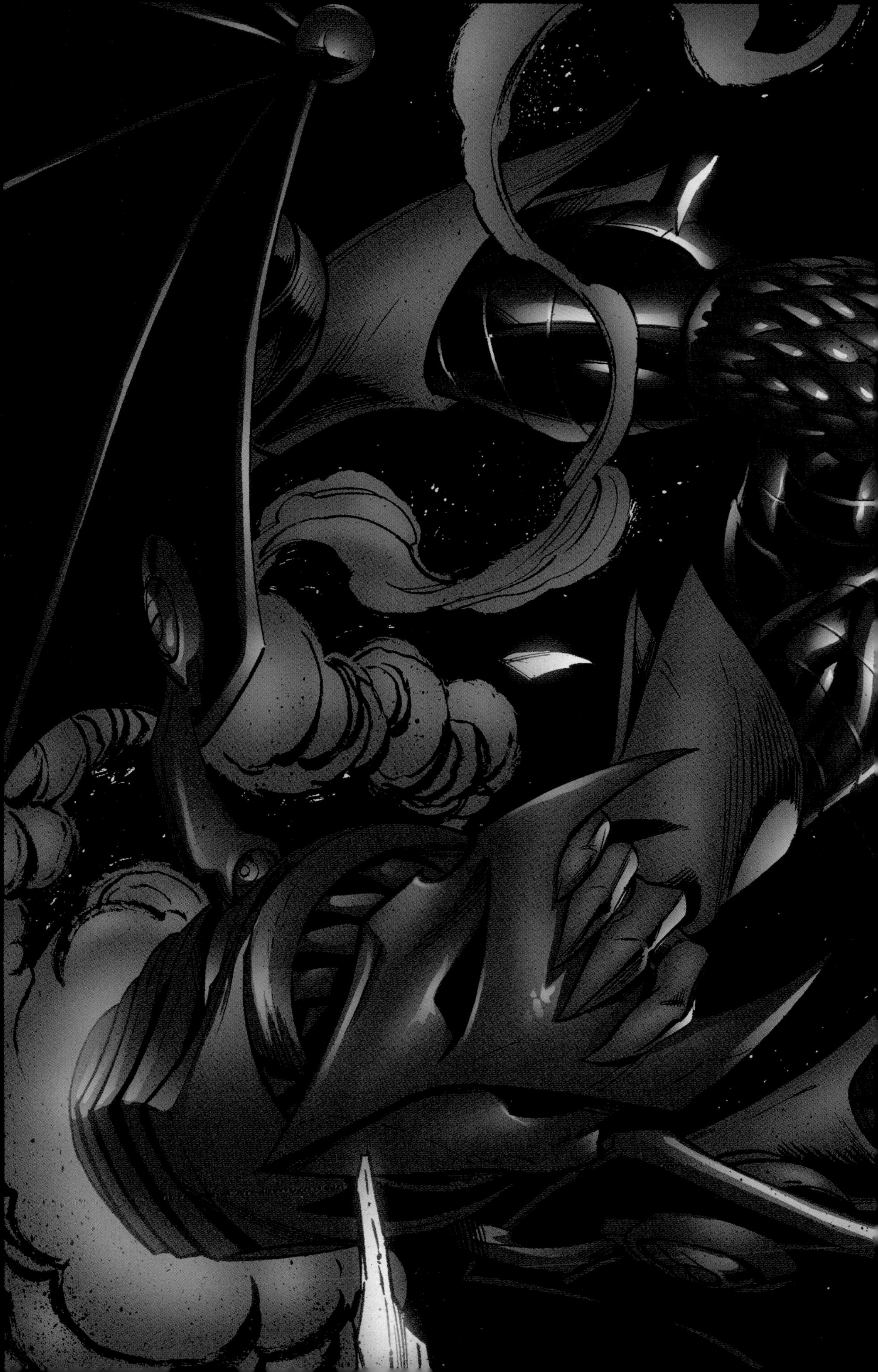

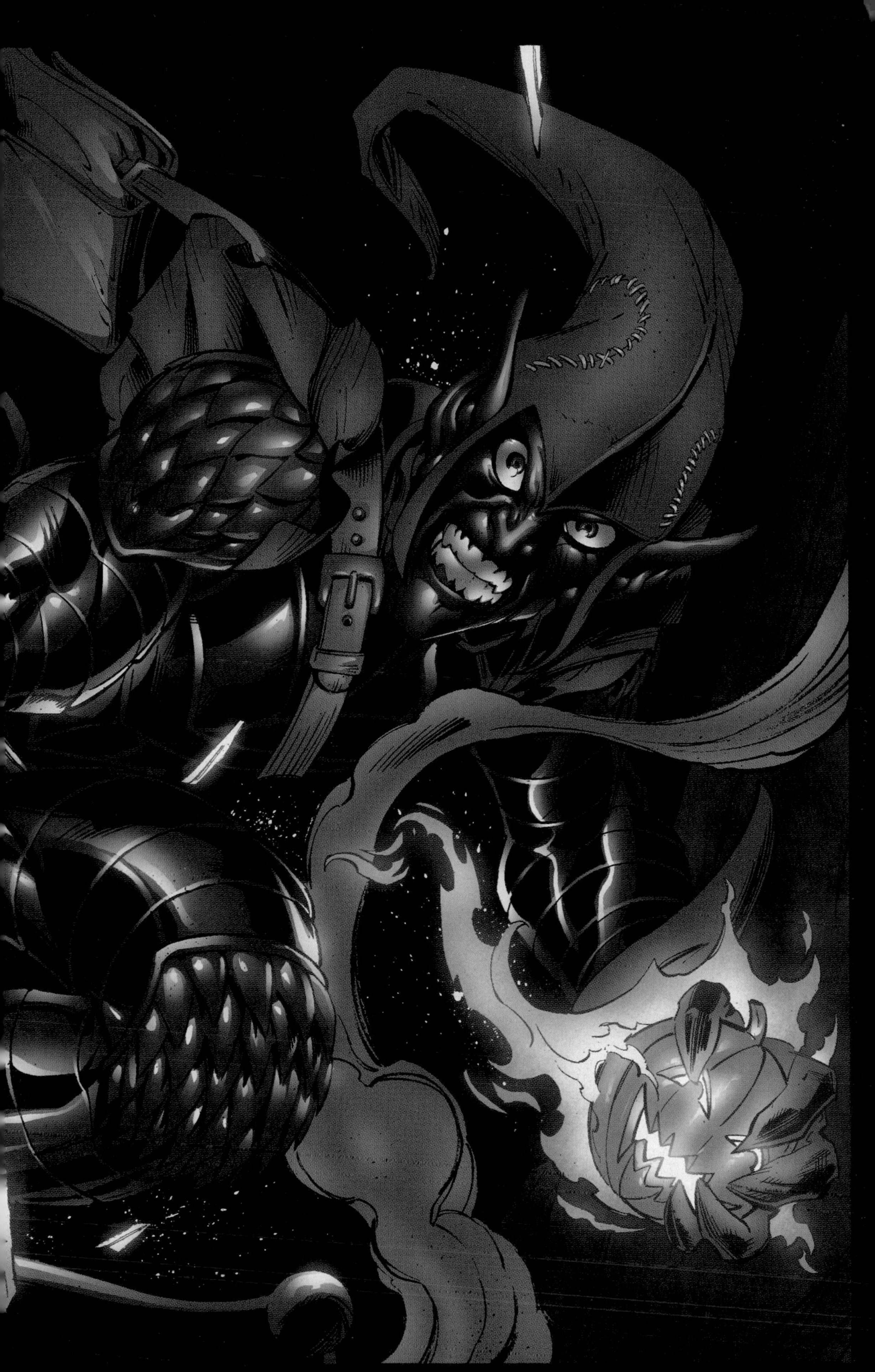

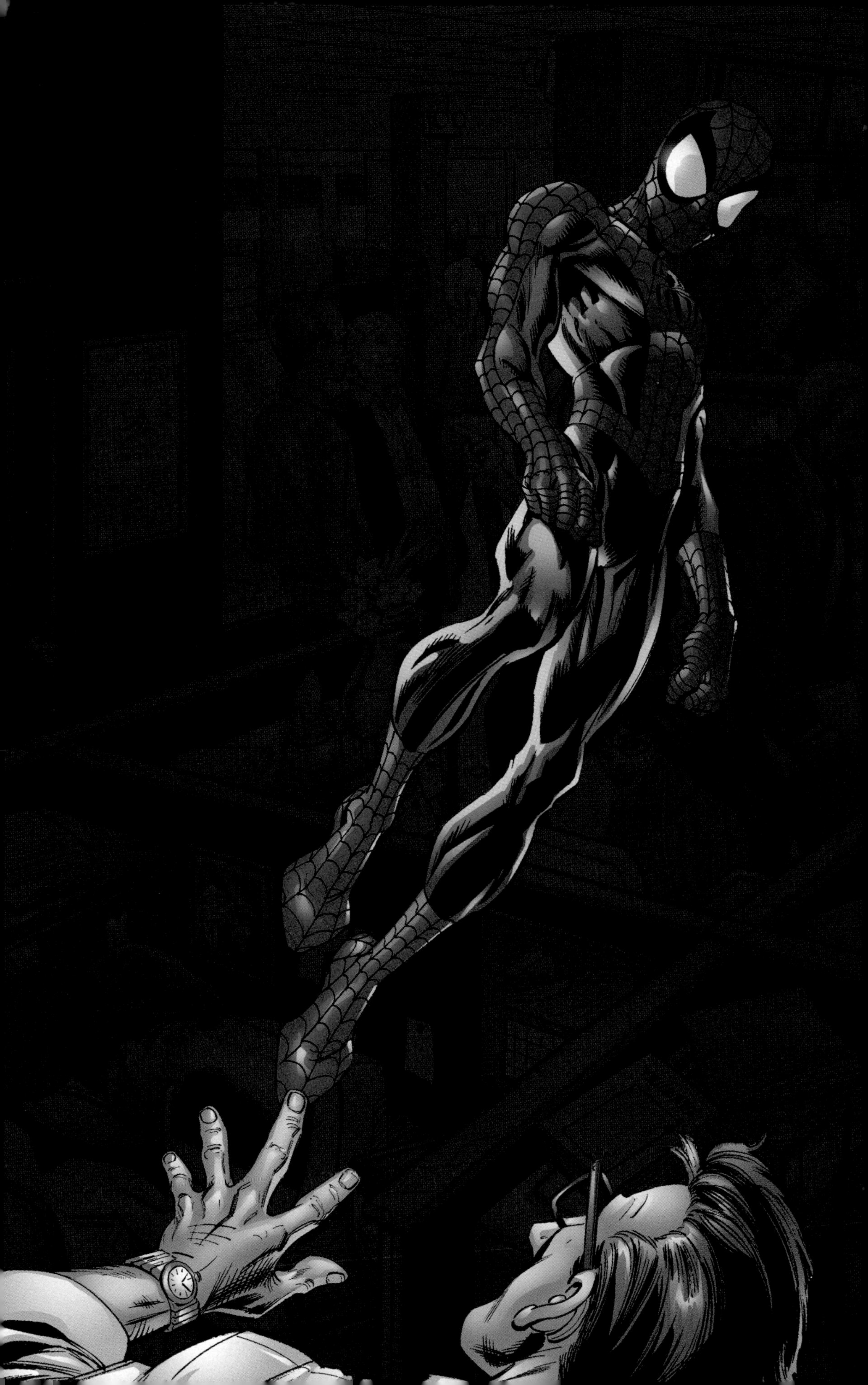

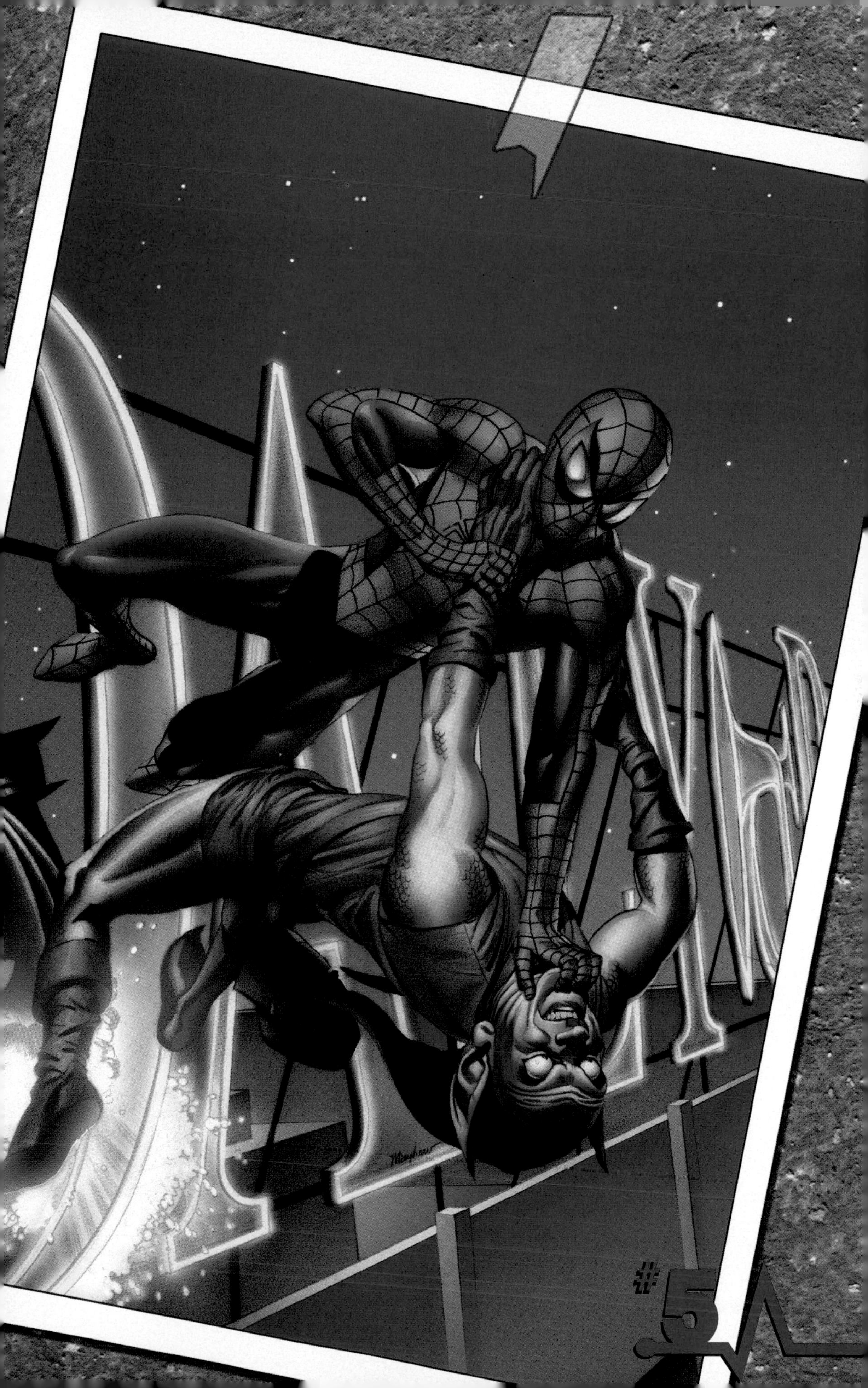
#5

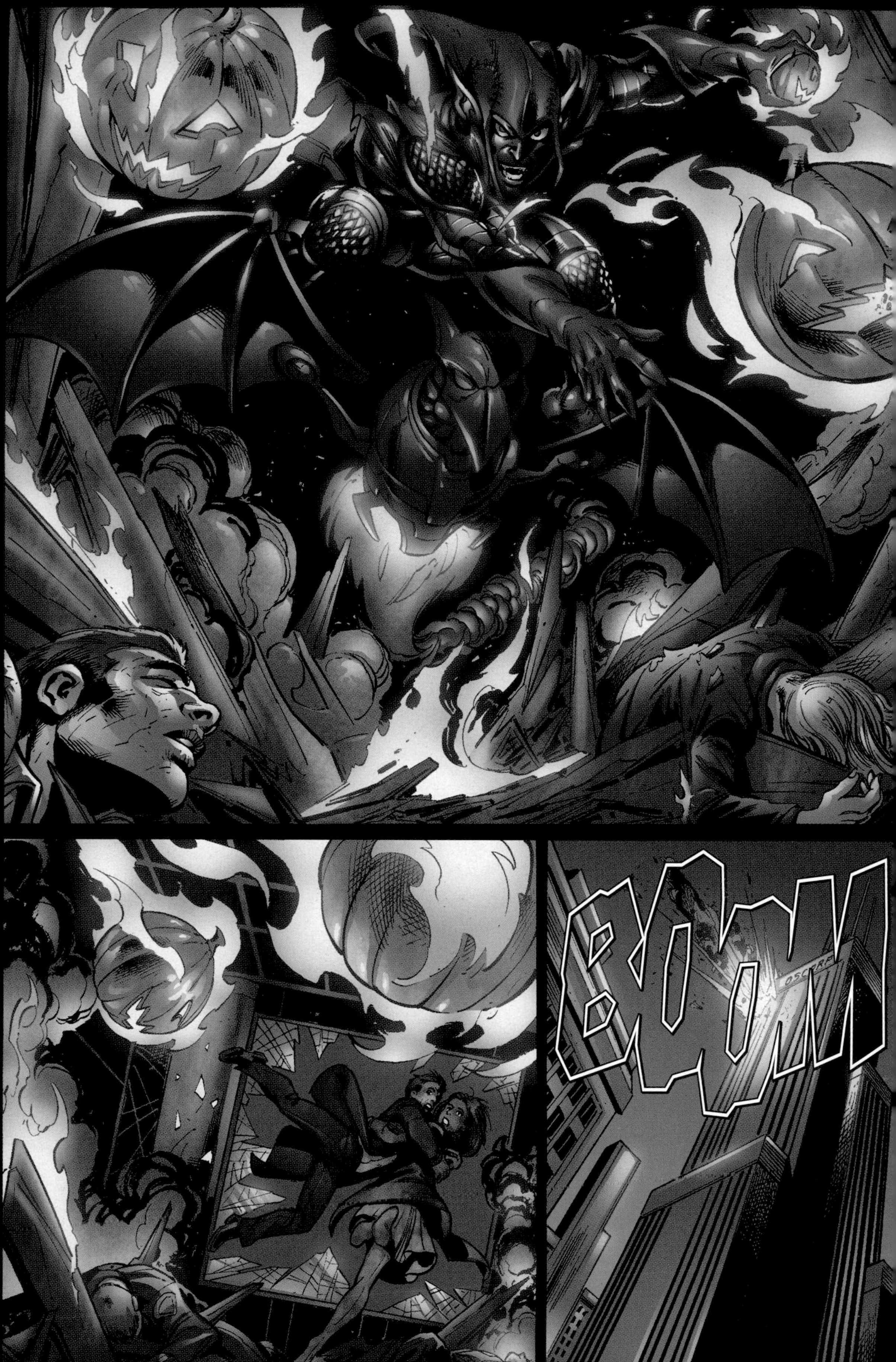
BOOM

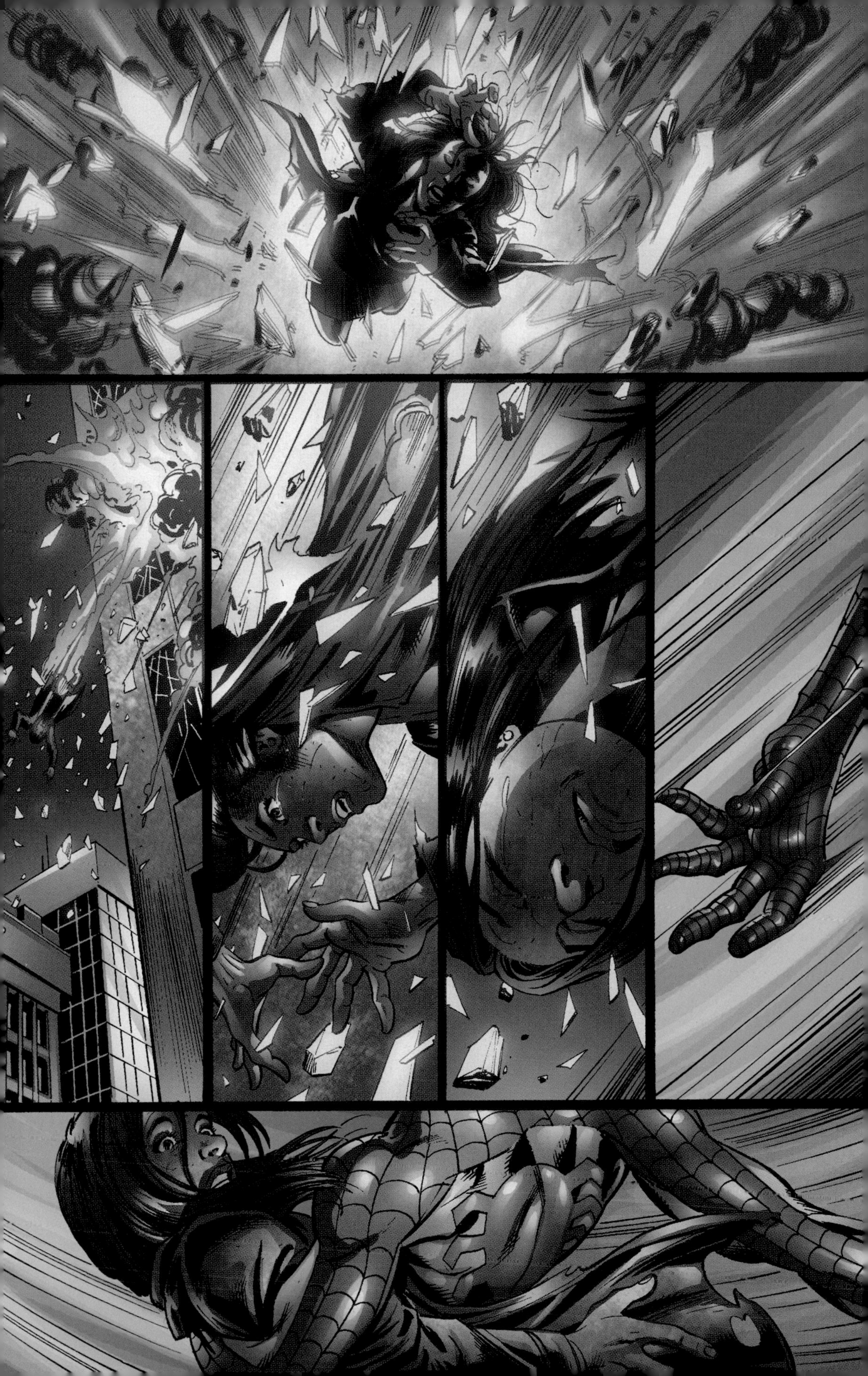

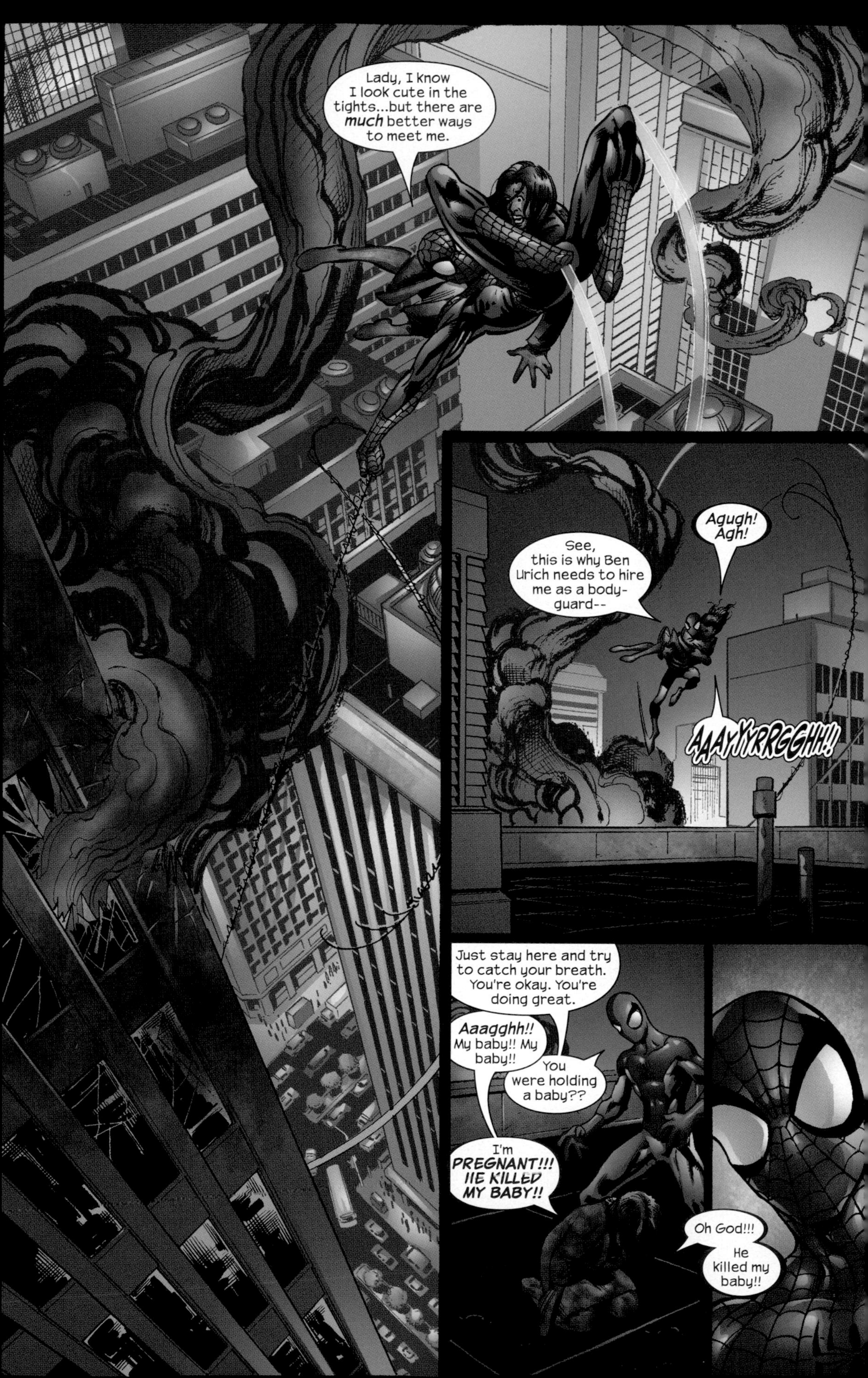

Lady, I know I look cute in the tights...but there are *much* better ways to meet me.
See, this is why Ben Urich needs to hire me as a body-guard--
Agugh! Agh!
AAAYYRRGGHH!!
Just stay here and try to catch your breath. You're okay. You're doing great.
Aaagghh!! My baby!! My baby!!
You were holding a baby??
I'm PREGNANT!!! HE KILLED MY BABY!!
Oh God!!!
He killed my baby!!

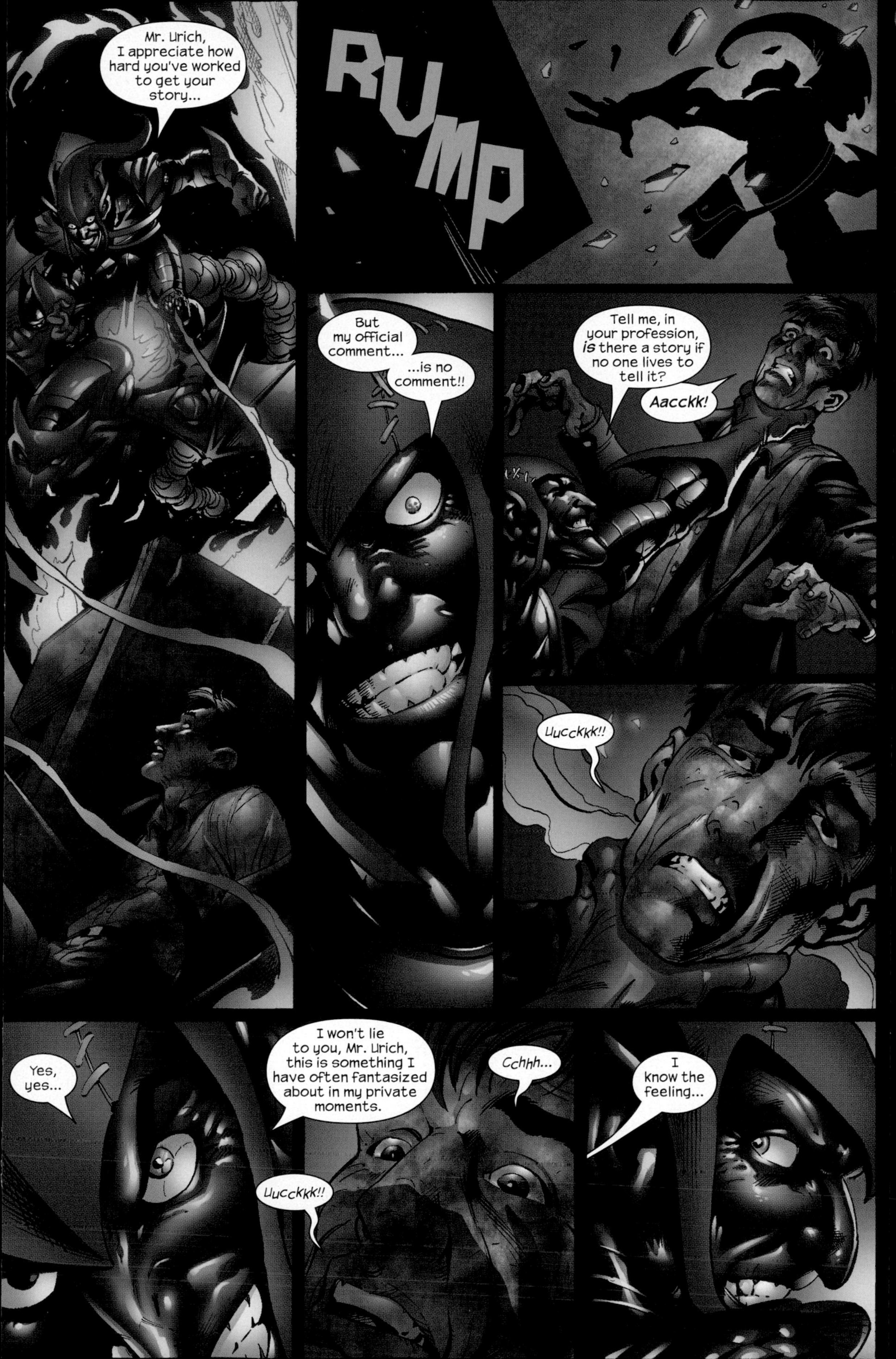
Mr. Urich, I appreciate how hard you've worked to get your story...
RUMP
But my official comment...
...is no comment!!
Tell me, in your profession, *is* there a story if no one lives to tell it?
Aacckk!
Uucckkk!!
Yes, yes...
I won't lie to you, Mr. Urich, this is something I have often fantasized about in my private moments.
Uucckkk!!
Cchhh...
I know the feeling...

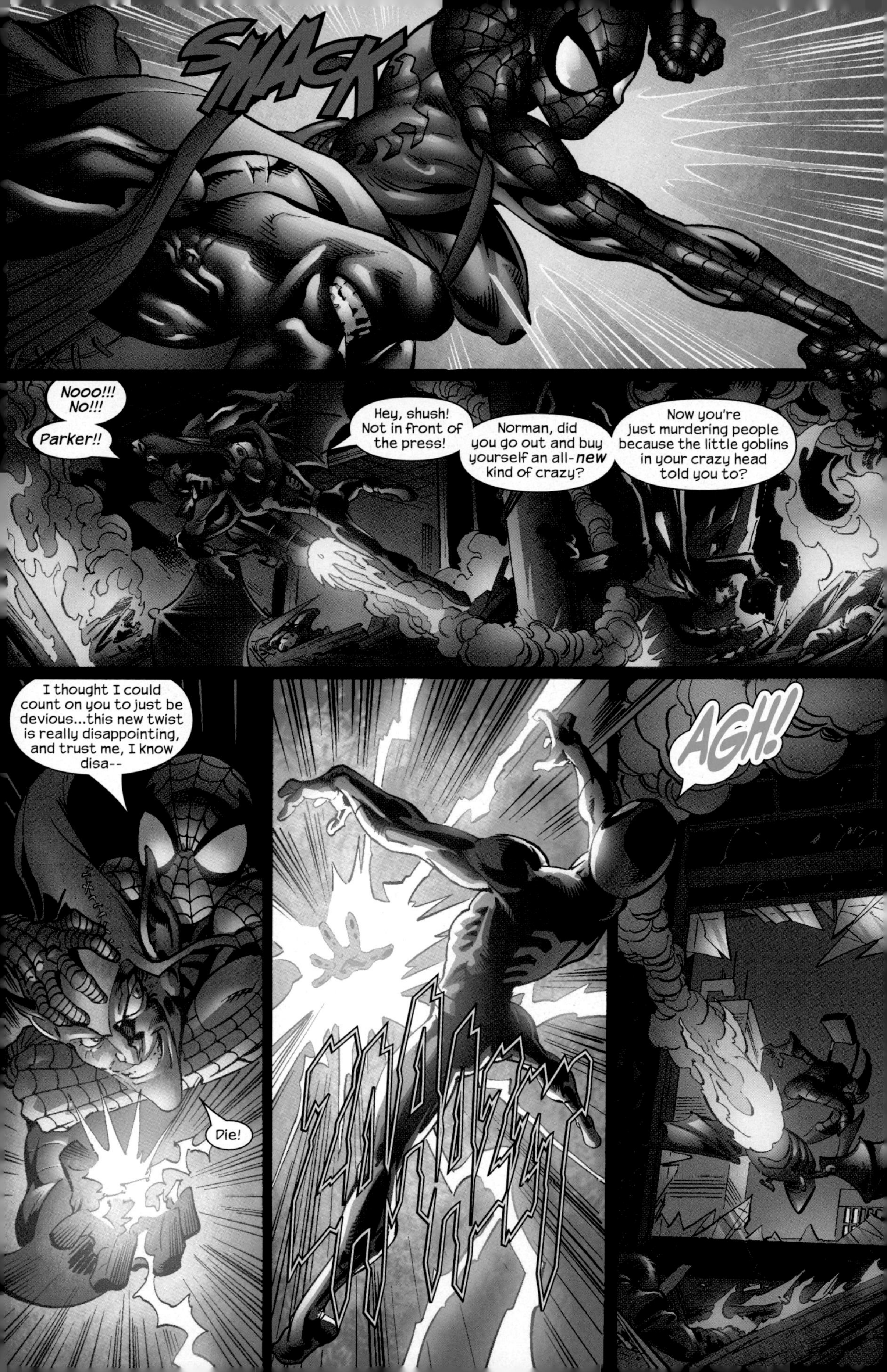
SHACK
Nooo!!! No!!!
Parker!!
Hey, shush! Not in front of the press!
Norman, did you go out and buy yourself an all-*new* kind of crazy?
Now you're just murdering people because the little goblins in your crazy head told you to?
I thought I could count on you to just be devious...this new twist is really disappointing, and trust me, I know disa--
Die!
AGH!

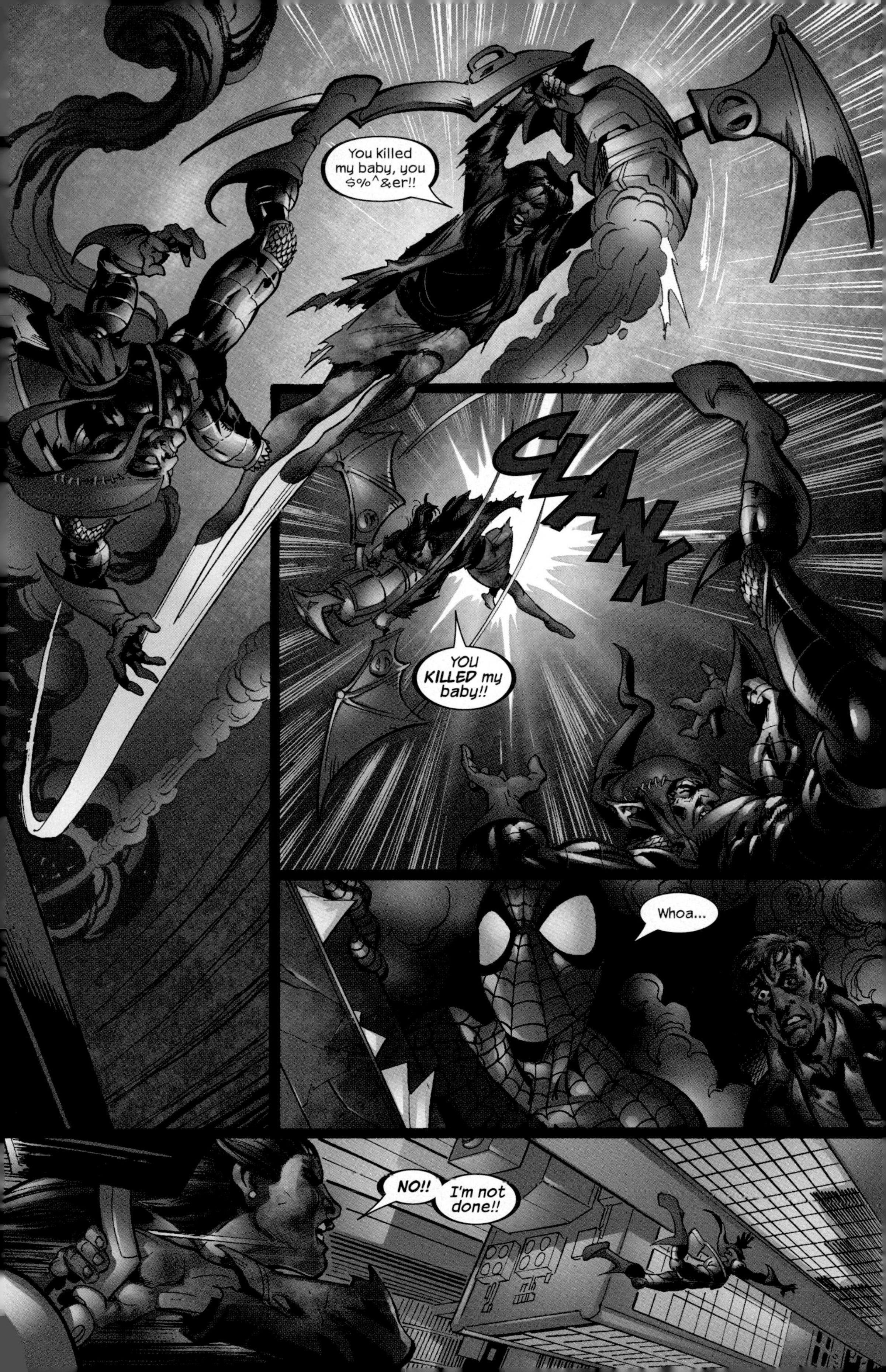
You killed my baby, you $%^&er!!
CLANK
YOU KILLED my baby!!
Whoa...
NO!!
I'm not done!!

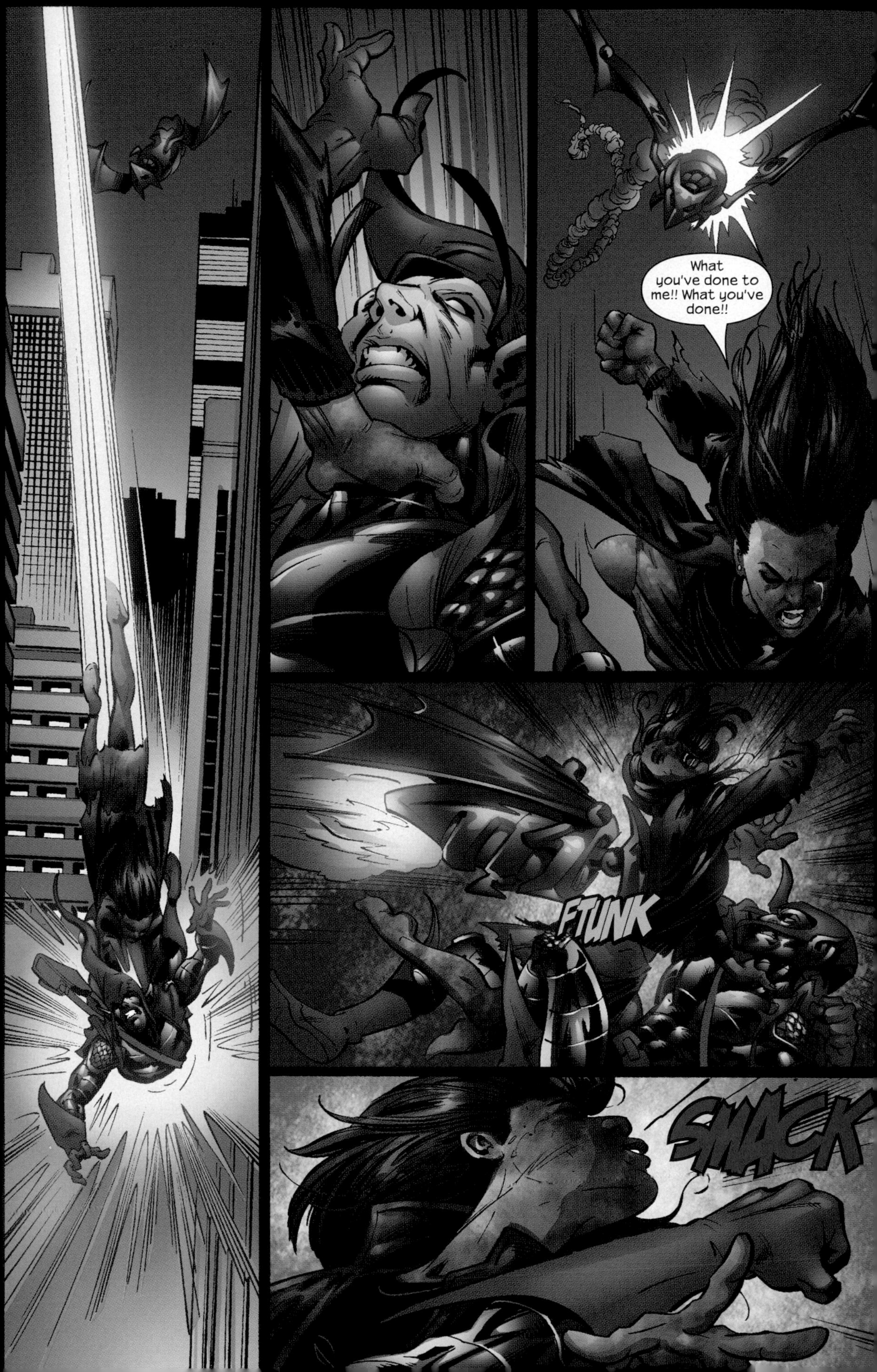
What you've done to me!! What you've done!!
FTUNK
SHACK

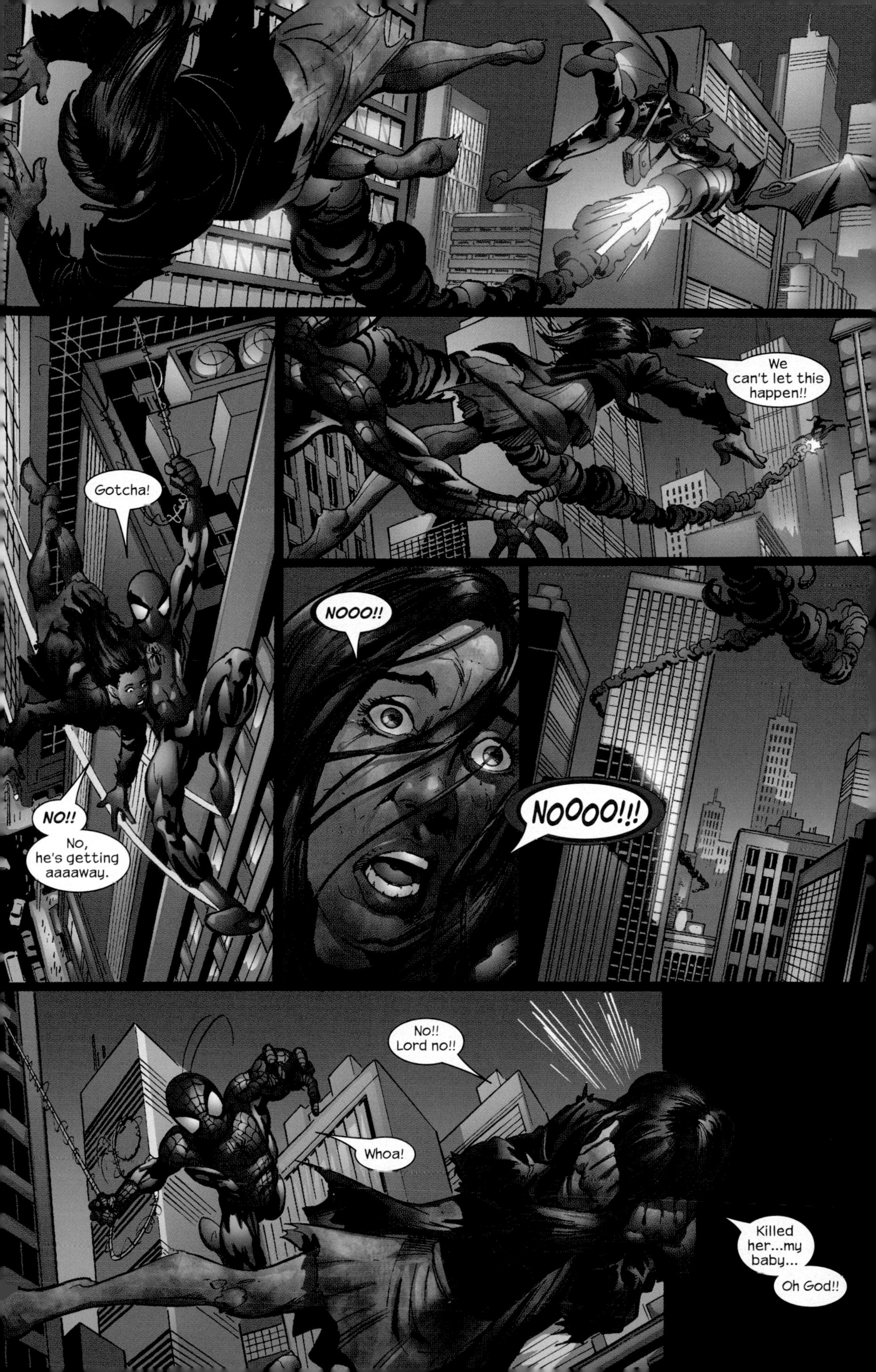
We can't let this happen!!
Gotcha!
NO!!
No, he's getting aaaaway.
NOOO!!
NOOOO!!!
No!! Lord no!!
Whoa!
Killed her...my baby...
Oh God!!

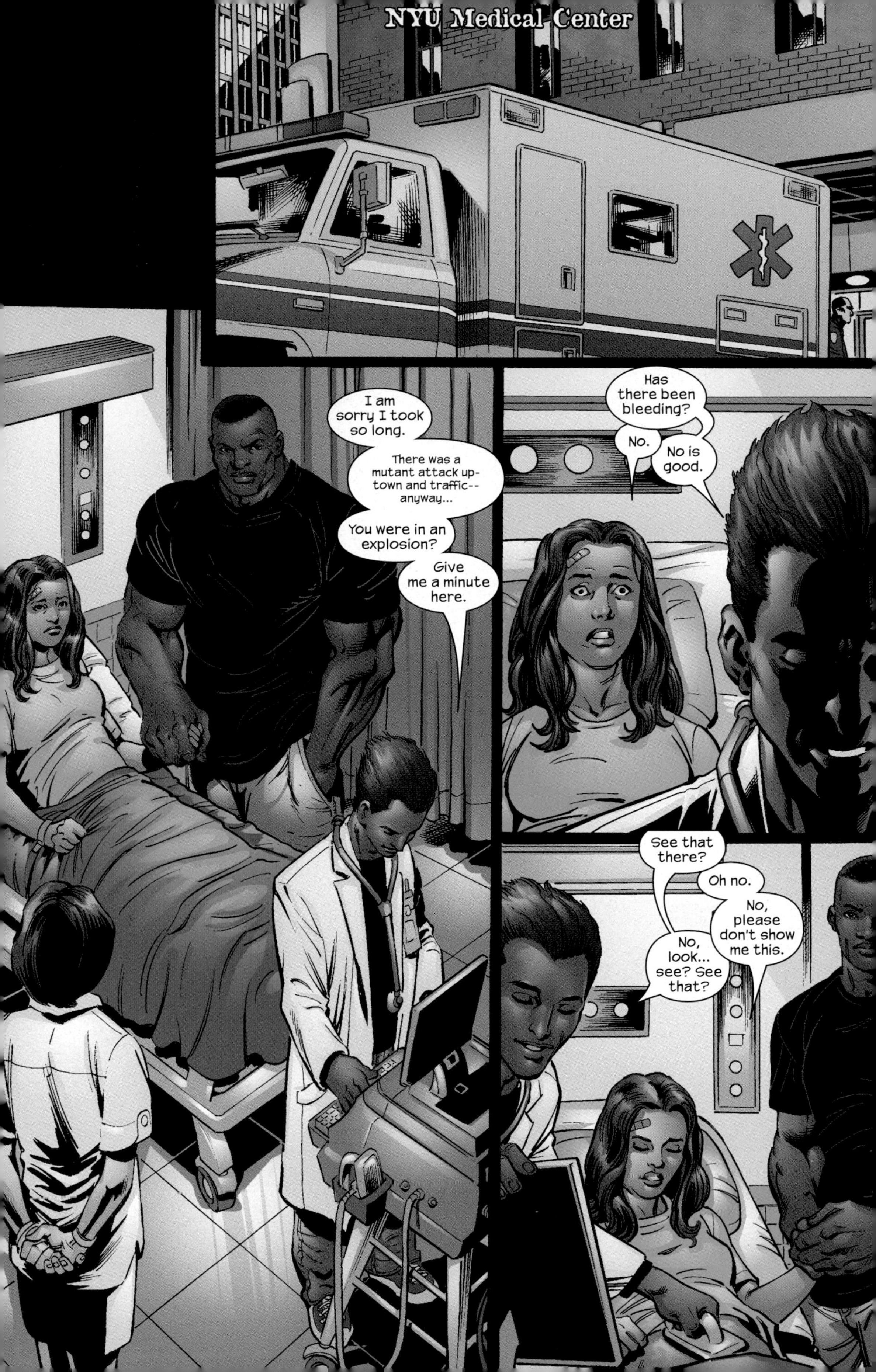
NYU Medical Center
I am sorry I took so long.
There was a mutant attack up-town and traffic-- anyway...
You were in an explosion?
Give me a minute here.
Has there been bleeding?
No.
No is good.
See that there?
Oh no.
No, please don't show me this.
No, look... see? See that?

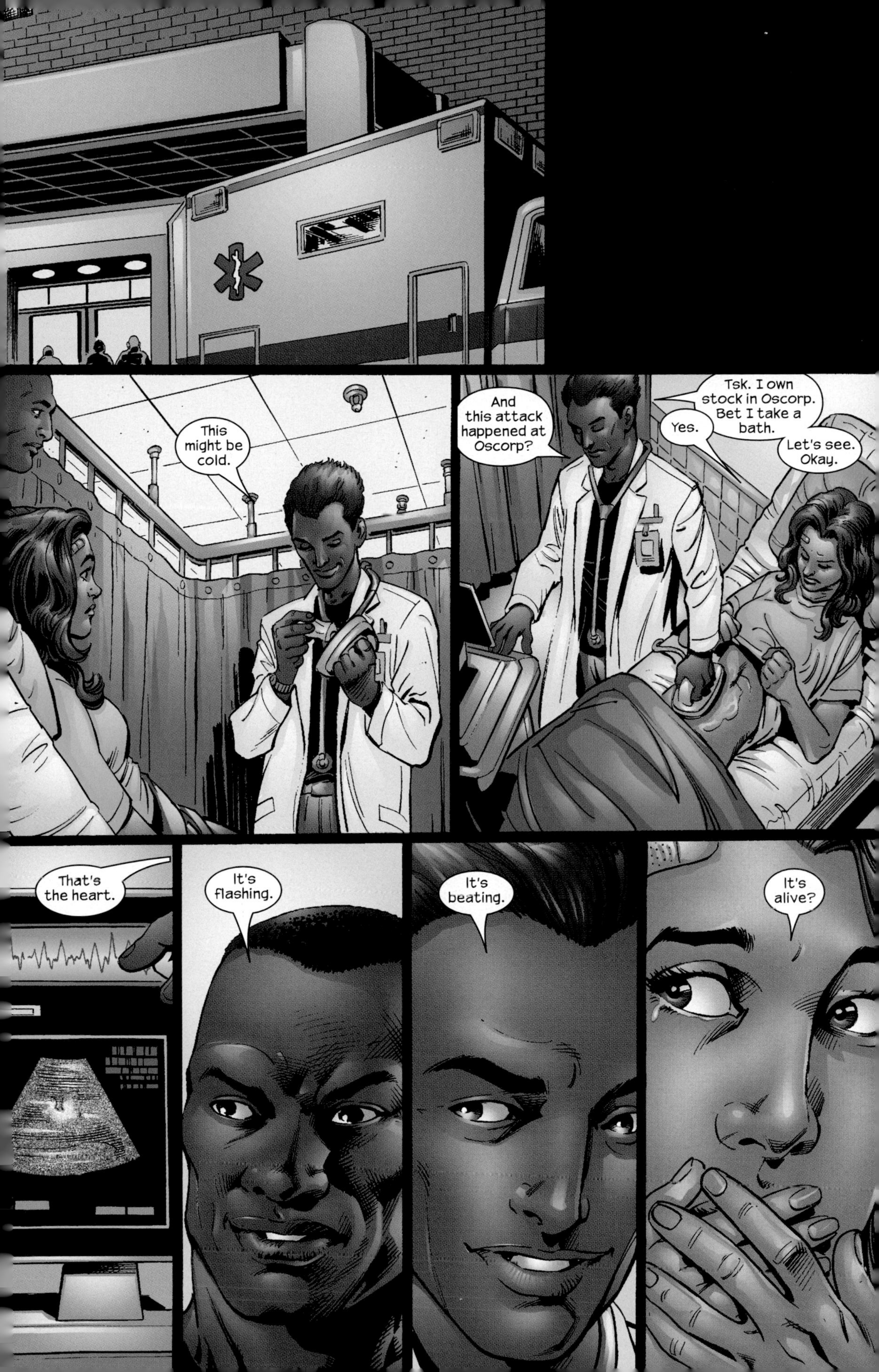
This might be cold.
And this attack happened at Oscorp?
Yes.
Tsk. I own stock in Oscorp. Bet I take a bath.
Let's see. Okay.
That's the heart.
It's flashing.
It's beating.
It's alive?

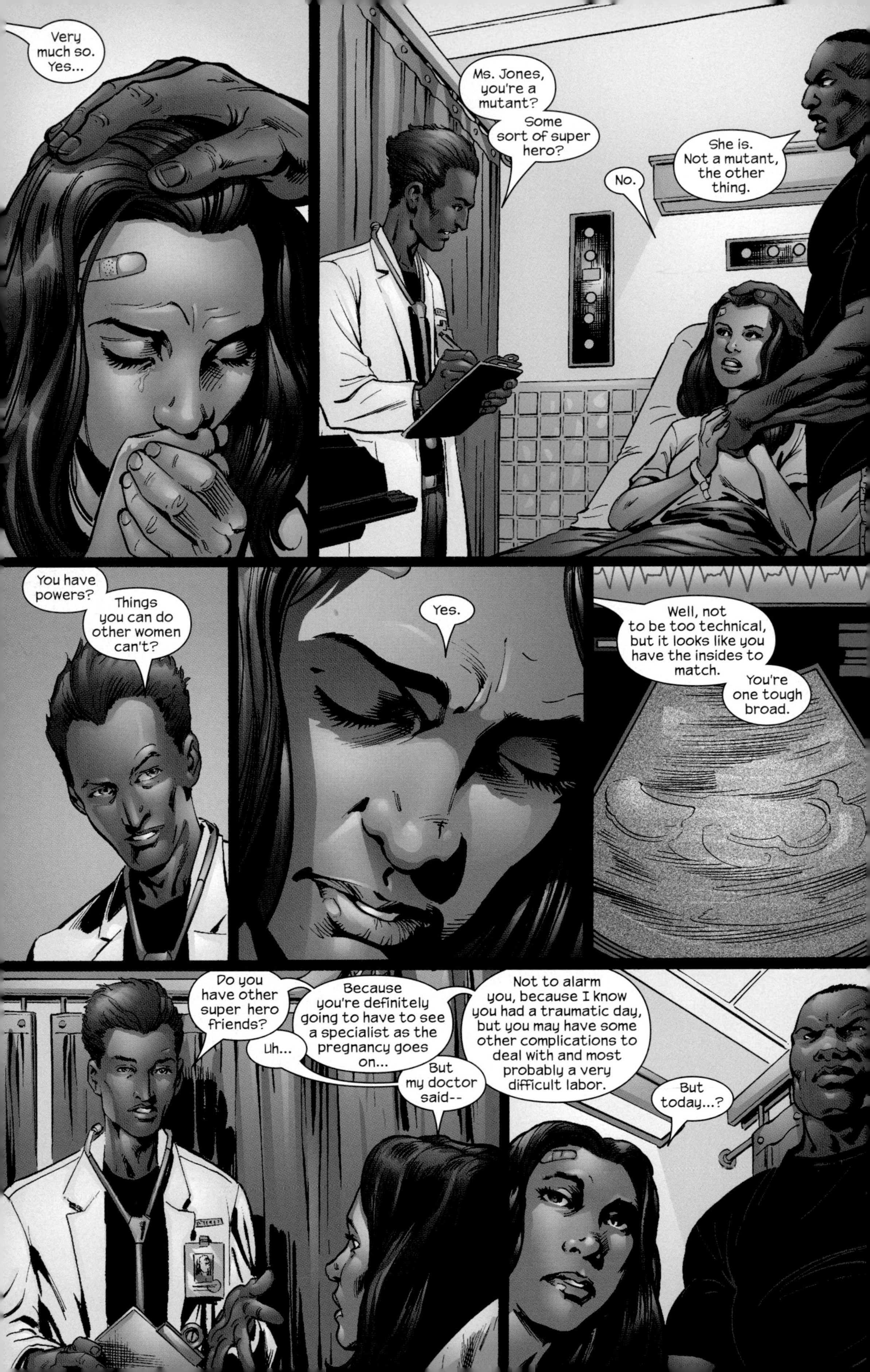
Very much so. Yes...
Ms. Jones, you're a mutant?
Some sort of super hero?
No.
She is. Not a mutant, the other thing.
You have powers?
Things you can do other women can't?
Yes.
Well, not to be too technical, but it looks like you have the insides to match.
You're one tough broad.
Do you have other super hero friends?
Uh...
Because you're definitely going to have to see a specialist as the pregnancy goes on...
But my doctor said--
Not to alarm you, because I know you had a traumatic day, but you may have some other complications to deal with and most probably a very difficult labor.
But today...?

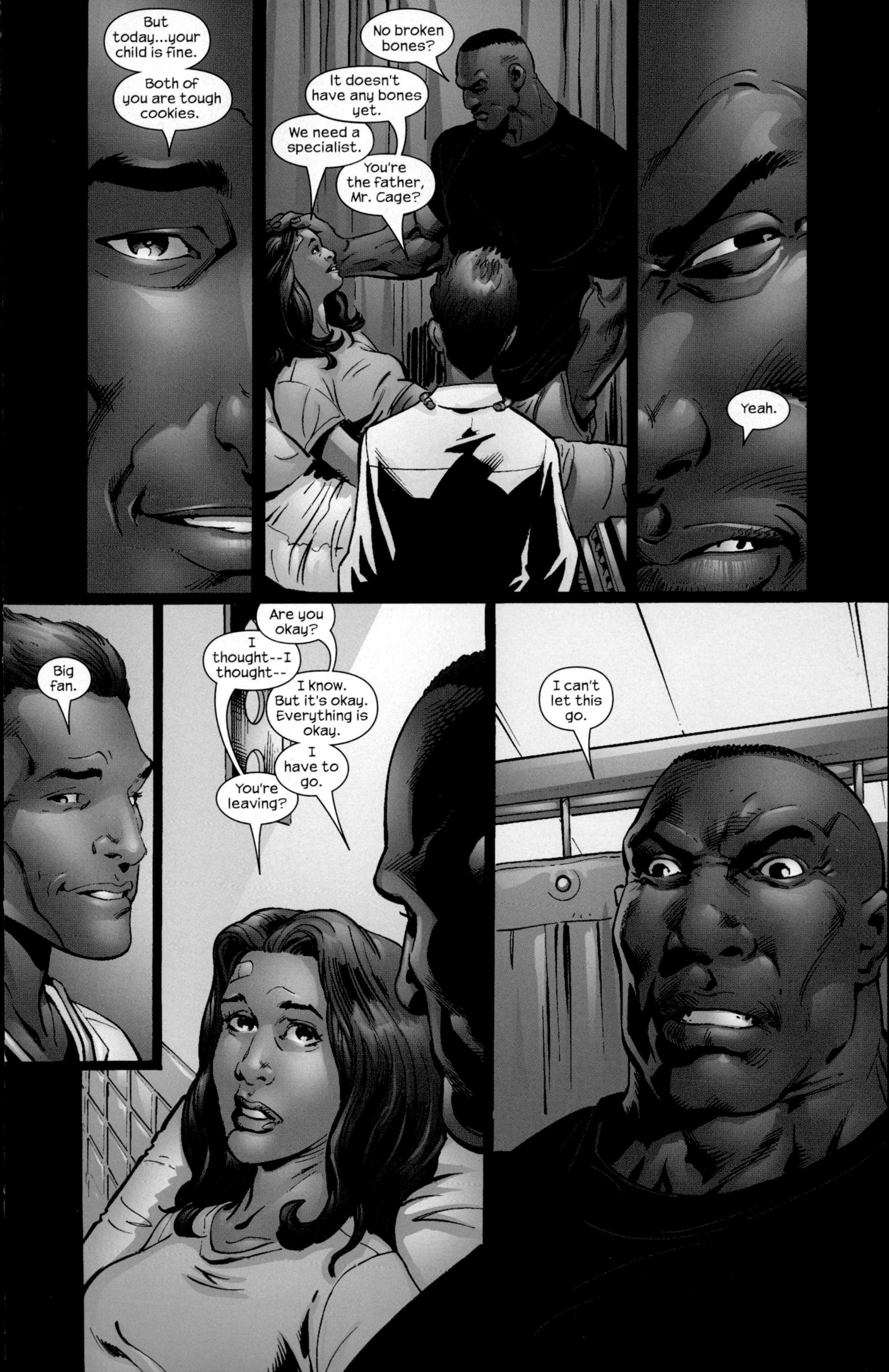

But today...your child is fine.
Both of you are tough cookies.
No broken bones?
It doesn't have any bones yet.
We need a specialist.
You're the father, Mr. Cage?
Yeah.
Big fan.
Are you okay?
I thought--I thought--
I know. But it's okay. Everything is okay.
I have to go.
You're leaving?
I can't let this go.

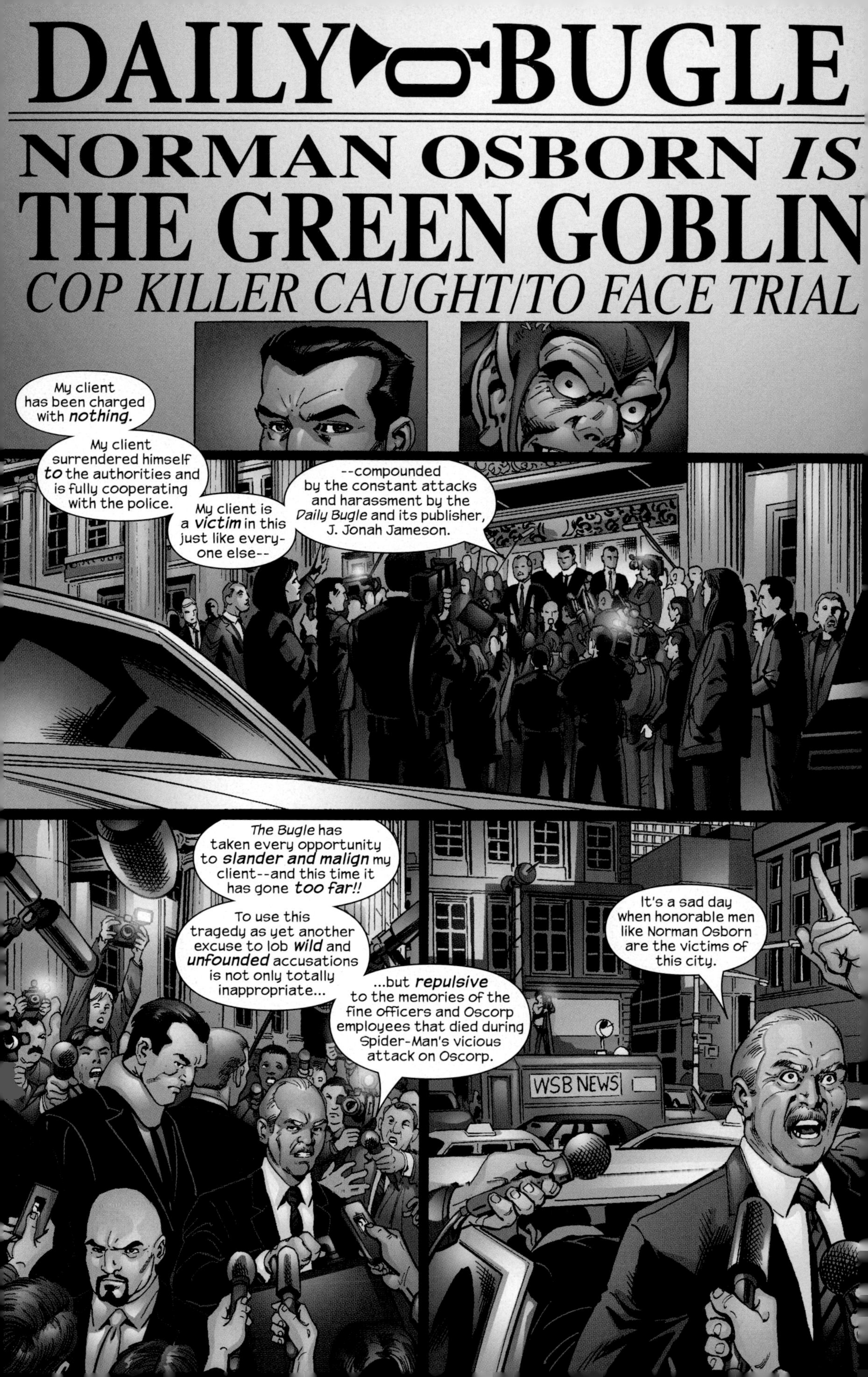

DAILY BUGLE
NORMAN OSBORN IS
THE GREEN GOBLIN
COP KILLER CAUGHT/TO FACE TRIAL
My client has been charged with nothing.
My client surrendered himself to the authorities and is fully cooperating with the police.
My client is a victim in this just like every-one else--
--compounded by the constant attacks and harassment by the Daily Bugle and its publisher, J. Jonah Jameson.
The Bugle has taken every opportunity to slander and malign my client--and this time it has gone too far!!
To use this tragedy as yet another excuse to lob wild and unfounded accusations is not only totally inappropriate...
...but repulsive to the memories of the fine officers and Oscorp employees that died during Spider-Man's vicious attack on Oscorp.
WSB NEWS
It's a sad day when honorable men like Norman Osborn are the victims of this city.

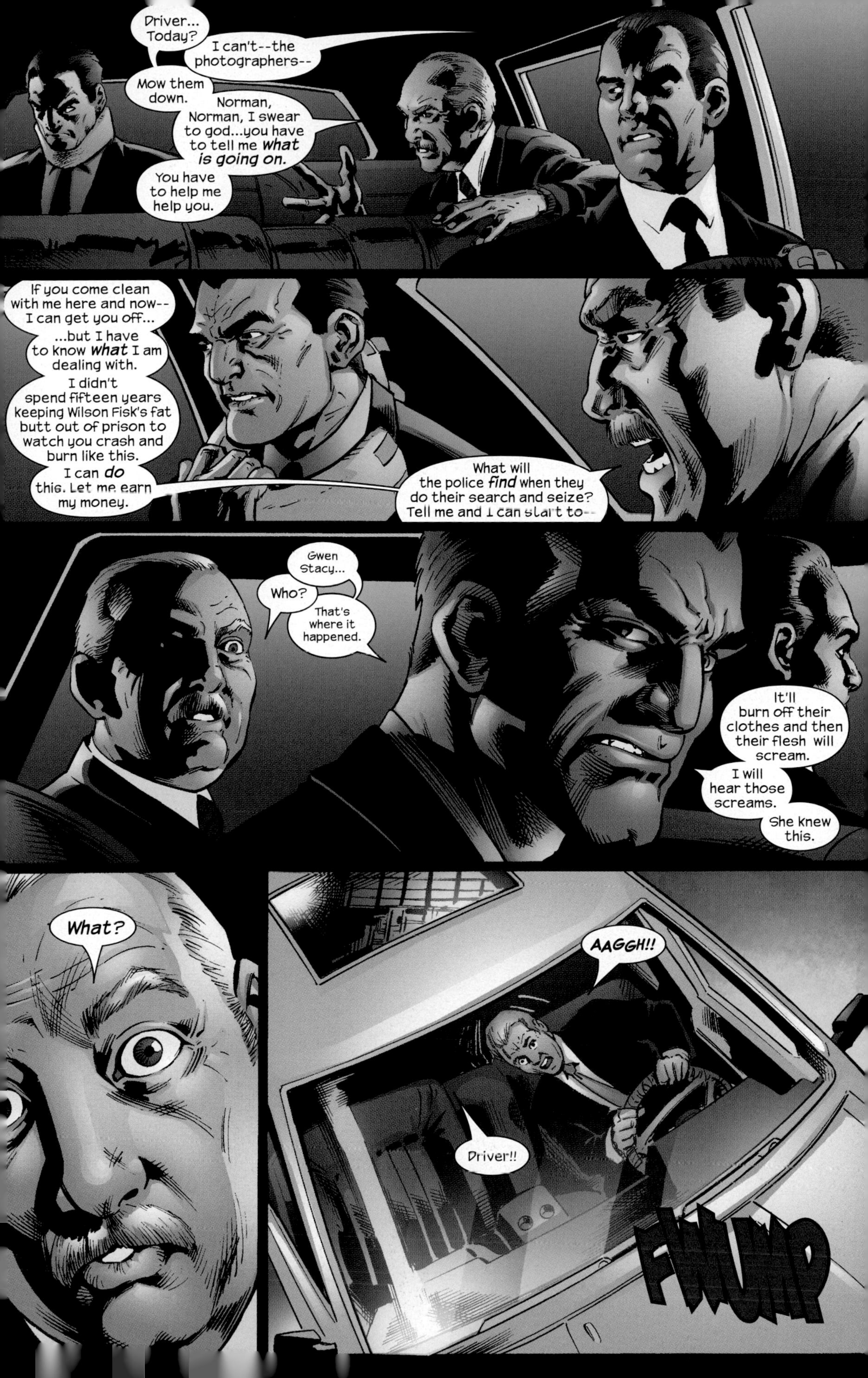

Driver... Today?
I can't--the photographers--
Mow them down.
Norman, Norman, I swear to god...you have to tell me what is going on.
You have to help me help you.
If you come clean with me here and now--I can get you off...
...but I have to know what I am dealing with.
I didn't spend fifteen years keeping Wilson Fisk's fat butt out of prison to watch you crash and burn like this.
I can do this. Let me earn my money.
What will the police find when they do their search and seize? Tell me and I can start to--
Gwen Stacy...
Who?
That's where it happened.
It'll burn off their clothes and then their flesh will scream.
I will hear those screams.
She knew this.
What?
AAGGH!!
Driver!!
FWUMP

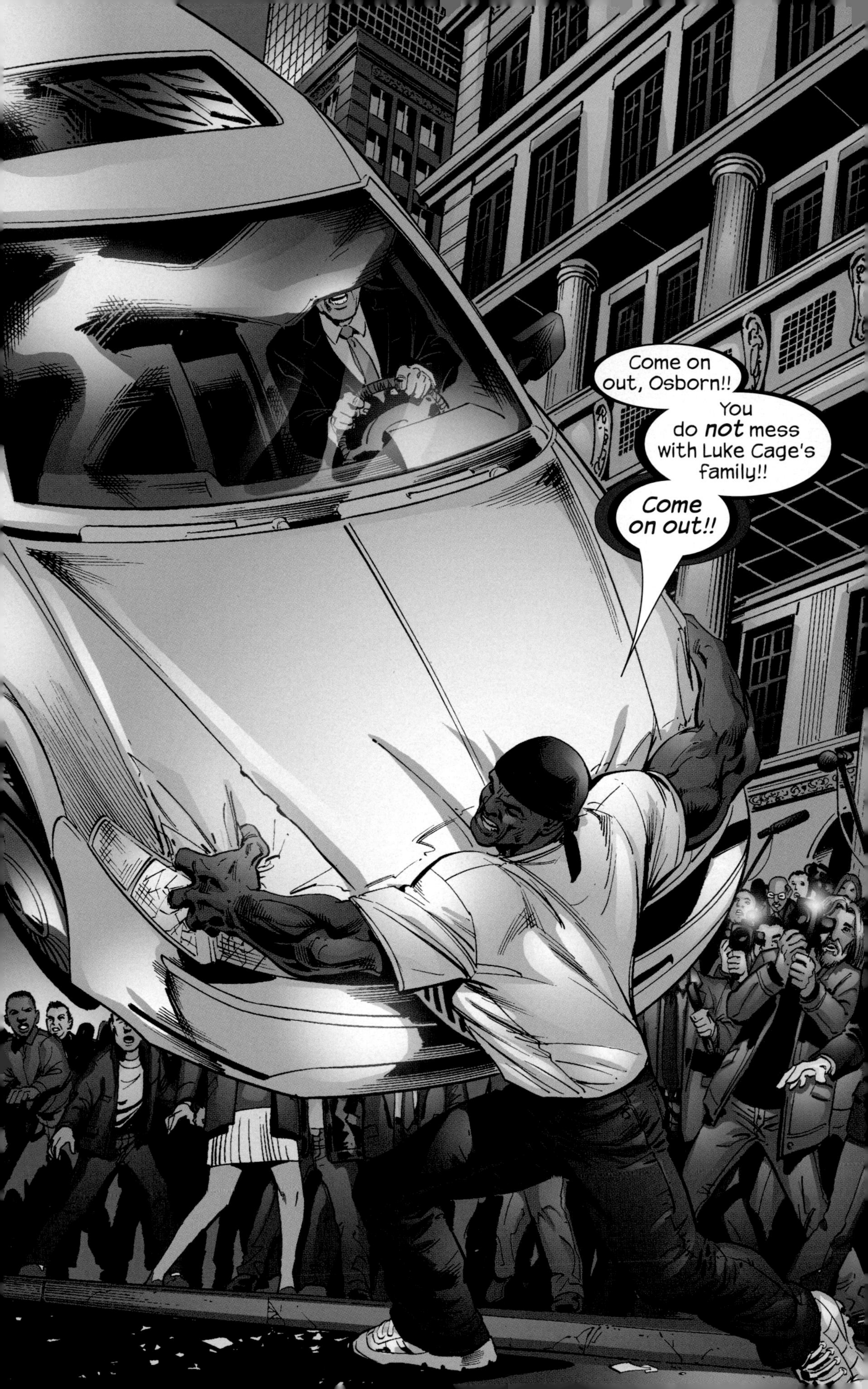
Come on out, Osborn!!
You do **not** mess with Luke Cage's family!!
Come on out!!

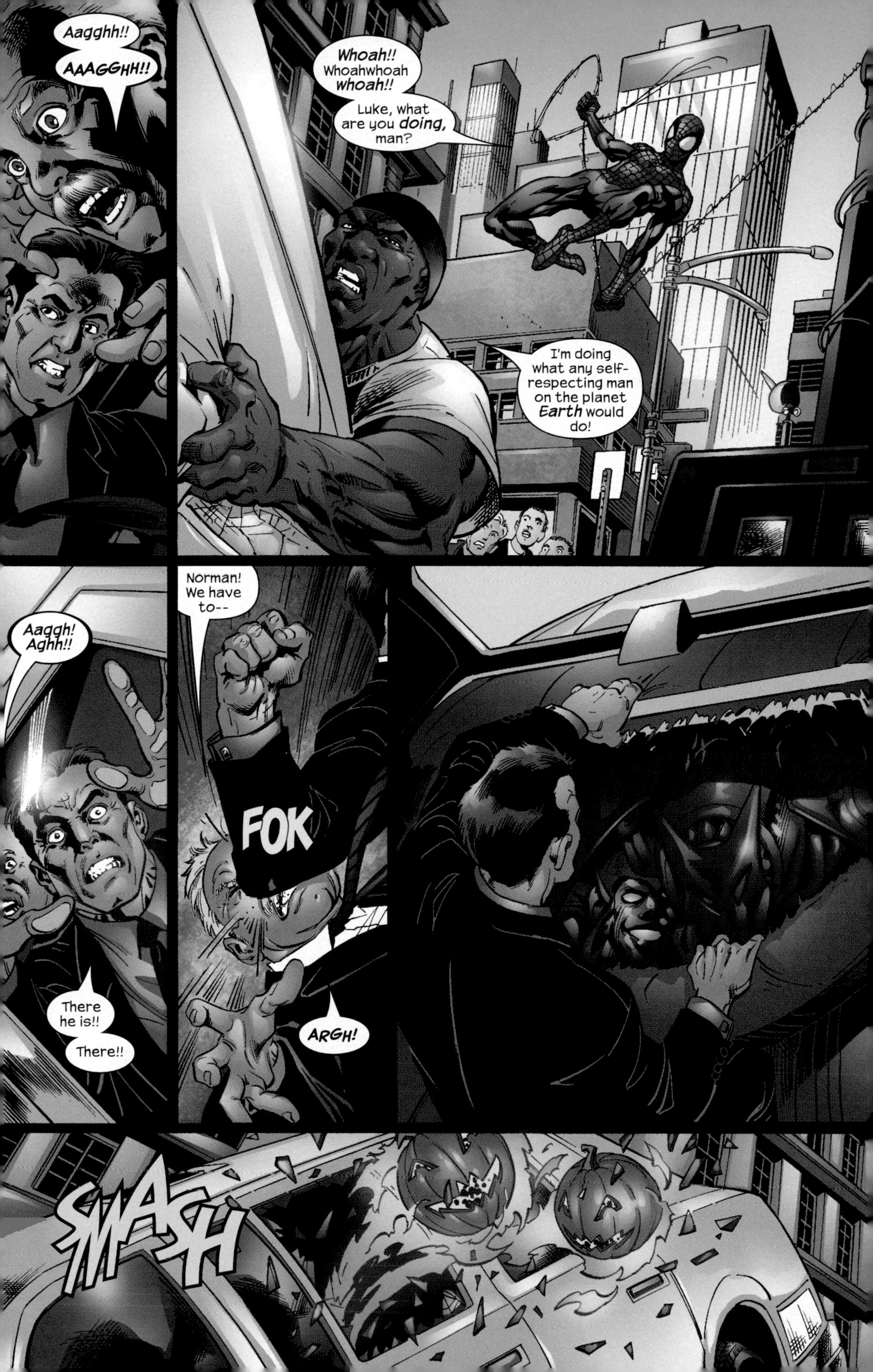
Aagghh!!
AAAGGHH!!
Whoah!! Whoahwhoah whoah!!
Luke, what are you doing, man?
I'm doing what any self-respecting man on the planet Earth would do!
Aaggh! Aghh!!
There he is!!
There!!
Norman! We have to--
FOK
ARGH!
SMASH

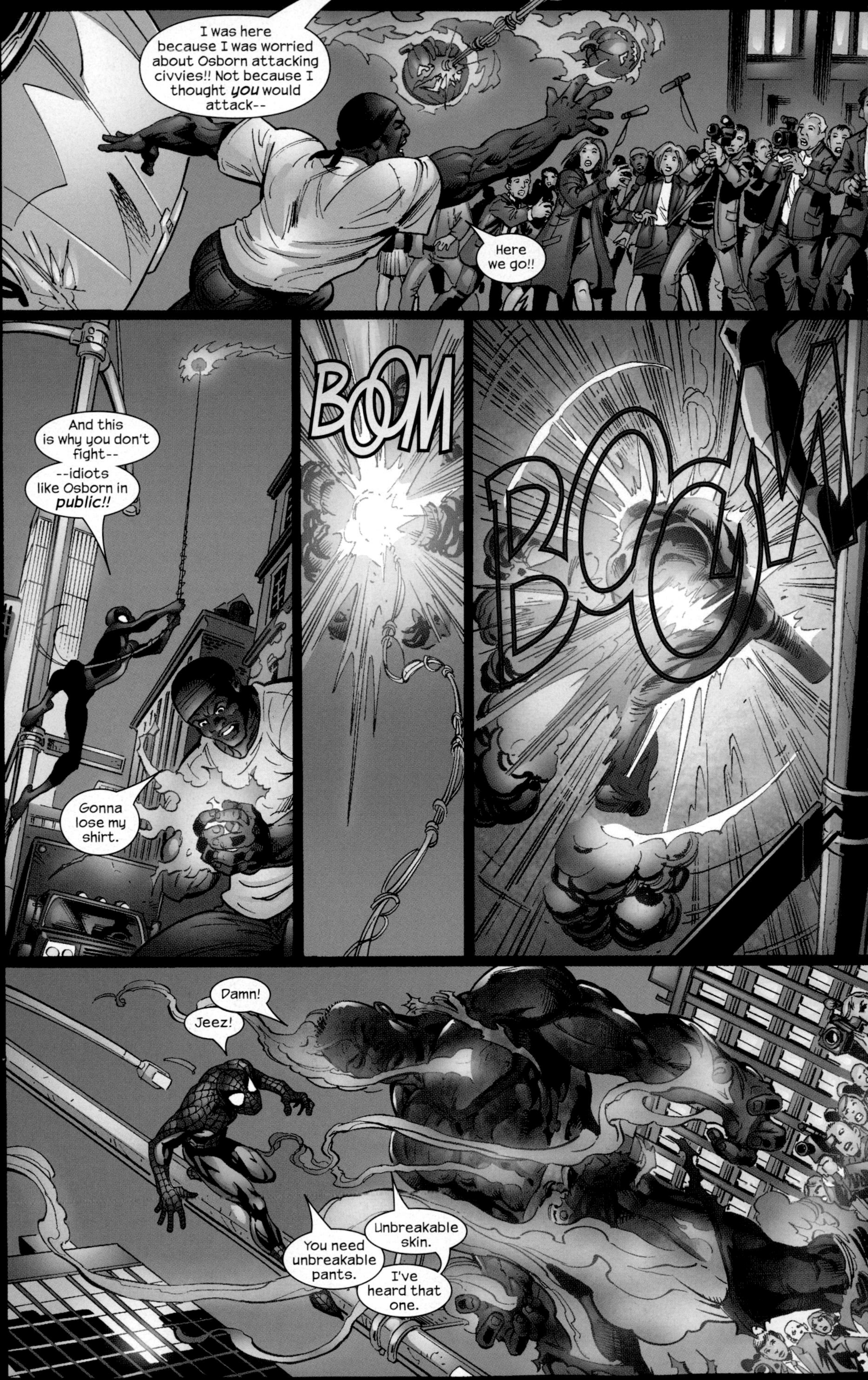
I was here because I was worried about Osborn attacking civvies!! Not because I thought *you* would attack--
Here we go!!
And this is why you don't fight--
--idiots like Osborn in *public!!*
Gonna lose my shirt.
BOOM
BOOM
Damn!
Jeez!
Unbreakable skin.
You need unbreakable pants.
I've heard that one.

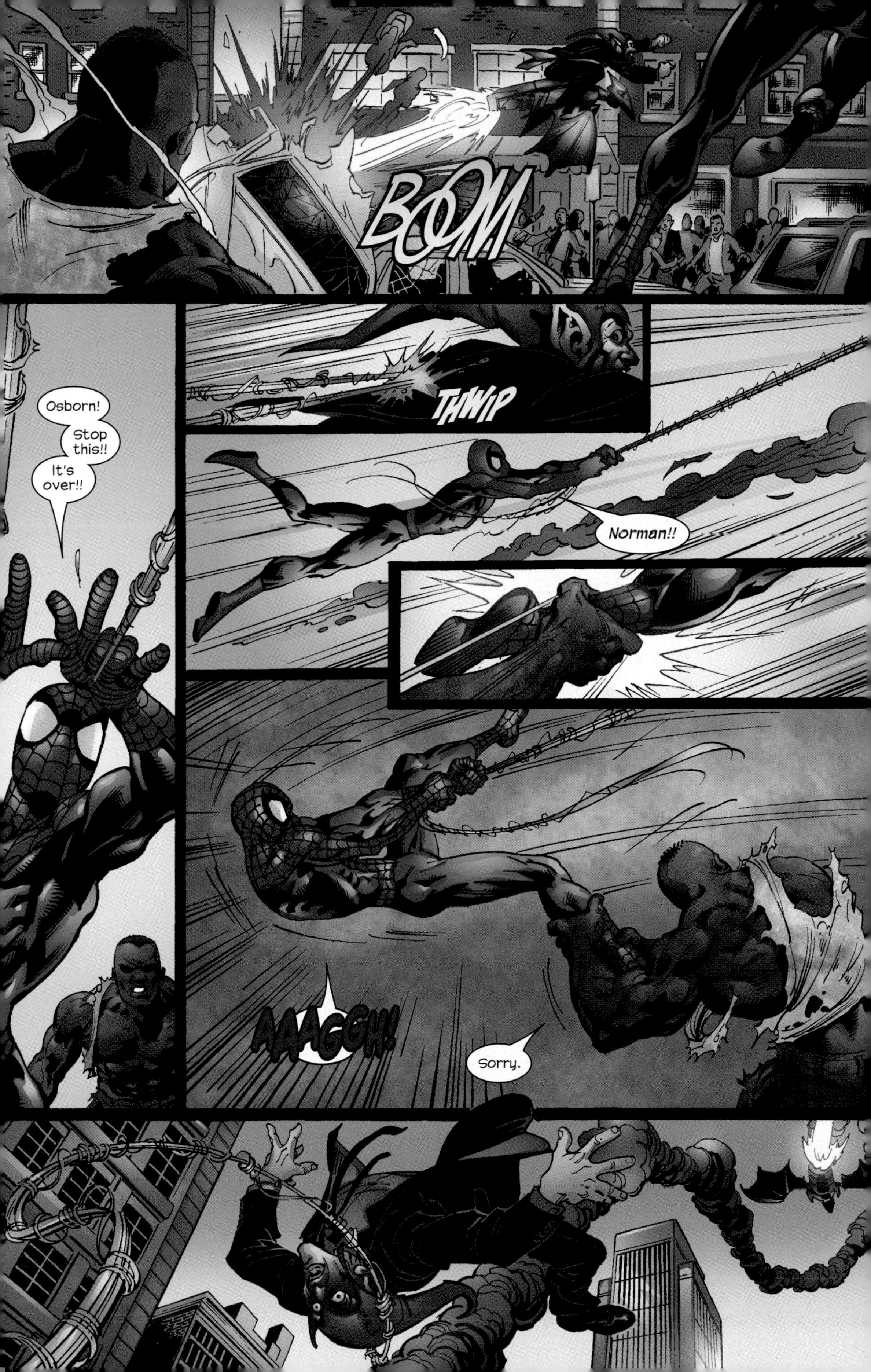
BOOM
THWIP
Osborn!
Stop this!!
It's over!!
Norman!!
AAAGGH!
Sorry.

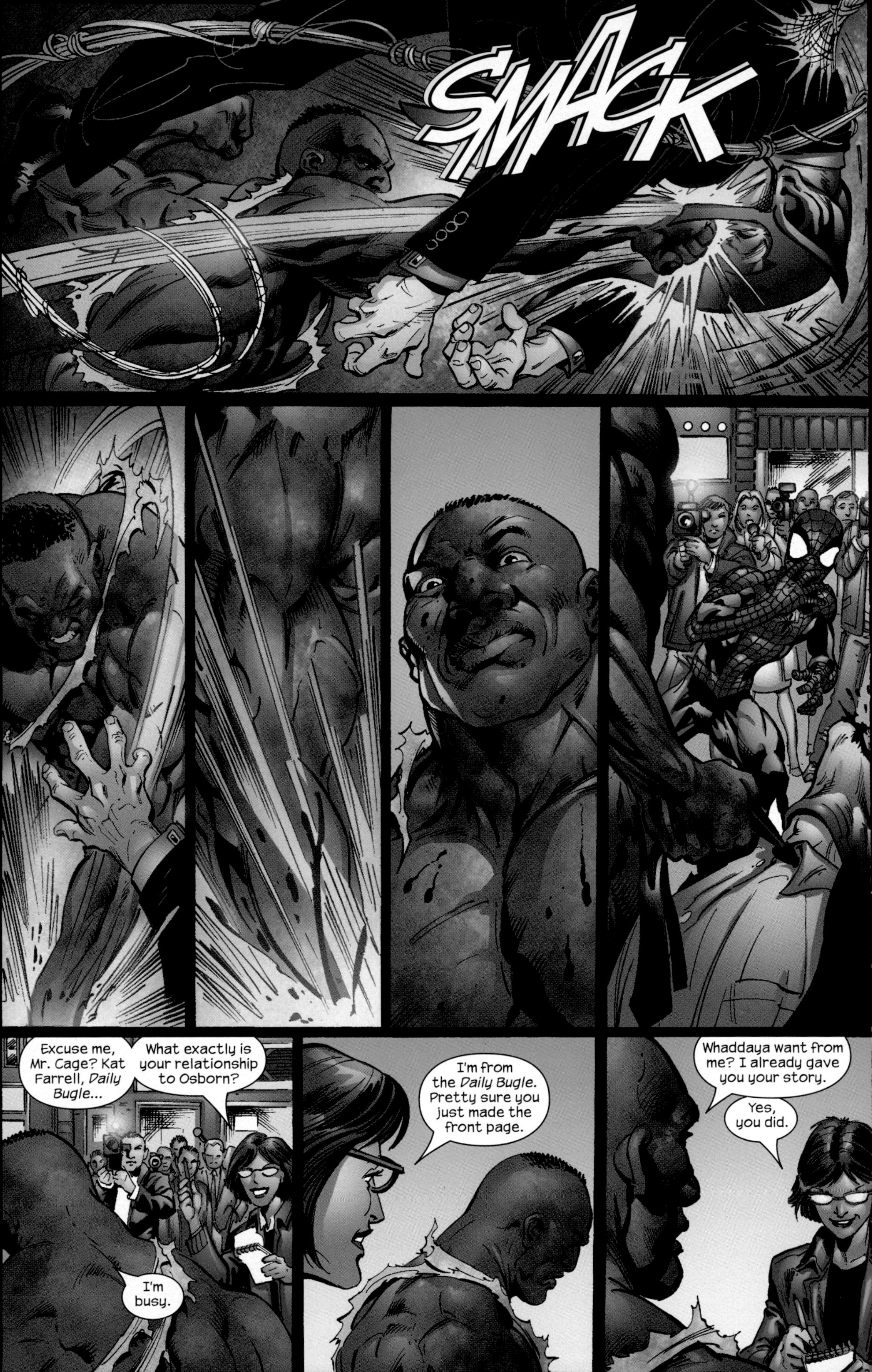
SMACK
Excuse me, Mr. Cage? Kat Farrell, *Daily Bugle*...
What exactly is your relationship to Osborn?
I'm busy.
I'm from the *Daily Bugle*. Pretty sure you just made the front page.
Whaddaya want from me? I already gave you your story.
Yes, you did.

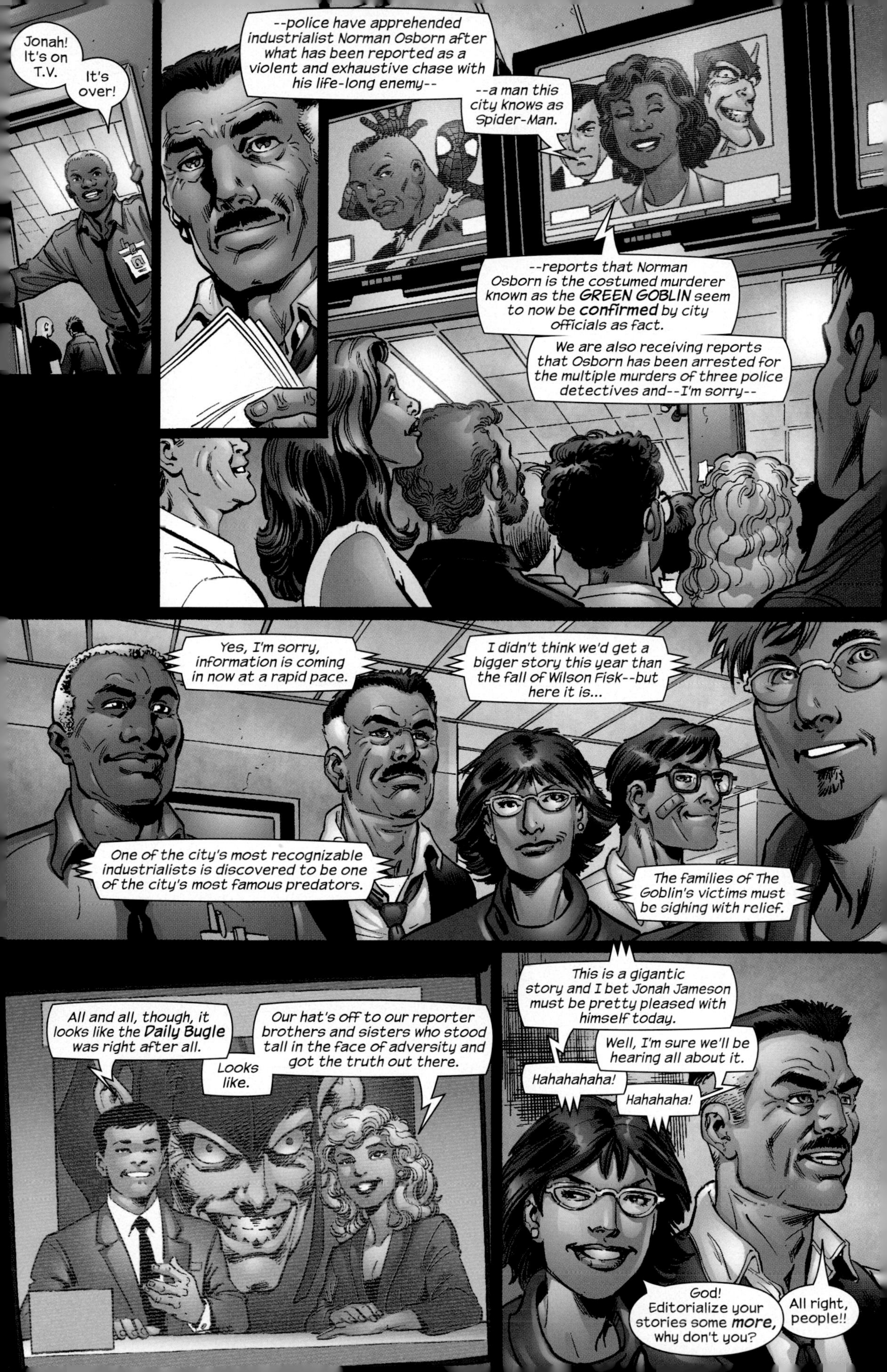
Jonah! It's on T.V.
It's over!
--police have apprehended industrialist Norman Osborn after what has been reported as a violent and exhaustive chase with his life-long enemy--
--a man this city knows as Spider-Man.
--reports that Norman Osborn is the costumed murderer known as the GREEN GOBLIN seem to now be confirmed by city officials as fact.
We are also receiving reports that Osborn has been arrested for the multiple murders of three police detectives and--I'm sorry--
Yes, I'm sorry, information is coming in now at a rapid pace.
I didn't think we'd get a bigger story this year than the fall of Wilson Fisk--but here it is...
One of the city's most recognizable industrialists is discovered to be one of the city's most famous predators.
The families of The Goblin's victims must be sighing with relief.
All and all, though, it looks like the Daily Bugle was right after all.
Looks like.
Our hat's off to our reporter brothers and sisters who stood tall in the face of adversity and got the truth out there.
This is a gigantic story and I bet Jonah Jameson must be pretty pleased with himself today.
Well, I'm sure we'll be hearing all about it.
Hahahahaha!
Hahahaha!
God! Editorialize your stories some more, why don't you?
All right, people!!

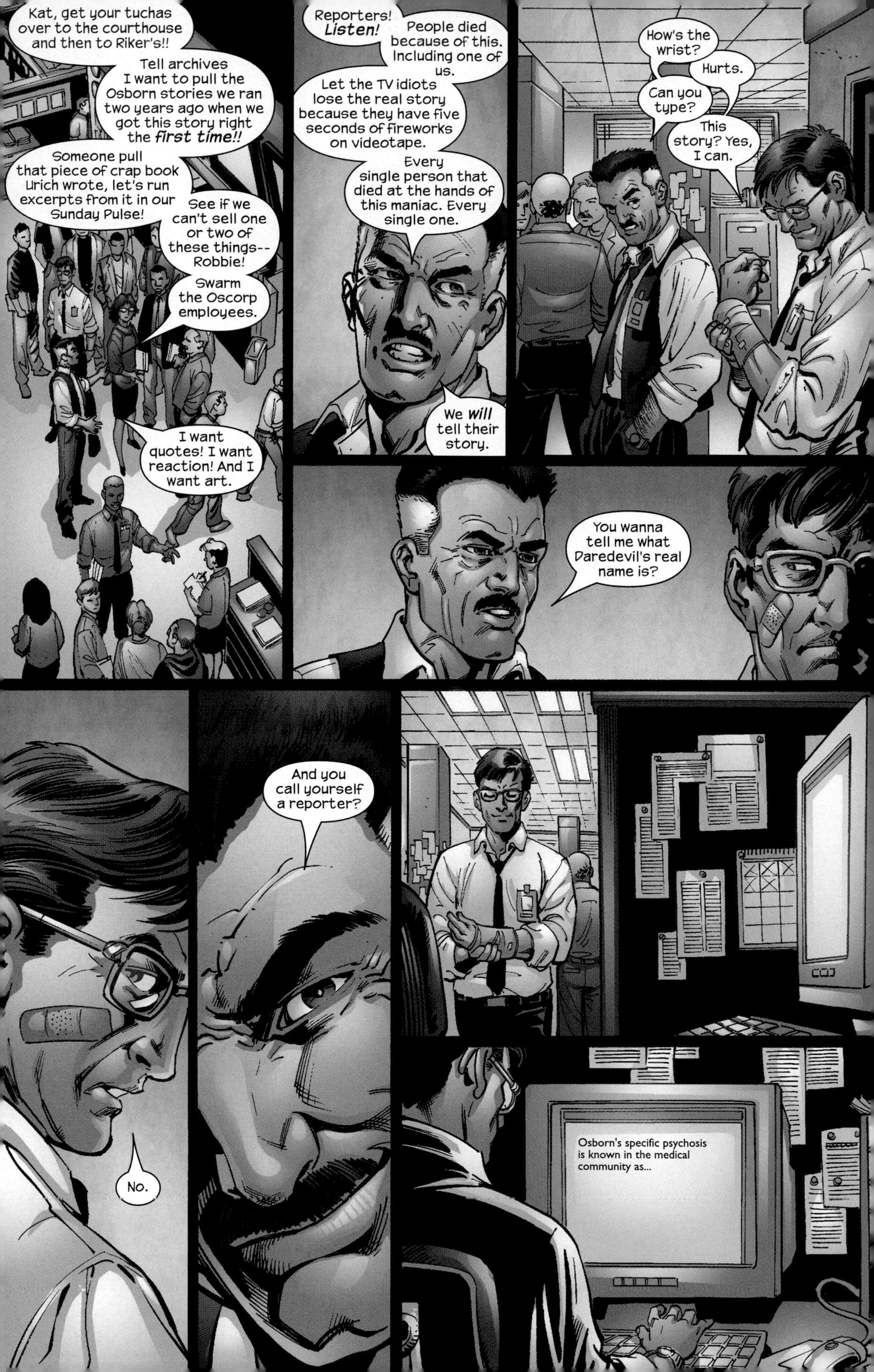
Kat, get your tuchas over to the courthouse and then to Riker's!!
Tell archives I want to pull the Osborn stories we ran two years ago when we got this story right the *first time!!*
Someone pull that piece of crap book Urich wrote, let's run excerpts from it in our Sunday Pulse!
See if we can't sell one or two of these things-- Robbie!
Swarm the Oscorp employees.
I want quotes! I want reaction! And I want art.
Reporters! *Listen!*
People died because of this. Including one of us.
Let the TV idiots lose the real story because they have five seconds of fireworks on videotape.
Every single person that died at the hands of this maniac. Every single one.
We *will* tell their story.
How's the wrist?
Hurts.
Can you type?
This story? Yes, I can.
You wanna tell me what Daredevil's real name is?
No.
And you call yourself a reporter?
Osborn's specific psychosis is known in the medical community as...

DAILY BUGLE

OSBORN JAILED!!

A BUGLE EXCLUSIVE.

Screw the rest of it...

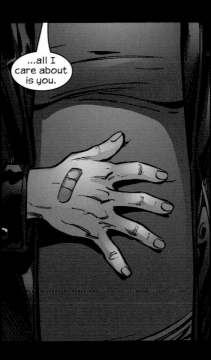

...all I care about is you.

Next: Secret War

Issue #1 Cover Layouts & Pencils

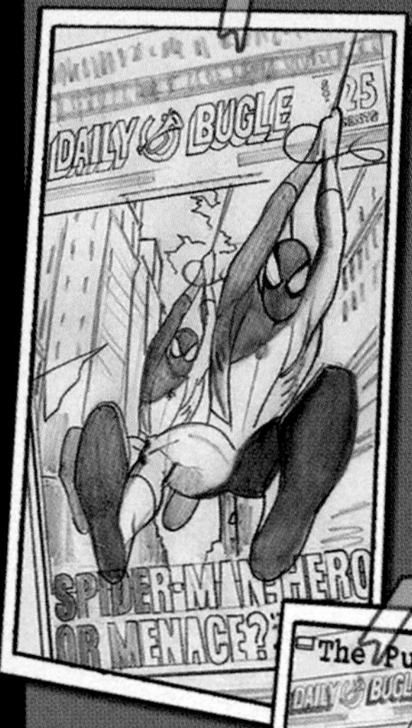
DAILY BUGLE
25
SPIDER-MAN: HERO
OR MENACE?

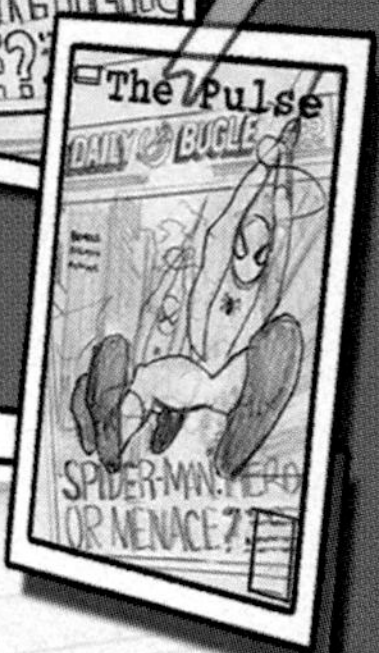
The Pulse
DAILY BUGLE
SPIDER-MAN: HERO
OR MENACE?

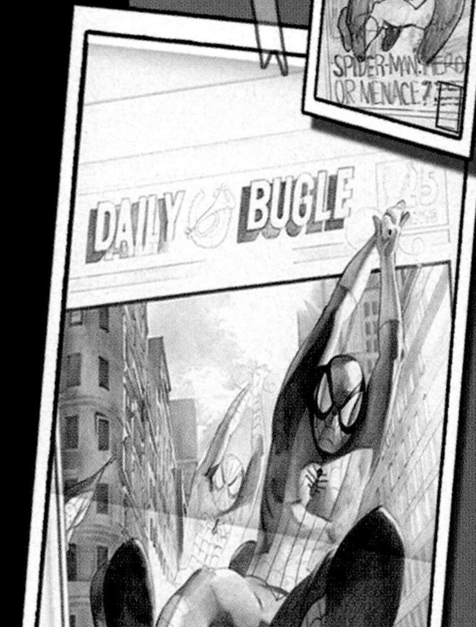
DAILY BUGLE
SPIDER-MAN: HERO
OR MENACE?

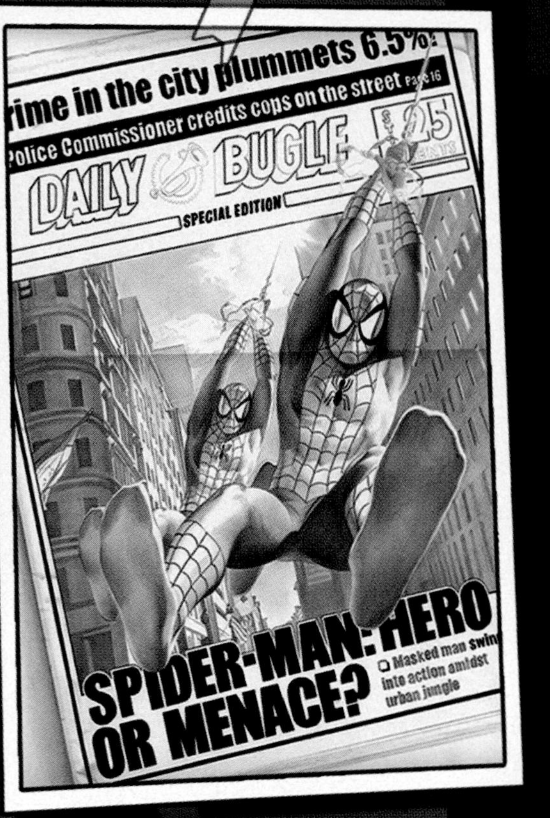
rime in the city plummets 6.5%!
Police Commissioner credits cops on the street Page 16
DAILY BUGLE
25 CENTS
SPECIAL EDITION
SPIDER-MAN: HERO
OR MENACE?
Masked man swin
into action amidst
urban jungle

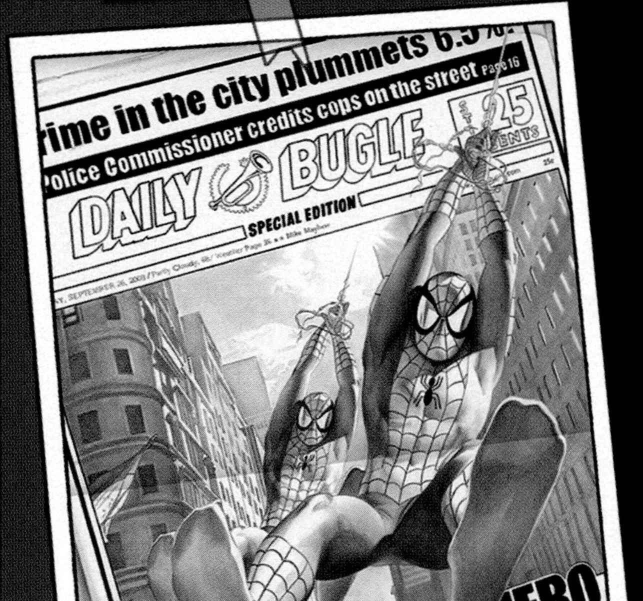
rime in the city plummets 6.5%
Police Commissioner credits cops on the street Page 16
DAILY BUGLE
25 CENTS
SPECIAL EDITION
SPIDER-MAN: HERO
OR MENACE?
Masked man swin
into action amidst
urban jungle

Issue #2 Cover
Layouts & Pencils

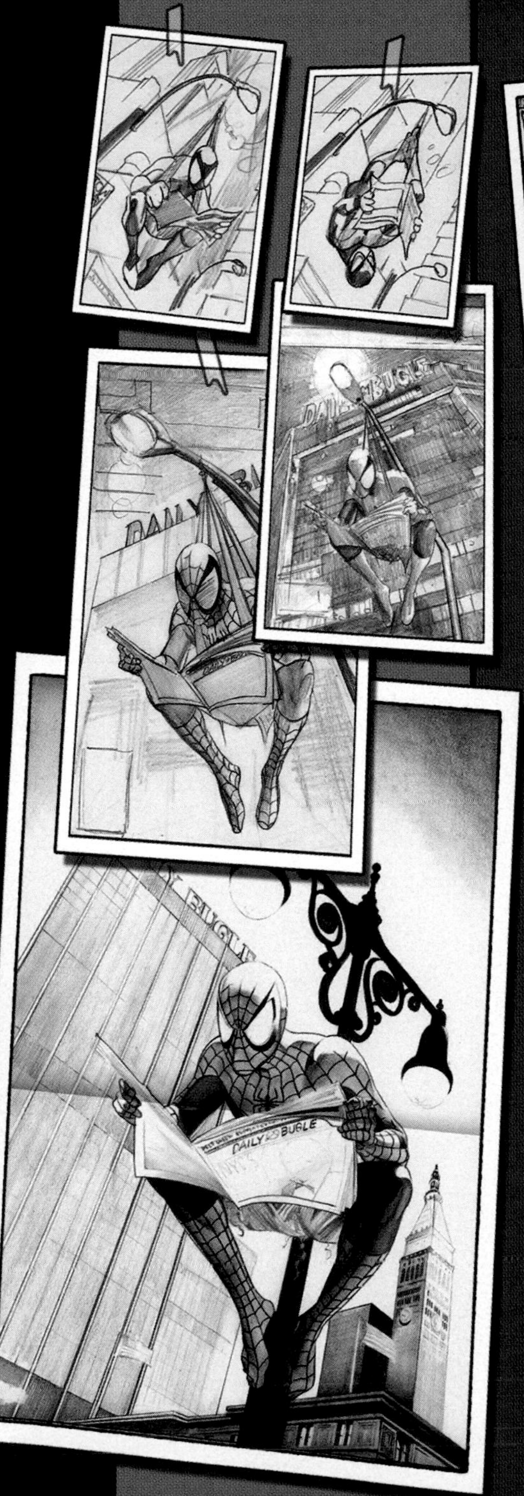
DAILY BUGLE

Issue #3 Cover
Layouts

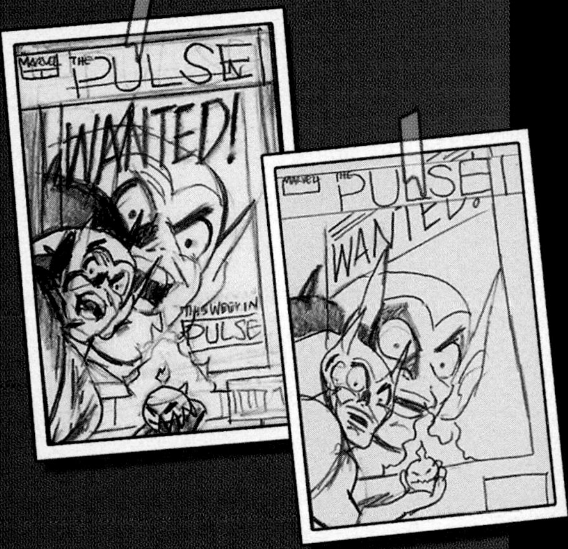
MARVEL THE PULSE
WANTED!
PULSE

Issue #5 Cover
Sketch

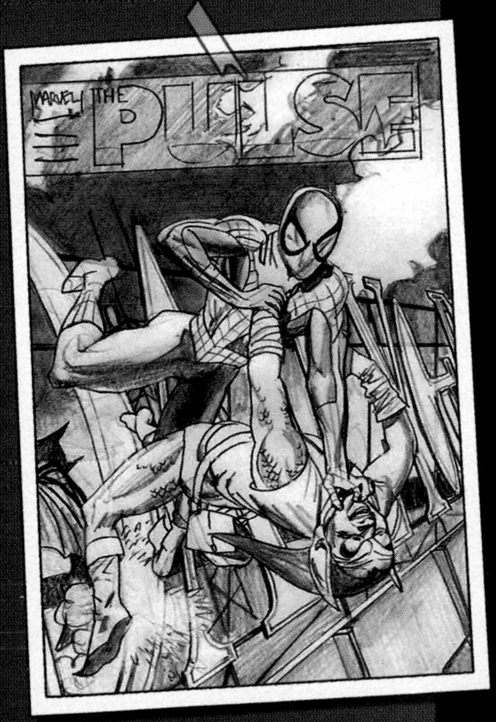
MARVEL THE PULSE

Unused Cover Layouts

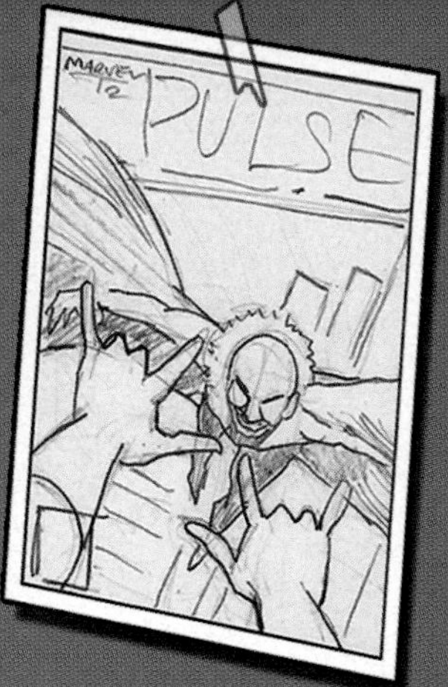
MARVEL
12
PULSE

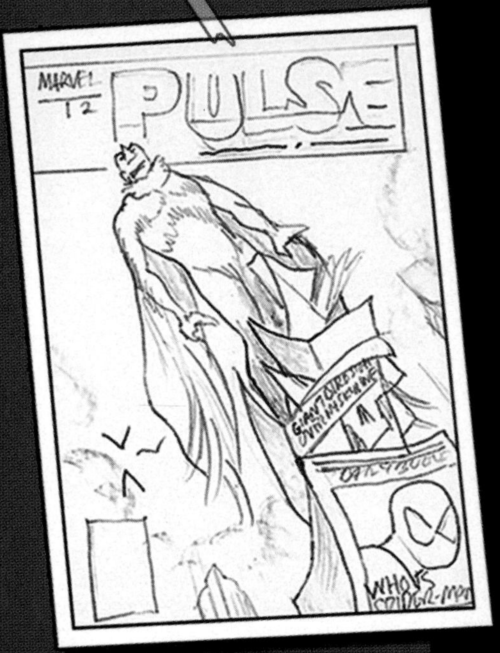
MARVEL
12
PULSE

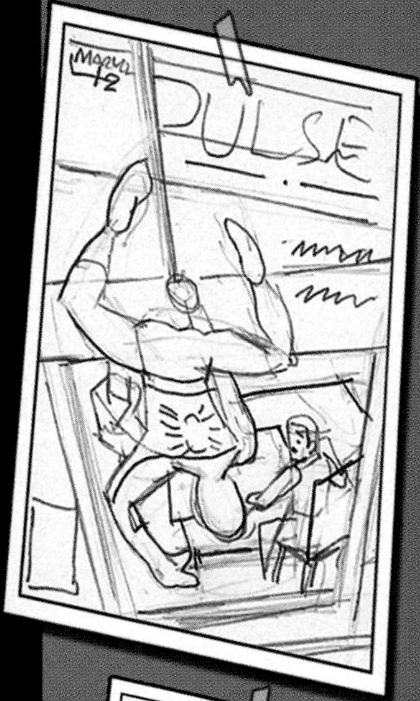
MARVEL
12
PULSE

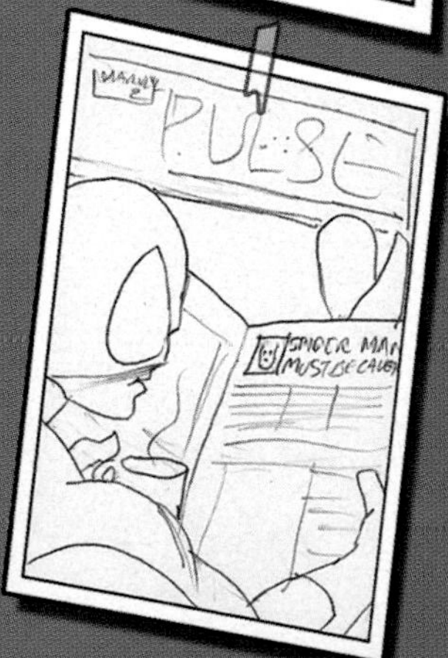
PULSE

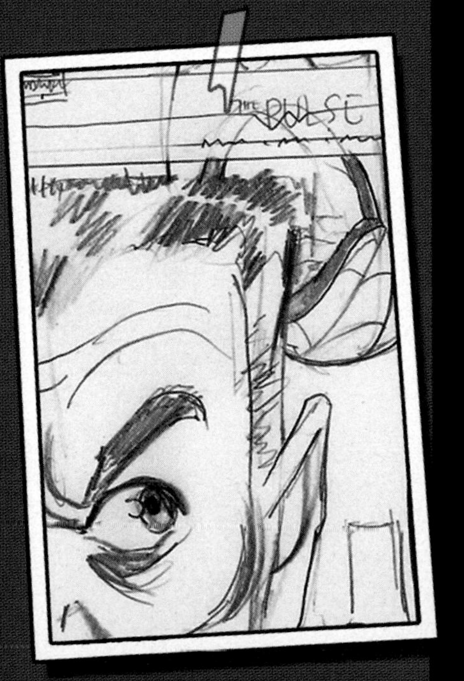
PULSE

Unused Cover

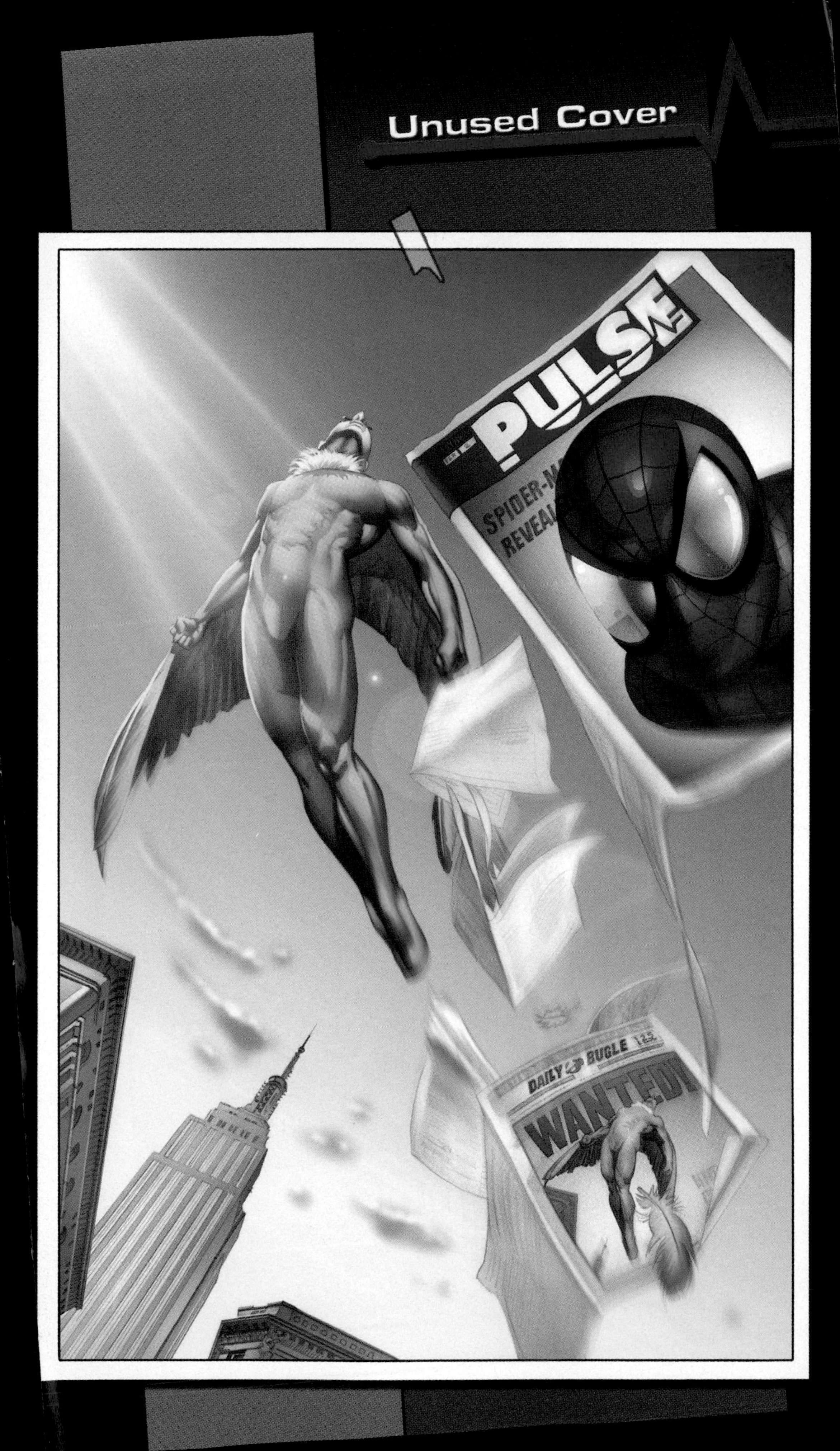
PULSE
DAILY BUGLE
WANTED!

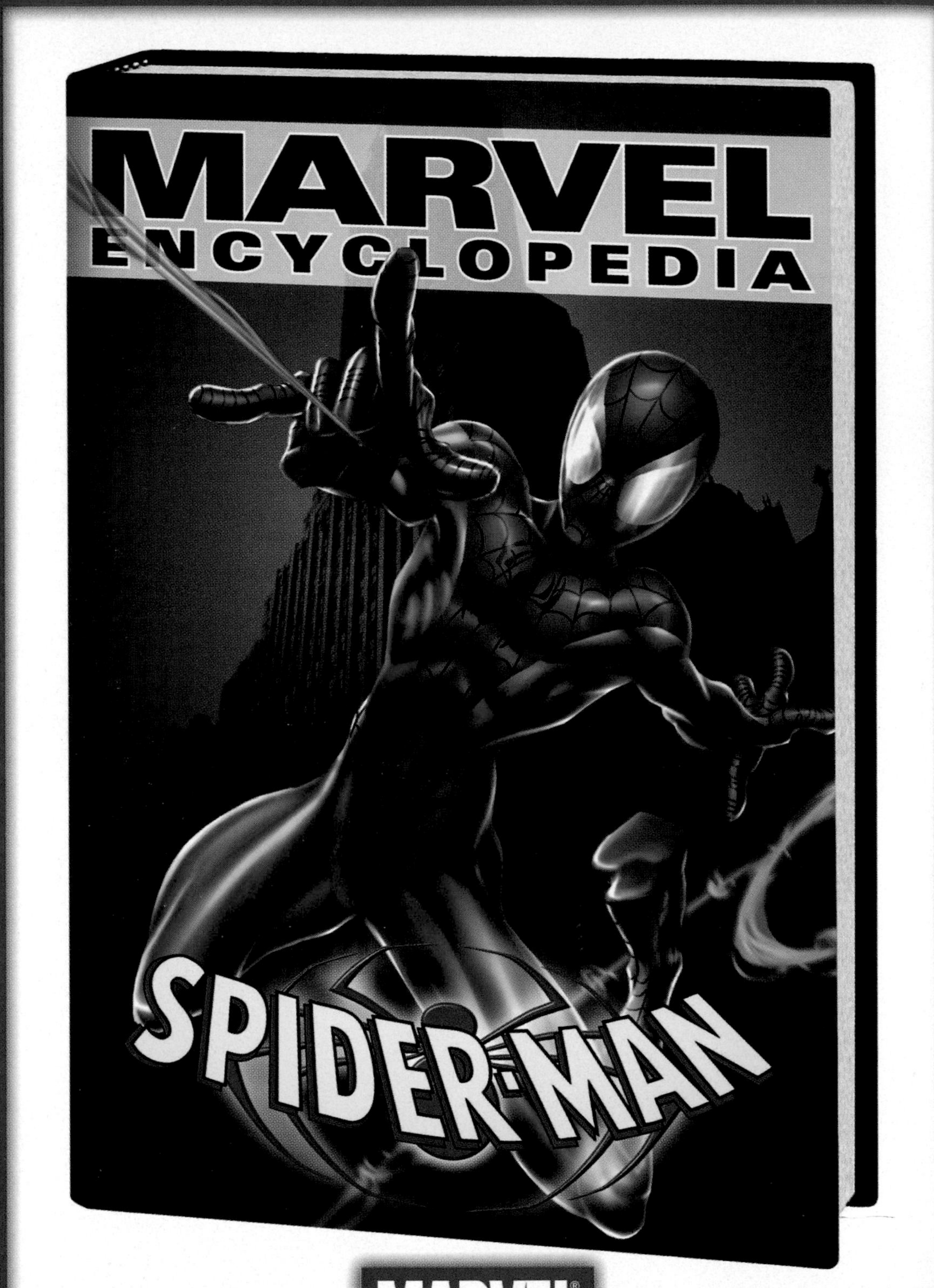
MARVEL ENCYCLOPEDIA
SPIDER-MAN